CRITICAL INSIGHTS

Martin Luther King Jr.

CRITICAL INSIGHTS

Martin Luther King Jr.

Editor
Robert C. Evans
Auburn University, Montgomery

SALEM PRESS
A Division of EBSCO Information Services, Inc.
Ipswich, Massachusetts

GREY HOUSE PUBLISHING

Cover photo: Martin Luther King Jr., LBJ Library Archive

Copyright © 2019 by Grey House Publishing, Inc.

Critical Insights: Martin Luther King Jr., published by Grey House Publishing, Inc., Amenia, NY, under exclusive license from EBSCO Information Services, Inc.

All rights reserved. No part of this work may be used or reproduced in any manner whatsoever or transmitted in any form or by any means, electronic or mechanical, including photocopy, recording, or any information storage and retrieval system, without written permission from the copyright owner. For information, contact Grey House Publishing/Salem Press, 4919 Route 22, PO Box 56, Amenia, NY 12501.

∞ The paper used in these volumes conforms to the American National Standard for Permanence of Paper for Printed Library Materials, Z39.48 1992 (R2009).

Publisher's Cataloging-In-Publication Data
(Prepared by The Donohue Group, Inc.)

Names: Evans, Robert C., 1955- editor.
Title: Martin Luther King Jr. / editor, Robert C. Evans, Auburn University, Montgomery.
Other Titles: Critical insights.
Description: [First edition]. | Ipswich, Massachusetts : Salem Press, a division of EBSCO Information Services, Inc. ; Amenia, NY : Grey House Publishing, [2019] | Includes bibliographical references and index.
Identifiers: ISBN 9781642650303 (hardcover)
Subjects: LCSH: King, Martin Luther, Jr., 1929-1968--Criticism and interpretation. | Speeches, addresses, etc., American--African American authors--History and criticism. | American literature--African American authors--History and criticism. | Civil rights in literature.
Classification: LCC E185.97.K5 M37 2019 | DDC 323.092--dc23

First Printing

PRINTED IN THE UNITED STATES OF AMERICA

Contents

About This Volume, Robert C. Evans   vii
On Martin Luther King: An Interview, Keith D. Miller   xv
Biography of Martin Luther King Jr., Simran Kumari   xxx

Critical Contexts

Marching, Singing, and Road Imagery in Martin Luther King's
    Involvement in the Civil Rights Movement, Raymond Blanton   3

The Traits and Impact of Martin Luther King's Speeches and Sermons:
    A Review of Reactions, Robert C. Evans   17

Martin Luther King's "I Have a Dream" Speech: A Pluralist Analysis,
    Jordan Bailey   33

Contraries and Progression in Martin Luther King, Nicolas Tredell   51

Critical Readings

Martin Luther King: The Uses of Intertextuality, Nicolas Tredell   71

Balanced Thinking and Balanced Phrasing in Martin Luther King's
    "Facing the Challenge" Speech, Robert C. Evans   88

How Samuel Smith and a Parade of Anthem Lovers Created
    the Conclusion of "I Have a Dream": Martin Luther
    King's Refusal to Extemporize, Keith D. Miller and Colleen Wilkowski   102

Precursors to Martin Luther King's 1963 "I Have a Dream" Speech
    at the Lincoln Memorial, Wolfgang Mieder   116

The Use of Proverbs in Martin Luther King's 1963 "I Have a Dream"
    Speech at the Lincoln Memorial, Wolfgang Mieder   132

"The Samaritan Way" in Martin Luther King's Final
    Public Address, Raymond Blanton   149

Martin Luther King and Whiteness: Reconsidering
    "Care for the Other" Rhetoric, Kristine Warrenburg Rome   163

Poems Inspired by Martin Luther King Jr.:
    A Series of Close Readings, Robert C. Evans   179

Critical Reactions to Abby Mann's Televised Miniseries
    on Martin Luther King Jr., Sam Dunton   197

Martin Luther King's *A Testament of Hope*: A Survey
    of Critical Reactions, Bryan Warren   214

Martin Luther King: An Interview with
    Charles Johnson, Marshall D. Buford   225

Martin Luther King: Interviews with People Who
    Personally Heard Him Speak, Donna Yvette Smith   233

Resources

Chronology of Martin Luther King Jr.'s Life   247
Works by Martin Luther King Jr.   253
Bibliography   255
About the Editor   259
Contributors   261
Index   265

About This Volume

Robert C. Evans

Martin Luther King Jr. is remembered today not only as one of the most important political and cultural figures in American history but also as one of America's most effective public speakers. This volume, then, is especially concerned with King the rhetorician and writer. Various essays examine a number of King's most significant speeches in detail, studying his use of metaphors, proverbs, contrasting phrases, balance, imagery, allusions, and numerous other techniques as well as the ethical, racial, and social dimensions of his work. The book also explores the impact King had on people who knew, heard, and read his words while he was still living as well as the influence he has had on later writers, including poets and novelists. All in all, the volume seeks to offer a comprehensive approach to numerous facets of King's accomplishments as an author and an orator.

The book opens with an introductory self-interview with Keith D. Miller, perhaps the most noteworthy student of King's oratory. Miller asks and answers numerous questions likely to be of interest to both first-time and veteran readers of King. His accessible, wide-ranging comments help explain the impact previous authors and speakers had on King's own writing and rhetoric. Miller also charts important developments in scholarship dealing with King as a master of words. In addition, he notes opportunities for significant new scholarship, both in relation to King and in relation to less famous figures from the civil rights era. Miller's interview is followed by a brief biography of King prepared by Simran Kumari, who charts the major developments in King's life.

Critical Contexts
As in all volumes in the Critical Insights series, the introductory pieces are followed by four contextual essays dealing, respectively, with historical contexts, critical reception, a particular analytical

perspective, and comparative analysis. Raymond Blanton's essay in this section sets King within the historical context of the developing civil rights movement, arguing that "by 1957 King had delivered more than two hundred speeches and sermons a year, and then delivered even more as the movement progressed." It is no wonder, Blanton argues, "that King's sermonic discourse was preeminently concerned with the archetype of the road: he himself was constantly, and quite literally, on the road and on the move, and his speeches and sermons were filled with references to the road."

Robert C. Evans then offers an overview of varied "reactions to King's speaking and preaching by many people who actually heard him speak or preach." He next surveys "some of the scholarly literature dealing with the stylistic, rhetorical, and structural traits that made King's speeches and sermons so memorable as pieces of writing." In fact, several of the most important analysts of King's rhetoric Evans discusses (especially Keith Miller and Wolfgang Mieder) are themselves contributors to the present volume.

In one of various essays concerned with King's famous "I Have a Dream" speech, Jordan Bailey presents the results of a pluralist approach to that speech—an approach conducted by a number of students in an upper-level college course in literary theory. Bailey explains that pluralism "is less an individual approach to literary criticism than a way of dealing with all other approaches." Pluralism, she notes, "suggests that different kinds of literary theory are like different kinds of tools: a hammer differs from a screwdriver, a wrench differs from a saw, a drill differs from a pair of pliers. No single tool is superior to another; instead, each is designed to do a different job." Moreover, "each tool must be used competently if the job is to be done well." Bailey reports how roughly twenty different students used roughly twenty distinct critical approaches (from the most ancient to the most current) to analyze the "I Have a Dream" address.

Finally, in the comparative analysis essay that concludes the Critical Contexts section, Nicolas Tredell not only compares and contrasts King with various other writers but also argues that King's prose itself "is structured around contraries, binary oppositions such as conformity/nonconformity, courage/cowardice, divine/human, joy/sorrow, optimism/pessimism, realism/idealism, and violence/nonviolence." According to Tredell, King's "texts sometimes state these contrasts explicitly and at other times assume or imply them." Often King makes use of contrasts by "juxtaposing different qualities that are not exactly opposites but that may come into conflict, such as expedient/ethical: expedient and ethical courses of action may sometimes happily, or suspiciously, coincide." However (Tredell continues), "they may also diverge and clash and when they do it is necessary to make a judgment, which may or may not be consciously formulated, as to whether expediency or ethics—and what kind of expediency or ethics—should prevail."

Critical Readings

The Critical Readings section—the longest portion of the book—offers a deliberately diverse group of essays that use many different methods. The section opens, for instance, with a second essay by Nicolas Tredell, who this time explores King's works in relation to the theme of intertextuality. Tredell notes that "King's published sermons, speeches, public letters, and articles are packed with intertextual references in the form of direct quotations from, allusions to, or echoes of classical, biblical, early modern and nineteenth- and twentieth-century literary, political, philosophical, and theological writings." He mentions, "for example, those of Plato, Aristotle, and Epictetus; the Old and New Testaments; Shakespeare and Donne; Tennyson and Arnold; James Russell Lowell, Emerson and Thoreau; Frederick Douglass and Paul Dunbar; and T. S. Eliot." Tredell's essay examines "a selection of significant intertextual references in key King texts."

An essay by Robert C. Evans then looks at one of King's earliest significant speeches, a 1957 address entitled "Facing the Challenge of a New Age." Evans argues that in this and many other works, and in "almost every way imaginable, King achieves a kind of verbal and intellectual balance that makes him sound like an eminently rational man, even when he is addressing topics that inspired great and sometimes violent emotions." Far more than some other potential leaders of the civil rights movement (according to Evans), King "was able to command respect both for the substance of his message and for the style of his writing and delivery. With his baritone voice, his unhurried pace, his complete sense of self-control, and his almost entirely serious manner (although occasionally leavened with humor)," King "came across to many white Americans as the perfect example of the kind of person who had been treated unfairly." In numerous respects and at many different levels, his phrasing was balanced in ways that seemed to imply persuasively balanced thinking.

In one of several essays on the famous 1963 "I Have a Dream" speech, Keith D. Miller and Colleen Wilkowski challenge the still-common (but incorrect) assumption that King improvised the conclusion of that address. Instead, they demonstrate the ways King drew on various predecessors, especially in his use of the song titled "America," with its famous opening line "My Country 'Tis of Thee." Next, Wolfgang Mieder—one of the world's leading scholars interested in proverbs and the author of a massive book on King's proverbial language—shows how "King had been using many of the same words and phrases in various other speeches that preceded his most famous address in 1963 as he stood before the Lincoln Memorial and spoke to hundreds of thousands of people." The "I Have a Dream" speech, Mieder shows, resulted from a long series of previous efforts to articulate many of the same ideas. Finally, in a related essay, Mieder argues that the "I have a dream" phrase was "just one of the "quotational and proverbial leitmotifs" that made King's "sermons, speeches, letters, essays, and books such effective and memorable statements in the cause of civil and human rights." According to Mieder, "quotations turned proverbs, as well as Bible proverbs, folk proverbs, and a plethora of proverbial expressions, are an intrinsic part of King's rhetorical prowess" and helped provide "his messages with colorful metaphors and authoritative strength."

In his second essay in this volume, Raymond Blanton now turns to what is perhaps King's other most famous speech: the "I See the Promised Land" address he delivered on the night before he died. In this particular essay, Blanton explores King's use of the metaphor involving the so-called "Samaritan Way" that "appears in the speech King delivered to striking sanitation workers in Memphis, Tennessee, on the evening of April 3, 1968." Blanton shows how the "Samaritan Way" metaphor was crucial to King's concept of morality. Also concerned with King's ethic as it appears in King's final speech is an ensuing essay by Kristine Warrenburg Rome. She examines King's "ethic of 'care for the other,' a term associated with the French philosopher Emmanuel Levinas." But she situates that ethic in relation to another important concept—the idea of the so-called racial contract—in order to show how King sought a "color-blind" society in ways that were not blind to the dark realities of racism.

Next, Robert C. Evans looks at the ways King has been presented in writings by others—particularly in a large new collection of poetry by numerous authors, entitled *The Mighty Stream*. Various poems in that anthology either "explicitly mention King or allude to him in less obvious ways." Evans offers close readings of a number of such poems to show how King, skillful in his own use of words, has now become of the focus of the literary skill of many others. Similarly, Sam Dunton examines the 1978 televised miniseries titled *King*, which was one of the first docudramas to deal with the career of the slain civil rights leader. Dunton notes that this film "is widely available on an inexpensive DVD and is, therefore, still likely to be viewed by anyone looking for a well-produced film about King and the civil rights movement." In addition, Dunton reports, "the film is also easily accessible on the internet and can thus be viewed for free or at a very minimal cost." Therefore, "the film is still likely to be used by teachers and students in classroom discussions concerning Martin Luther King Jr. and his legacy." Dunton surveys some typical 1978 reviews of *King*, "beginning with negative assessments, then moving to mixed reactions, and finally ending with positive responses to Mann's film." By doing so, Dunton seeks "to provide students, teachers, and other viewers of the film with some sense of the kinds of reception the series first aroused and the kinds of responses it can still arouse today."

Also concerned with the critical reception of an important work dealing with King is Bryan Warren's survey of reactions to a massive but inexpensive anthology of King's writings. This book, entitled *A Testament of Hope* and edited by James M. Washington, was first published in 1986 and remains in print today. Running to more than seven hundred pages and very reasonably priced, Washington's anthology was sanctioned by the King family and has been widely praised for reprinting so many of King's most important works. However, the book has also been accused of various flaws that readers, and teachers, should keep in mind. Warren's survey calls attention both to the praise the book has elicited and to the criticism it has provoked.

The next two pieces in the present book consist of interviews. The first, conducted by Marshall D. Buford in conversation with Charles Johnson, gives Johnson a chance to discuss not only King's works but also his own writings *about* King. Johnson, winner of a MacArthur Genius Grant and of the 1990 National Book Award, is also the author of a novel entitled *Dreamer*—one of the fullest depictions of King in American fiction. Johnson explains why he considers King such an important figure in the nation's culture and how and why he chose to depict King as he did in *Dreamer*, which deals with King's final years, especially his campaign in Chicago. In a second interview, Donna Yvette Smith, a resident of Tuskegee, Alabama, converses with various African American people who lived in the Tuskegee/Montgomery area during King's lifetime and who were personally familiar with his speaking and his crusades. The now-elderly interviewees discuss the impact King had on their own lives and how he was regarded by members of their local communities.

Resources

Like the other volumes in the Critical Insights series, this one closes with various resources, including a chronology of King's life, a listing of his works, a secondary bibliography, profiles of the editor and the contributors, and a comprehensive index. Taken all together, these resources and the preceding essays will, ideally, provide readers with a diverse, up-to-date, and suggestive guide to King's speeches and writings and to the responses they have evoked from others.

On Martin Luther King: An Interview

Keith D. Miller

Editor's note: Keith D. Miller is one of the world's leading experts on Martin Luther King Jr. In this self-interview, Miller answers some basic questions about his pioneering scholarship.

Q: You've written a lot about Martin Luther King Jr. What got you interested in him?

A: My father, Ernest Miller, was a liberal Protestant minister. When I was a child, he and my mother took me and my brothers to Dallas for an international convention of their denomination, the Disciples of Christ. There, in a large, filled auditorium, I heard King give a speech. Later I read everything I could find on the Vietnam War, and appreciated King's courage in opposing it. But I didn't focus on him. Let me tell a story. Texas Christian University once invited Isaac Bashevis Singer, a renowned writer, to campus for a week. I volunteered to drive him around in my twenty-year old rust bucket, which fortunately did not crash and kill him before, a couple of years later, he won the Nobel Prize for Literature. Recreating the Polish village of his Jewish childhood, he populated his fiction with a gallery of conniving liars and rare saints, whose lives were filled with mysticism and sex, with demons lurking nearby. He eschewed modernist stream of consciousness, relying instead on traditional narrative forms, like those of, say, Dickens and Tolstoy. In a small circle of students and professors, I asked him what he thought of James Joyce. He dryly replied, "No one reads him except PhD students in literature." I brashly responded, "Well, I read him and I'm not a PhD student!" He calmly stated, "You will be." At the time I didn't anticipate that I would enroll in a PhD program, but later I did. So he was right. Even though he hadn't met me before, he somehow understood me better than I understood myself!

During that PhD program, I was required to study Old English and to read a huge amount of British literature. But I only fell in love with Shakespeare and a few other British writers, not most of British literature. I decided to do a dissertation on King's sermons because my interests in religion, American history, African American culture, dissent, and rhetoric seemed to converge on him.

Q: How did your dissertation develop?

A: Dad gave me an advantage. He attended seminary at Texas Christian at the same time that King matriculated at Crozer Theological Seminary outside Philadelphia. They never met, but they studied the same curriculum, reading the same biblical scholars and the same theologians, such as Walter Rauschenbusch, Reinhold Niebuhr, and Paul Tillich. I heard my father talk about them at home, in church, and while fishing in mountain streams in New Mexico. He mingled their names with those of stellar Protestant preachers such as Harry Emerson Fosdick, George Buttrick, J. Wallace Hamilton, and Halford Luccock.

A seminar student at Vanderbilt, my friend Bob Hill, found a sermon by Hamilton that overlapped with a later King sermon. One day, in my father's office, I absentmindedly took books of sermons off his shelves. Flipping through a table of contents in a book by Luccock, I found a sermon title that closely resembled the title of a later King sermon. The sermons both opened with the same anecdote about Rip van Winkle. From reading biographies, I realized that King crisscrossed the nation constantly. I also knew that his sermons invariably seemed perfect. Suddenly, I wondered: could King have borrowed sermons regularly? I talked more to my dad about preachers and, upon returning to campus, started rifling through books of sermons in the seminary library. I found more correspondence, especially with material from Fosdick, Buttrick, and Hamilton. Sometimes I would read a passage and it would sound familiar, but I couldn't remember the source. As it turned out, different ministers echoed each other's sermons, leaving me confused and dizzy trying to keep track of who took what from whom. I realized that I needed to practically memorize King's book of sermons so I could identify a passage from someone else that he reiterated. At different points, King mirrored sermon titles, biblical cornerstones for homilies, the three- or four-point structure (or skeleton) of the homily, illustrations, and literary quotations.

Q: What happened after your dissertation?

A: I applied everywhere, but no university would hire me for a tenure-track job, so I took a position as an instructor at Ohio State, under a three-year contract that, at the start, they told me was nonrenewable. On the quarter system, I taught 13 classes per year, all but one of them for basic writers who needed more preparation before taking the regular first-year writing course. When not grading stacks of papers, I kept tracking down more sources at the Ohio State library, the Library of Ohio, and two nearby seminaries. I also visited the King archive in Atlanta again and then explored the King papers at Boston University and other salient material at the Schomburg Center in Harlem and the archive at Howard University in Washington, D.C. When I finally arrived at the Library of Congress, the librarians let me roam through the stacks in their underground floors—something that they now forbid. I was disappointed when I realized that I had already seen almost all their books of sermons somewhere else. Then my disappointment surged into happiness: I decided that, if the Library of Congress held nothing new, my four-year search for sources had ended. At some point I understood that I needed to grasp the African American preaching that King heard as a child and teen. So I read everything I could find and listened to black sermons distributed on a blues record label. I initially felt that I wouldn't be able to comprehend this tradition very well, especially the animated folk preaching of King's father and grandfather. But then I decided that the scholarship about folk sermons was so patronizing and so terrible that I couldn't possibly do worse. I interviewed older people in King's church, including the Reverend J. H. Edwards, who had served on the committee that ordained King as a minister. In his old, dented Chevrolet, he kindly drove me over the Martin Luther King Freeway while escorting me back in time several decades. Finally, I published my first essay, in a journal called *College English*.

By then, I had applied for many tenure-track jobs; but, nearing the end of my third year at Ohio State, I still couldn't land one. Stress threw me into the hospital. Meds allowed me to leave in time for an on-campus job visit at Arizona State, one of the only schools with any interest in me. After I returned, I waited two months but heard nothing and thought I'd never hear anything. Finally, one month before my stint at Ohio State ended, Arizona State rescued me by calling with a tenure-track job offer. I was ecstatic: I wouldn't have to work as a professional writer for the electric company in rainy Columbus, Ohio.

Q: Then how did your work develop?

A: In the library at Arizona State, I stumbled on a previously unknown source for the conclusion of "I Have a Dream": Archibald Carey's "Address to the Republican Convention" from 1952. I published three more articles and mailed one of them to someone I didn't know, King's biographer David Garrow. He contacted me and asked how he could help. I told him I needed a publisher for my book *Voice of Deliverance*. Fortunately, he lived in New York City, knew people, and found me a publisher!

For my book, I documented many preachers' tendency to borrow liberally from each other. Sometimes a literary quotation would float into as many as seven or eight sermons by seven or eight different authors. They were schizoid about the whole process. In the seminary libraries, one book would admonish preachers never to borrow anything. But the next book on the same shelf would be titled *A Thousand Illustrations for Your Sermons*. Ministers would give the impression that they stayed up all night reading Shakespeare to find the proper quotation to pluck for a homily, but they actually got that quotation from someone else's homily. Even the greatest preachers did that. But, given that they had to preach virtually every Sunday of the year, borrowing material was better than delivering a bad original sermon. Also, African American folk preachers were still giving (and recording) sermons during the 1940s and 1950s that were first delivered during slavery. I found the whole process fascinating.

Q: Can you talk about a source that you found for some of King's sermons?

A: King leaned heavily on George Buttrick's *The Parables of Jesus*. George Buttrick's son, David Buttrick, told me that his father took that book out of print because too many preachers were echoing it. Yet, in my second book, *Martin Luther King's Biblical Epic: His Great, Final Speech*, I show that George Buttrick himself, without acknowledgment, borrowed lines from a preacher who was tied to a long string of sources that dated back to the nineteenth century. Some of those lines showed up in King's "I've Been to the Mountaintop" (sometimes called "I See the Promised Land"). Yes, without knowing it, at least one nineteenth-century writer composed part of one of the most significant speeches in American history.

Q: Why didn't King mention the names of the preachers very often?

A: King sometimes credited his reading of philosophers and theologians even for passages that he actually replayed from other pulpits. He regularly credentialed himself by citing the most famous sources he could—Shakespeare, Donne, Emerson, Thoreau, Lincoln, Marx, Niebuhr, Gandhi, etc.—while usually failing to mention the names of the homilists. The preachers proved way more useful to him, but he omitted their names because those names carried little cultural capital. To black and white audiences alike, his ability to reference important ideas and figures of Western civilization refuted racist stereotypes about African Americans' supposed inferiority. But, had he actually quoted philosophers and theologians very much, he would have sounded stuffy and pretentious; listeners would have neither understood nor liked him.

Q: Someone attacked your first book for supposedly disparaging King. Others attacked it for supposedly excusing King's unacknowledged use of sources. How do you respond?

A: I wasn't trying to defend King or attack King. I was—and still am—trying to comprehend how his language worked, how it proved persuasive. To me, that is *by far* the most important question to ask about his language. His big contribution was to *help change America*. His lack of original language helped him because he repeatedly inserted his protest against racism inside road-tested sermonic rhetoric that his Northern, liberal Protestant audiences had already heard and approved. That made his protest sound way more mainstream and way more acceptable. I urge others to pursue the same question: What made King so persuasive? Starting during his lifetime and continuing into the present, some people keep trying to define him as a philosopher. They often claim that he followed Niebuhr or the Boston Personalists, almost as if he were a robot, making no original contributions himself. To me, his biggest rhetorical and religious intervention—and the biggest rhetorical and theological innovation of the civil rights movement—was to simultaneously instantiate and explain what I call a Judeo-Christian rhetoric and theology of the body, consisting of marches, songfests, sit-ins, integrated bus rides, stints in jail, and suffering from beatings, stabbings—and even murder. He exemplified the theology that he was explicating. This simultaneously orated and embodied theology, if you will, contrasts with the erudite but safe theology of the seminar room. My question is: How and why did that succeed? Despite his frequent use of sources, many people still paint him as a solitary genius. Unfortunately, by mythologizing and fetishizing him in that way, they prompt people to long for another solitary genius and thereby make future, positive social change far less likely. *The greatest tribute people can pay to King is simply to understand him.* As Gardner Taylor and some of King's other friends realized, mythologizing and fetishizing him serves no useful purpose.

Q: Have you changed your mind about anything in *Voice of Deliverance*?

A: Yes. I am too busy with other projects to redo that book. But, if I were to rework it, I would portray African American Protestantism in a more pluralistic way. I would certainly make a bigger distinction between, on the one hand, the folk sermons of King's grandfather and father and, on the other hand, the oratory of formally educated African American leaders, such as Benjamin Mays, Howard Thurman, and Mordecai Johnson. Mays, Thurman, and Johnson were simultaneously academics and preachers, and all three served as extremely important mentors and exemplars for King, as did other African American ministers, such as William Holmes Borders and J. Pius Barbour. Mays, Thurman, and Johnson actually traveled to India to talk to Gandhi in person about using nonviolence and civil disobedience in the African American struggle. In an excellent new book, Gary Dorrien lucidly explains the enormous impact that Mays, Thurman, Johnson, and Barbour exerted on King.

In addition, Drew Hansen (in an unpublished essay), Patrick Parr, and Dorrien persuaded me that King's education at Crozer Seminary and Boston University was not as perfunctory as I claimed in *Voice of Deliverance*. I now agree with them that King actually did engage intellectually with many of the topics he studied in graduate school. He sank his teeth into many of his course readings and avidly participated in class discussions. Although white preachers such as Buttrick, Fosdick, and Hamilton gave him sources to mine, I still strongly maintain that the African American pulpit and African American community served as the wellspring for his oratory, theology, politics, and leadership. The son and grandson of African American preachers, he packaged the centuries-old African American demand for freedom into homiletic packages that Northern liberal white audiences had already approved. Unlike African American ministers whom he heard as a child and adolescent, his professors in graduate school seldom discussed race. I continue to strongly disagree with the often-repeated argument that Reinhold Niebuhr greatly impacted King. Niebuhr was so conservative about race that he refused to support the Montgomery Bus Boycott.

Q: You also write about King's interpretation of the Bible.

A: Yes. King's decision to write his dissertation on theology spurs many to write about his relationship to theology rather than his interpretation of the Bible. But he was obviously exposed to the

Bible while growing up in his parents' church, and he took quite a few courses in the Bible. And he routinely interprets the Bible in his sermons and speeches. During his years in seminary, his professors taught him to study biblical texts in a quasi-scientific fashion—an approach that grew out of the Enlightenment. Attempting to strip the Bible of its mythology and folklore, the professors explained that it was ancient literature and that Moses was a fictional character, not a historical figure. They assumed that only experts in ancient Middle Eastern languages and archeology knew enough to probe the Bible intelligently. In his own seminary papers, King imitated them by explicating the Bible in a quasi-scientific manner. But, throughout the civil rights movement, he explained the Bible quite differently. Failing to treat the Pentateuch as an ancient document, he instead interpreted the Exodus as an ongoing drama that kept spiraling through history. Gandhi, he maintained, acted as another Moses and the Supreme Court, in its *Brown* decision, also served as a Moses. The civil rights movement, he claimed, served as a later chapter in the Exodus. Not only were ordinary African Americans qualified to interpret the Bible, he asserted, they were living inside a biblical drama that they needed to comprehend in order to grasp their own lives. This entire form of interpretation sprang from African American folk religion, beginning with slavery, when slaves sometimes identified Harriet Tubman or Abraham Lincoln as a new Moses and Southern plantation owners as Pharaohs.

Q: After completing *Voice of Deliverance*, you linked King to the political oratory of Frederick Douglass and others.

A: Yes; in an article co-authored with Elizabeth Vander Lei and another article co-authored with Emily Lewis, the three of us argue that "I Have a Dream" is a classic example of an African American jeremiad developed and reiterated by generations of black orators, dating back at least to Frederick Douglass's "What to the Slave Is the Fourth of July?" in 1852. In a recent article, I identify orators who argued for racial equality by citing Acts 17:26 ("God hath made of one blood all nations of men to dwell on all the face of the earth") as early as the seventeenth century in England. Many later abolitionists in both Britain and the U.S. —including such prominent figures as Douglass, John Woolman, and Wendell Phillips—cited the same scripture for the same purpose. Treating this biblical passage like a baton, they handed it down until it eventually reached Mays, Vernon Johns, King, and Fannie Lou Hamer—all of whom proffered it as a biblical repudiation of white supremacy. Over literally three hundred years, racial progressives strengthened their arguments by brandishing this line from *Acts*—an astonishing strand of rhetorical continuity. But the recalcitrance of white supremacy over so many centuries is utterly heartbreaking and tragic beyond words.

Q: How do you see the current state of research about the civil rights era?

A: During the last twenty years or so, Elizabeth Jacoway, Raymond Arsenault, Charles Eagles, Charles Payne, and other scholars have decentered the movement away from King, focusing on civil rights episodes in which his involvement was either peripheral or nonexistent: the Little Rock Nine, the Freedom Rides, Ole Miss, and Delta protests. David Holmes examines civil rights orators in Birmingham. Barbara Ransby, Maegan Parker Brooks, Cynthia Fleming, and others contributed outstanding biographies of important figures, many of whom were women, and all of whom have been overshadowed by King in popular memory. During the 1950s and 1960s, the almost entirely male reporters bird-dogged Medgar Evers, Malcolm X, and (especially) King, while ignoring female leaders on the mistaken assumption that they did not exist. Historians have worked assiduously and commendably to remedy these omissions and widen the lens for viewing the movement. Fortunately, in 2011, Davis Houck and Brooks assembled a sterling collection of speeches by the indomitable Fannie Lou Hamer. Curiously, during recent decades, the popular memory of the movement, I think, has shrunk more and more to King, King, King. For example, when President Obama spoke of the freedom struggle of the 1950s and 1960s, he almost always celebrated King and usually "I Have a Dream" or Selma. The nation needs to ponder many other torchbearers, including Hamer, Pauli Murray, JoAnn Robinson, Ella Baker, Fred Shuttlesworth, Daisy Bates, Diane Nash, and on and on. Fortunately, Rosalind Rosenberg recently published the first biography of Murray, a pioneer with jaw-dropping accomplishments.

Q: Along with Gary Dorrien, is anyone else writing anything interesting about King?

A: Patrick Parr recently reconstructed King's seminary education far better than anyone else, interviewing his now-octogenarian former classmates. Fortunately, he also located King's white sweetheart, whom no one else had been able to find, and, soon before her death, coaxed her to talk about her youthful romance with King. Marc Perrusquia generated an excellent new book on FBI spying in Memphis during the 1960s. In addition, I value W. Jason Miller's nuanced treatment of Langston Hughes's impact on King—an analysis that appeared in 2015. Nassir Ghaemi is working on a book about King that seems promising, though it may give some people heartburn. I am also working with Holly Fulton, Colleen Wilkowski, and Anjanette Griego on an essay about "Letter from Birmingham Jail" that might create controversy. A number of other recent books about King amount to the same old same old.

Q: What else needs to be done?

A: I predict that historians will dramatically reconfigure our understanding of Malcolm X. When his widow, Betty Shabazz, died during the 1990s, she had kept literally hundreds of pages of his handwritten and self-typed letters, speeches, diaries, and radio sermons in her home, without letting anyone outside her family see them. Through a bizarre and circuitous route, in 2002, they wound up at the Schomburg Center in Harlem, the best repository of African American documents. Schomburg archivists processed these manuscripts in 2004, and anyone who travels to the Schomburg can now read them on microfilm machines. With the exception of the diaries, the documents have never been published or digitized. Literally all researchers writing about Malcolm X before 2004 were handicapped because they had no chance to scrutinize these materials. Other extremely important primary documents about Malcolm X are housed at the Library of Congress, the University of Tennessee, Columbia University, New York University, and elsewhere. No one has written extensively about the columns he wrote for major African American newspapers in New York City and Los Angeles, or about his eighty radio sermons, or about his long trips to the Middle East and Africa in 1964.

Instead of scrutinizing the whole body of his addresses delivered both inside and outside mosques, people have long philosophized about a small number of his public speeches, some of which are badly edited. This tendency has led to skewed conclusions. Robert Terrill is the only scholar who has grappled with the black radical's apocalypticism. I am now researching a book about *The Autobiography of Malcolm X*, which editors changed dramatically in ways that have not been understood. People view his break with the Nation of Islam in 1963 as a drastic switch, and in some ways it was. But I see surprising threads of continuity in the speeches and interviews that he gave before and after he split from the Nation of Islam. Beginning in the 1950s, he chafed against the strictures of Elijah Muhammad by advocating international struggle—a cause that he continued to advance throughout his foreign sojourns in 1964 and in his final interviews.

Q: Anything else?

A: In addition, someone needs to write a detailed and trenchant biography of Alex Haley, a collaborator on *The Autobiography of Malcolm X* and author of the stupendously popular and hugely influential *Roots*. That would not prove an easy project because Haley frequently moved from one city to another and often traveled on freighters across oceans and on planes across continents. Even his wives and best friends sometimes didn't know where his wanderlust had carried him. Late in his life he often ventured to Seattle, where he died, but no one knows why he went there. It wouldn't be easy to track all his whereabouts or the reasons for his peripatetic life. He managed to charm almost everyone, yet not too many people knew him well.

Further, more people need to join Patricia Roberts-Miller in studying white supremacist rhetoric and demagogic language in order to comprehend why that utterly deplorable discourse persuades certain people, century after century. Kenneth Ladenburg has written an excellent dissertation on recent racist rhetoric, and I expect him to turn his dissertation into an incisive book.

Q: What further work should be done on King himself?

A: Coretta Scott King taped her husband's sermons in Montgomery but waited decades before revealing the existence of the tapes. Finally, she told Clayborne Carson and others at the Martin Luther King, Jr., Papers Project at Stanford about these sermons, and the project published them in their Volume VI. King took roughly ten or twelve of his favorite homilies on the road and preached variations of them on many occasions throughout most or all his career. Some of the taped sermons, however, are ones he decided not to recycle. Jonathan Rieder explores a few of them. But, as far as I can tell, some of these one-time-only—or at least rarely preached—sermons have *never* been discussed in print by literally anyone. Just as each of Shakespeare's poems and each of Lincoln's speeches is important, so is each of King's sermons. Who can doubt that? In addition to examining what they are like, it would be useful to wrestle with why he discarded some homilies and replayed others. Scholars should inquire about the subjects, themes, and tropes that he offered, then rejected. Researchers should ask: Why did he keep hammering the same ten or twelve homilies when he had others available that he chose not to pull from his files?

Q: Do you think your work has larger implications for English studies?

A: My tastes are eclectic: I have long appreciated Shakespeare, Tolstoy, Jane Austen, Pablo Neruda, William Carlos Williams, George Orwell, Maya Angelou, Ernest Gaines, Octavia Butler, Rachel Carson, Jim Corder, L. M. Montgomery, Daphne du Maurier, Elie Wiesel, Tony Hillerman, Amy Tan, Sandra Cisneros, Alberto Rios, and Simon Ortiz. Although wildly diverse, these authors all seek to reach large, public audiences. I like Isaac Bashevis Singer—and enjoyed driving him around—partly because I value his ability to engage a large readership, not simply a coterie of self-selected intellectuals. I hope that, one day, professors of English will more fully grasp that speaking or writing intelligently for masses of people usually means creating extraordinarily sophisticated feats of language under a mask of simplicity. Lincoln and Langston Hughes are perfect examples of rhetoricians who do that. So are King, Murray, Hamer, and Malcolm X. Not only are such figures worthy of study but I submit that elitist writers might do well to emulate them.

Works Cited or Consulted

Arsenault, Raymond. *Freedom Riders: 1961 and the Struggle for Racial Justice*. Oxford UP, 2011.

Books, Maegan Parker. *A Voice That Could Stir an Army: Fannie Lou Hamer and the Rhetoric of the Black Freedom Movement*. UP of Mississippi, 2014.

_____, and Davis W. Houck. *The Speeches of Fannie Lou Hamer: To Tell It Like It Is*. UP of Mississippi, 2011.

Buttrick, George Arthur. *The Parables of Jesus*. Harper, 1928.

Carey, Archibald. "Address to the Republican National Convention, 1952," in *The Rhetoric of Racial Revolt*. Edited by Roy Hill, Golden Bell, 1964, pp. 149-54.

Dorrien, Gary. *Breaking White Supremacy: Martin Luther King and the Black Social Gospel*. Yale UP, 2019.

Douglass, Frederick. "What to the Slave Is the Fourth of July?" TeachingAmericanHistory.org. teachingamericanhistory.org/library/document/what-to-the-slave-is-the-fourth-of-july. Accessed 6 Oct. 2018.

Eagles, Charles W. *The Price of Defiance: James Meredith and the Integration of Ole Miss*. U of North Carolina P, 2009.

Fleming, Cynthia Griggs. *Soon We Will Not Cry: The Liberation of Ruby Doris Smith Robinson*. Rowman and Littlefield, 1998.

Haley, Alex. *Roots: The Saga of an American Family*. 1974. Da Capo, 2007.

Holmes, David G. *Where the Sacred and Secular Harmonize: Birmingham Mass Meeting Rhetoric and the Prophetic Legacy of the Civil Rights Movement*. Wipf and Stock, 2017.

Jacoway, Elizabeth. *Turn Away Thy Son: Little Rock, the Crisis That Shocked the Nation*. Simon & Schuster, 2007.

King, Martin Luther, Jr. "I See the Promised Land." In Washington, pp. 279-86.

_____. *The Papers of Martin Luther King, Jr., Volume VI: Advocate of the Social Gospel, September 1948 March 1963*. Edited by Clayborne Carson et al, U of California P, 1992.

Miller, Keith D. "All Nations, One Blood, Three Hundred Years: Martin Luther King, Jr., Fannie Lou Hamer, and Civil Rights Rhetoric as TransatlanticAbolitionism." *Rhetoric across Borders*. Edited by Anne Demo, Parlor, 2015, pp. 71-82.

_____. *Martin Luther King's Biblical Epic: His Great, Final Speech*. U of Mississippi P, 2013.

_____. *Voice of Deliverance: The Language of Martin Luther King, Jr. and Its Sources*. Free, 1992.

_____, and Emily Lewis. "Touchstones, Authorities, and Marian Anderson: The Making of 'I Have a Dream.'" In *The Making of Martin Luther King and the Civil Rights Movement*. Edited by Brian Ward and Tony Badger, Macmillan, 1996, pp. 147-61.

Miller, W. Jason. *Origins of the Dream: Hughes's Poetry and King's Rhetoric*. UP of Florida, 2016.

Parr, Patrick. *Seminarian: Martin Luther King Jr. Comes of Age*. Chicago Review, 2018.

Payne, Charles. *I've Got the Light of Freedom: The Organizing Tradition and the Mississippi Freedom Struggle*. U of California P, 2007.

Perrusquia, Marc. *A Spy in Canaan*. Melville House, 2018.

Ransby, Barbara. *Ella Baker and the Black Freedom Movement: A Radical Democratic Vision*. U of North Carolina P, 2003.

Rieder, Jonathan. *The Word of the Lord Is Upon Me: The Righteous Performance of Martin Luther King, Jr*. Harvard UP, 2009.

Roberts-Miller, Patricia. *Fanatical Schemes: Proslavery Rhetoric and the Tragedy of Consensus*. U of Alabama P, 2010.

Rosenberg, Rosalind. *Jane Crow: The Life of Pauli Murray*. Oxford UP, 2017.

Terrill, Robert E. *Malcolm X: Inventing Radical Judgment*. Michigan State UP, 2007.

Vander Lei, Elizabeth, and Keith D. Miller, "Martin Luther King, Jr.'s 'I Have a Dream' in Context: Ceremonial Protest and African American Jeremiad," *College English*, vol. 62, 1999, pp. 83-89.

Washington, James M., editor. *A Testament of Hope: The Essential Writings and Speeches of Martin Luther King, Jr.* 1986. HarperOne, 1991.

X, Malcolm. *The Autobiography of Malcolm X*. Random House, 2015.

Biography of Martin Luther King Jr.

Simran Kumari

Martin Luther King Jr. was born around noon on January 15, 1929, in Atlanta, Georgia. Originally his name, like that of his father, was Michael King, but in 1934 the father changed both his own name and that of his firstborn son to Martin Luther King. (A daughter, Willie Christine, had been born in 1927.) Explanations of this change differ: some claim the alteration of the boy's name was made to correct an error on his birth certificate, but the most obvious reason for both changes was the elder King's desire to honor the memory of the great German theologian Martin Luther, the sixteenth-century founder of Protestantism who broke decisively with the Catholic church. Young Martin's father was "a prominent local [Baptist] preacher and civil-rights leader," and his mother, Alberta, was "a former schoolteacher" (Lee). According to one account, his childhood was "comfortable" and he excelled "in school, skipping the ninth and twelfth grades," but he had first become "conscious of racism at age 6, when a white friend's father prohibit[ed] his son from playing with Martin" (Lee).

In 1943, King entered Booker T. Washington High School. However, because he was accepted early to Atlanta's Morehouse College under a program for advanced placement, he did not complete his high school graduation. Instead, in 1944, at fifteen, he enrolled as a freshman at Morehouse. Four years later, in February 1948, he was appointed an assistant pastor at his father's church, Ebenezer Baptist, in Atlanta. In June of that year, at the age of nineteen, King completed his undergraduate studies at Morehouse with a bachelor of arts degree in sociology. He then began working toward a bachelor of divinity degree at Crozer Theological Seminary in Pennsylvania, from which he graduated in May 1951. Next, in September of that year, he began graduate studies in systematic theology at Boston University's School of Theology.

In January 1952, King met Coretta Scott, younger daughter of Obadiah and Bernice McMurray Scott, in Boston ("Martin"). Coretta was an aspiring singer and activist from Alabama who studied at the New England Conservatory of Music (Lee). After one year of dating, King and Coretta got married in June 1953 at her parents' home near Marion, Alabama ("Martin"). King's father conducted their wedding ceremonies ("Timeline: The Life"). In that same month, the first massive African American boycott of segregated public buses began in Baton Rouge, Louisiana, an action that eventually inspired the far more famous Montgomery bus boycott in 1955-1956 ("Martin"). King, of course, would lead that later boycott, which propelled him to national and international fame.

It was in September of 1954, however, that King began his pastorate at Dexter Avenue Baptist Church in Montgomery, the capital city of Alabama ("Timeline: The Life"). For a while, his leadership there was relatively uneventful. But following the arrest on December 1, 1955, of a black woman named Rosa Parks for refusing to give up her bus seat to a white man, the former head of Alabama's NAACP called King and asked him to join the Montgomery bus boycott, which he would soon be asked to lead. King, in fact, was highly regarded among local blacks because of his "leadership ability" and "wonderful speaking voice" (Lee). On December 5, 1955, therefore, he became the official spokesperson for the boycott, after having been appointed president of the Montgomery Improvement Association ("Timeline").

In the late evening of January 27, 1956, King received a threatening phone call ("Martin"). This led him to a spiritual revelation that helped give him the strength to continue his fight despite any hurdles and persecution ("Martin"). Three days later, at 9:15 P.M., his home was bombed while he was away giving a speech at a mass meeting. Fortunately, his wife and daughter suffered no injuries. Outside his damaged home that evening, he addressed an outraged crowd, appealing for nonviolence ("Martin"). Finally, on November 13, 1956, the U.S. Supreme Court struck down the segregation laws the public bus system had been following, thus ensuring an important victory for the boycott and for the larger cause of civil rights ("Timeline"). By December of that same year, Montgomery buses offered full, nondiscriminatory service on all routes. In fact, King was one of the first black passengers to occupy seats previously reserved for whites ("Martin"). In January 1957, notable Southern ministers prominent in the civil rights movement met in Atlanta to share strategies in their battle against segregation. They met with the chairman of the Southern Negro Leaders Conference on Transportation and Nonviolent Integration, which later became known as the Southern Christian Leadership Conference (SCLC) ("Martin"). Soon, King was elected that organization's president (Lee).

In February 1957, King's growing fame was acknowledged by *Time* magazine, which put a photo of him on its cover. He was now, obviously, a man of national importance. In the following month, he visited Ghana in West Africa to attend celebrations of the formation of a new nation, headed by Prime Minister Kwame Nkrumah ("Major King Events"). In May, he delivered "Give Us the Ballot," his first national address, at the Prayer Pilgrimage for Freedom, which was held at the Lincoln Memorial in Washington, D.C. ("Timeline: The Life"). King and Ralph D. Abernathy met with Vice President Richard M. Nixon the following month and issued a statement about their meeting ("Major King Events"). In September 1957, the U.S. Congress passed the Civil Rights Act ("Martin").

In June 1958, King, along with Roy Wilkins, A. Philip Randolph, and Lester Grange, met with President Dwight D. Eisenhower to discuss civil rights. In September of that year, King's first book, *Stride toward Freedom: The Montgomery Story*, was published ("Major King Events"). On September 20, during a book signing at Blumstein's Department Store in Harlem, King was brutally stabbed with a letter opener by a mentally ill black woman named Izola Ware Curry ("Major King Events"; "Timeline: The Life"). He was rushed to a nearby hospital, where a team of doctors removed the seven-inch blade from his chest ("Major King Events"). His doctors told him that if he had coughed or sneezed while the letter opener was stuck into his side, he could easily have died.

In February 1959, at the invitation of Indian Prime Minister Jawaharlal Nehru, King and his wife, Coretta, embarked on a monthlong visit to India. There, he met many Indian social reformers, government officials, and associates of the late Mahatma Gandhi, whose philosophy of nonviolence deeply inspired King's own approach to defeating racial discrimination (Lee). After this visit, King wrote, "I left India more convinced than ever before that nonviolent resistance is the most potent weapon available to oppressed people in their struggle for freedom" (Lee; "Timeline"). In the same year, King resigned as pastor of Dexter Avenue Baptist Church to devote more time to his struggle for civil rights ("Timeline").

In February 1960, King moved to Atlanta to direct the activities of the SCLC ("Timeline"). He also became assistant pastor to his father at Ebenezer Baptist Church ("Major King Events"). On October 19, he was arrested during a sit-in demonstration at Rich's department store in Atlanta after deliberately breaking Georgia's trespassing law ("Major King Events"; "Martin"). He was also sentenced to four months of hard labor "for violating a suspended sentence he had received in a 1956 traffic violation." A week later, however, he was released on $2,000 bond ("Major King Events").

On May 4, 1961, an integrated group of freedom riders left Washington, D.C., on Greyhound buses. Upon arriving in Alabama, the riders were beaten and one bus was burned ("Martin".) King, to honor the riders, soon addressed "a mass rally at a mob-besieged Montgomery Church" ("Major King Events"). Later that year, on October 16, King met with President John F. Kennedy to gain his support for the civil rights movement and to urge him to "issue a second Emancipation Proclamation to eliminate racial segregation" ("Major King Events"; "Martin"). During the following month, the Interstate Commerce Commission banned segregation in interstate travel thanks, in part, to the work of King and the freedom riders ("Timeline"). On December 16, King, along with Ralph Abernathy, "Albany Movement president William G. Anderson, and other protesters" were arrested by the Albany police chief, Laurie Pritchett, "during a campaign in Georgia" ("Major King Events"). On September 28, 1962, "at the closing session of the SCLC conference in Birmingham, Alabama," King was struck twice in the face by a member of the American Nazi Party ("Major King Events"). Two days later, rioting occurred on the campus at the University of Mississippi ("Martin").

On Good Friday, April 12, 1963, King was arrested along with Abernathy by Birmingham "Police Commissioner Eugene 'Bull' Connor for demonstrating without a permit" ("Timeline"). The so-called Birmingham Campaign began the very next day and later proved to be a "turning point in the war to end segregation in the South" ("Timeline"). During the eleven days he spent in jail, King penned his concerns about civil rights for black Americans in his famous "Letter from Birmingham Jail" ("Timeline"; "Martin"). On May 7, the situation in Birmingham became especially intense when Connor employed high-pressure fire hoses, dogs, clubs, and cattle prods "to disperse four thousand demonstrators in downtown Birmingham" ("Major King Events"; "Martin"). Three days later, the Birmingham Agreement was announced, under which stores, restaurants, and schools were desegregated and the hiring of African Americans began ("Timeline").

During the following month, King led 125,000 people on a freedom walk in Detroit ("Timeline"). On August 28, 1963, at the important March on Washington for Jobs and Freedom, King addressed an estimated of 250,000 people on the National Mall (Lee). His powerful call for racial justice came to be known as the "I Have a Dream" speech, which is seen both as a "rhetorical masterpiece" and as a "defining moment of the civil rights movement" (Lee). The following month, King delivered the eulogy at the funerals of three of the four young girls killed during a September 15 bombing of the 16th Street Baptist Church in Birmingham. The fourth victim was buried in a separate ceremony ("Major King Events"). Later that year, President John F. Kennedy was assassinated in Texas ("Timeline").

On January 3, 1964, King appeared as Man of the Year on the cover of *Time* magazine ("Timeline"). Later that month, President Lyndon B. Johnson met with King, Roy Wilkins, Whitney Young, and James Farmer and sought their support for his fight against poverty ("Major King Events"). During the following month, the leader of the civil rights movement in St. Augustine, Florida, Robert Hayling, invited King and the SCLC to join the struggle there ("Major King Events"). On March 26, King met Malcolm X, a leader of the Black Muslim movement (and another prominent advocate for black rights) in the nation's capital "for the first and only time" ("Major King Events"). During that summer, King experienced "his first hurtful rejection by black people" when he was "stoned by Black Muslims in Harlem" ("Timeline"). In June, King and seventeen others were arrested for trespassing after they demanded service at a whites-only restaurant in St. Augustine, Florida ("Timeline: The Life"). The following month, King was invited to the White House while President Johnson signed the Public Accommodation and Fair Employment sections to the Civil Rights Act of 1964 ("Martin").

On July 20, a people-to-people tour of Mississippi was launched by King and SCLC staff to assist the Student Nonviolent Coordinating Committee (SNCC) and the Congress of Racial Equality (CORE) in the Freedom Summer Campaign ("Major King Events"). In November, J. Edgar Hoover, director of the FBI, denounced King as "the most notorious liar in the country" after he criticized the agency's failure to protect civil right workers ("Major King Events"). A week later, Hoover claimed that the SCLC was "spearheaded by Communists and moral degenerates" ("Major King Events"). On December 10, 1964, King received the Nobel Peace Prize at the age of 35, making him the youngest recipient of the prestigious award so far (Lee). He declared his intention to use the $54,000 award to advance the ongoing civil rights struggle ("Major King Events").

In March 1965, the SCLC and other civil rights groups demanded voting rights for blacks during "a 54-mile march from Selma, Alabama, to the state capital of Montgomery" in response to the "continued disenfranchisement of millions of black people across the South" (Lee). After the marchers were attacked and beaten by the police at the Edmund Pettus Bridge in Selma, King, James Forman, and John Lewis peacefully led another group of marchers from Selma to Montgomery ("Major King Events"; "Timeline: The Life"). On August 6, President Johnson signed the 1965 Voting Rights Act ("Martin"). After this act became law, King began to shift more of his attention to the socioeconomic problems blacks faced ("Timeline").

In January 1966, King and his wife moved into a Chicago slum tenement to attract people's attention to the living conditions of the poor ("Timeline"). During the following month, he met Elijah Muhammad, leader of the Nation of Islam, in Chicago ("Major King Events"). In June, after the civil rights activist James Meredith was shot and wounded near Memphis, King, Floyd McKissick of CORE and Stokely Carmichael of SNCC resumed Meredith's "March Against Fear" from Memphis to Jackson ("Major King Events"). King initiated a new campaign the following month to prohibit discrimination in housing, employment, and schools in Chicago ("Timeline"). On April 4, 1967, King delivered a speech entitled "Beyond Vietnam" at Riverside Church in Manhattan, in which he openly expressed his opposition to the Vietnam War (Lee). Although he had "publicly criticized the war two months earlier, in a speech at the Nation Institute," his "widely publicized Riverside Church speech" disturbed many supporters. They blamed him for hurting the cause of civil rights by alienating President Johnson and conservative members of the public (Lee). But King, undeterred, expanded his call for social justice at home into a "much broader, pacifist message" (Lee).

King urged an end to riots in the summer of 1967 that resulted in forty-three deaths. On November 27, he announced the commencement of a Poor People's Campaign to focus on providing freedom and sources of employment to the poor of all races ("Timeline"). In early December, he unveiled plans to lead a march on Washington, D.C., to demand a $12 billion economic bill of rights ("Timeline"). By undertaking this march, he aimed to guarantee employment for the able-bodied, income for those who could not work, and a complete halt to housing discrimination ("Timeline"). This step was intended to expand civil rights activities into the area of economic rights ("Timeline: The Life"). On March 28, 1968, King led a march of six thousand protesters to support striking sanitation workers in Memphis, Tennessee ("Major King Events"). The march gradually descended into violence and looting, and King had to be rushed from the scene ("Major King Events"). This was the first time ever that one of King's events had turned violent ("Timeline"). Six days later, King returned to Memphis, determined to lead a peaceful march ("Major King Events"). During an evening rally at Memphis's Mason Temple (the national headquarters of the Church of God in Christ), he delivered what would be his last speech: "I See the Promised Land" ("Martin"; "Major King Events").

The very next day, on April 4, 1968, King was shot as he stood on a balcony at the Lorraine Motel; he was declared dead within an hour. The murderer, James Earl Ray, fled the country and was arrested two months later at Heathrow Airport in London (Lee). Ray was sentenced to ninety-nine years in prison but died of liver failure in 1998 ("Martin"). Although Ray was known to be a racist, his exact motives for killing King were never made clear (Lee). King's assassination sparked riots in more than a hundred cities in the United States (Lee). His mourners viewed his body on the campus of Spelman College in Atlanta. On April 9, his funeral was held at the Ebenezer Baptist Church, Atlanta. More than 300,000 people marched through the city with his mule-drawn coffin, and King was buried in South Cemetery in Atlanta, Georgia. In 1977, King was posthumously awarded the Presidential Medal of Freedom by President Jimmy Carter ("Martin"). On November 2, 1983, President Ronald Reagan signed legislation to commemorate King's birthday with a federal holiday every third Monday in January. In 1986, Martin Luther King Jr. Day was celebrated nationwide, and in 2004, King was posthumously honored with a Congressional Gold Medal ("Martin").

Works Cited or Consulted

Lee, Eli. "Martin Luther King Jr. Changed a Nation in Only 13 Years: A Timeline." www.theatlantic.com/magazine/archive/2018/02/martin-luther-king-jr-timeline/552548/. Accessed 22 Oct. 2018.

"Major King Events Chronology 1929-1968." The Martin Luther King Jr. Research and Education Institute, Stanford University. kinginstitute.stanford.edu/king-resources/major-king-events-chronology-1929-1968. Accessed 22 Oct. 2018.

"Martin Luther King Timeline." Dates and events.org. www.datesandevents.org/people-timelines/28-martin-luther-king-timeline.htm. Accessed 22 Oct. 2018.

"Timeline of Martin Luther King, Jr.'s Life." Louisiana State University Libraries.guides.lib.lsu.edu/c.php?g=353667&p=2385247. Accessed 22 Oct. 2018.

"Timeline: The Life of Martin Luther King, Jr." *USA Today*. www.usatoday.com/story/news/nation-now/2018/02/02/martin-luther-king-jr-timeline/1061525001/. Accessed 22 Oct. 2018.

CRITICAL CONTEXTS

Marching, Singing, and Road Imagery in Martin Luther King's Involvement in the Civil Rights Movement

Raymond Blanton

In the twentieth century, millions of African Americans were actively moving, geographically and substantively, along the Upward Way, migrating from the South to the North and looking for better opportunities and living conditions (see Gregory). Such movement allows us to situate the mythic archetype of the road as a rhetorical encounter with the other in the American civil rights movement. As blacks migrated to Northern cities, not only were they met with limited opportunities for employment, but the ones they did have were reduced; in Detroit, for instance, they were consigned to the foundry, the dirtiest place at the Ford Motor Company. After Pearl Harbor, when assembly lines were finally integrated, racial tensions continued to swell, resulting in the Detroit race riots of 1943, which were eerily similar to the Tulsa race riots of 1921.

Nevertheless, many African Americans pressed their struggle for freedom by serving in the war. In fact, blacks had fought on the front lines since the Civil War, but to no avail. One visceral example of the hardships of travel in midcentury America comes in the story of Army Sergeant Isaac Woodard, who in February 1946 asked if he could use the bathroom on a bus but was denied. At the next stop, two officers beat Woodard and blinded him, driving the end of their nightsticks into his eyes. At age twenty-seven, having returned from service to his country, he was blind for the rest of his life. In his political radio broadcast, the actor and director Orson Welles asked, "What does it cost to be a Negro? In Macon, South Carolina, it cost a man his eyes. Officer X: All America is ashamed of you. If there is room for pity you can have it for you are far more blind than he" (see Bertelsen). Many African Americans, despite all of the progress they had witnessed in the twentieth century, from fame on the stage and screen to success on the baseball diamond, still could not sit at the front of a bus or eat at a lunch counter (see Bertelsen).

In January of 1954, a young Martin Luther King visited Montgomery, Alabama, to preach for Dexter Avenue Baptist Church, which was without a pastor. In his Sunday morning sermon, titled "The Three Dimensions of a Complete Life," King (in a version of the sermon published in 1960) instructs the Dexter congregants about the Jericho Road—a vision he would return to repeatedly throughout his public life.

The Road Metaphor and the Act of Marching

As everyone knows, some of the most important features of the civil rights movement involved the literal movement of marching. Various marches are worth exploring, but here I will focus on only two: the ones involving Montgomery and Birmingham, both in Alabama. The events leading up to the Montgomery march are worth outlining. A few months after King arrived in Montgomery, after accepting the call to become Dexter Avenue Baptist Church's pastor, a fifteen-year-old high school girl named Claudette Colvin was pulled off a bus, handcuffed, and jailed for refusing to give up her seat for a white passenger (King, *Stride* 41). Months later, Mary Louise Smith, eighteen years old, was subjected to similar abuse. Continually troubled by such mistreatment, the African American community began talk of boycotting the buses in protest. In response, a citizens committee, on which King served, was formed to discuss possible action. Such action became even more probable on December 1, 1955, when Rosa Parks, a forty-two-year old seamstress, weary from a day's work, boarded the Cleveland Avenue Bus in downtown Montgomery and sat in the front row of the "colored" section. As the bus moved along Montgomery Street, white passengers began filling its front rows. As was customary, when the bus became full, blacks were expected to give up their seats for white passengers. "Are you going to stand up?" the driver (J. F. Blake) demanded. "No," Park replied. Flustered, he responded, "Well, I'm going to have you arrested." "You may do that," Parks softly replied (qtd. in Brinkley 166). The driver instructed Parks and other black passengers to move to the back so the white passengers could sit down. Three blacks got up and went to the back. Rosa Parks did not. The driver got off the bus, walked to a pay telephone, and called police for help. Parks was arrested. Her arrest, though now considered a key moment in the history of the struggle for civil rights, was then just a four-paragraph story on the bottom of page 9A of a Montgomery newspaper. Four days later, Parks was convicted and fined in a Montgomery city court. In response, a one-day boycott of the city buses was staged. The Montgomery Improvement Association (MIA) was formed and King was elected its leader. After some deliberation, it was decided that the MIA should hold a citywide mass meeting on Monday, December 5, at Holt Street Baptist Church to express their support of the bus boycott. A leaflet succinctly stated the purpose of the meeting and the protest:

> Don't ride the bus to work, to town, to school, or any place Monday, December 5. Another Negro woman has been arrested and put in jail because she refused to give up her bus seat.
> Don't ride the buses to work, to town, to school, or anywhere on Monday. If you work, take a cab, or share a ride, or walk.
> Come to a mass meeting, Monday at 7:00 P.M., at the Holt Street Baptist Church for further instructions. (qtd. in King, *Stride* 48)

Throughout December, the MIA and black citizens of Montgomery negotiated with the city on a proposal for a more reasonable seating policy. On December 13, the MIA began to operate a car pool, using station wagons and the like to transport black citizens to work. Negotiations with the city continued into January but came to a halt when Mayor W. A. Gayle ended them. Several days later, King was charged with speeding and was jailed by Montgomery police. Later the next week, his house was bombed while his wife and infant daughter were inside, though they were unharmed. On February 10, 1956, the White Citizens Council rallied in Montgomery to express its support of city officials' opposition to bus desegregation. For three hundred and eighty-one days, the black citizens of Montgomery stood their ground, walking to work or using other means of transportation.

More than a year after the first protest, on December 21, 1956, the Montgomery buses were desegregated after a thirteen-month boycott and legal action brought by civil rights lawyers. Of course, though official policies might have changed, many personal attitudes had not. For example, on Christmas Eve, five white men attacked a fifteen-year-old girl at a Montgomery bus stop. In the ensuing days, Rosa Jordan, a black woman riding a Montgomery bus, was shot in both legs; a sniper fired into a city bus just a week later; and various churches and homes were bombed or subjected to attempted bombings (for instance, a bundle of dynamite left on King's porch failed to explode).

It is important to remember that the bus boycott was a local effort. The movement King led was part of the larger opposition to a much more extensive and troubling history of segregated travel in America. The Montgomery bus boycott helped prepare the way for the modern civil rights campaign, but it did not eliminate the difficulties of bridging long-standing divisions and struggles between blacks and whites. By the 1960s, local buses had been desegregated in forty-seven Southern cities, but more than half of the region's local bus lines remained legally segregated. In the Deep South, Jim Crow transit still prevailed. In early 1957, King and others predicted that the Montgomery experience would serve as a catalyst for a regionwide movement of nonviolent direct action (Arsenault 46-47). Strategically, in the 1960s, civil rights leaders were even able to use the Cold War to their advantage by warning of the "international vulnerability of a nation that failed to practice what it preached on matters of race and democracy" (Arsenault 43).

Birmingham

In the years that followed the Montgomery bus boycott, King's public persona and his role as the movement's central voice became more distinct. In many of his early speeches and sermons, he used road imagery as one means of explaining the nature of the struggle. Addressing the annual Institute on Nonviolence and Social Change in Montgomery, King noted, "The road from the Egypt of slavery to the Canaan of freedom is an often lonely and meandering road surrounded by prodigious hilltops of opposition and gigantic mountains of evil" (King, "Address at the Fourth" 338). In an address delivered on September 23, 1959, King further accentuated this idea when he noted that "the flight from the Egypt of slavery to the glorious promised land is always temporarily interrupted by a bleak and desolate wilderness with its prodigious mountains of opposition and gigantic hilltops of evil" ("Address at Public" 281). "Keep moving," King urged students at Spelman College in Atlanta on April 10, 1960: "Move out of these mountains that impede our progress . . . we must keep moving" ("Keep Moving" 418-19). Images of roads and movement were key to King's understanding and explanations of the progress needed in civil rights.

Building on the momentum of the Montgomery bus boycott, protestors staged sit-ins in Greensboro, North Carolina, and freedom rides in 1961. And in April and May of 1963, the Birmingham marches became the "climactic moment in the history of the civil rights movement" (Selby 137). The marches challenged the city's economic interests and its political leadership, provoking Birmingham's racist commissioner of public safety, Theophilus Eugene "Bull" Connor. In turn, his vicious treatment of the marchers aroused the moral outrage of the nation as people watched Connor's police force use water cannons and dogs on nonviolent protestors. Once again, King turned to road imagery, particularly by relating the modern civil rights movement to the biblical exodus. He equated the marchers' experiences of opposition with the wilderness experience of the ancient Israelites: "You don't get to the Promised Land without going through the wilderness" (King, "Address to MIA" 200). Selby also positions the significance of Birmingham around the theme of the journey, built around a collection of words such as *climbing, walking, rolling, moving,* and *going* (Selby 137).

Progressively, the term *march* came to define the movement. The first official march had occurred on Saturday, April 6, and had included around thirty volunteers, all of whom were arrested. On April 7, leaders led a second march to the downtown section, where Connor's police dogs met them, resulting in a violent confrontation that received substantial television coverage and national attention.

One of the truly defining marches of the campaign occurred on May 2, 1963, when hundreds of children, some young enough to attend elementary school, joined the marches, resulting in the arrest of more than a thousand people. The overcrowding in the jails forced Connor to desperate measures, such as using water cannons and more police dogs to turn back protestors. Selby succinctly, and aptly, describes the fortitude of the people by saying, "All told, the protestors managed to stage a march every day from the beginning of the campaign until the city leaders finally capitulated to their demands just over one month later" (142). More importantly, for Selby, the Birmingham campaign represented the defining moment in the movement's *rhetorical* history (138). Similarly, I argue that the march, the road, was the most defining rhetorical feature of the movement.

Let Freedom Ring

In addition to the marches, the soul of the movement might also be located in the freedom songs. Here I hope to illustrate how the themes of movement and the road were prominent rhetorical features of the freedom songs in a manner similar to the imagery found in old Negro spirituals. In the spirituals, which were powerful mythic tools for the slaves and which were deeply connected to themes of bondage and deliverance, the theme of movement became ubiquitous:

> When slaves sang of movement, tentative or bold, they sang of moving away from the place of their slavery. The essential message was one of determination and inevitability. They sang, "I can't stay behind," asked "who will rise and go with me," warned "no man can hinder me," [and] promised "I ain't got long to stay here," and "I don't expect to stay much longer here." The message was "I'm bound to go." Slaves proclaimed themselves willing, according to their songs, to travel under difficult conditions. (qtd. in Selby 37)

Like the spirituals, the freedom songs became a form of rhetorical resistance, the songs functioning both as individual poetic and ritual expressions of mythic meaning and at the same time as communal expressions of collective identity. The marches and the freedom songs were synecdoche: figures of speech that use a part to represent the whole (e.g., *hired hands* to denote *workers*) or the whole for the part (e.g., "the world has mistreated me"). They were more than metaphoric or casual rituals of passing time. Similar to the mythic nature of the blues, the freedom songs were social tools, myths around which the people cohered and acted, with the road serving as an especially revolutionary symbol. King, in an interview, attributed part of the success of the movement to its music:

> In a sense the freedom songs are the *soul* of the movement. Consider, in World War II, *Praise the Lord and Pass the Ammunition,* and in World War I, *Over There* and *Tipperary,* and during the Civil War, *Battle Hymn of the Republic* and *John Brown's Body.* A Negro song anthology would include sorrow songs, shouts for joy, battle hymns, and anthems. Since slavery, the Negro has sung through his struggle in America. *Steal Away* and *Go Down, Moses* were the songs of faith and inspiration, which were sung on the plantations. For the same reasons the slaves sang, Negroes today sing freedom songs, for we, too, are in bondage. We sing out our determination that "We shall overcome, black and white together, we shall overcome someday." (King, "*Playboy* Interview" 348)

There is a hint of an ultimate order in King's reference to overcoming—a suggestion of a move from the dialectic of white and black toward a state of togetherness. Along the movement's metaphorical route, the freedom songs functioned *psychagogically* to lead the soul toward the good—the Promised Land. In a similar tone but with different words, King further substantiated the importance of song:

> In a sense the freedom songs are the soul of the movement.... I have stood in a meeting with hundreds of youngsters and joined in while they sang, "Ain't Gonna Let Nobody Turn Me Round." It is not just a song; it is a resolve. A few minutes later, I have seen those same youngsters refuse to turn around before a pugnacious Bull Connor in command of men armed with power hoses. These songs bind us together, give us courage together, and help us to march together. (qtd. in Morris 257)

King's language in the final quoted sentence reflects the tone of my own argument. Here, King clearly indicates the mythic role, in the sense (associated with Kenneth Burke) that I have set forth, of the marches and freedom songs. When one recalls Burke's essay "Revolutionary Symbolism in America," King's language gives further credence to the idea of the freedom songs as mythic by linking them to the mythic symbolism of marching. King notes, "They can stop the leaders, but they can't stop the people" (qtd. in Morris 258). To be more specific, I hope to demonstrate here the rhetorical significance of the road in the freedom songs, and therefore to the movement and the marches.

Moving and Singing

> Stand up and rejoice! A great day is here! We're fighting Jim Crow and the victory is near! Hallelujah! I'm-a-travelin', Hallelujah, ain't it fine. Hallelujah! I'm-a-travelin' down freedom's mainline!" (qtd. in Arsenault 61)

During the sit-ins in Greensboro, songs like "Moving On" made it clear that "Old Jim Crow's moving on down the track, he's got his bags and he won't be back" (qtd. in Carawan and Carawan 36). On the freedom rides, songs like "Freedom's Comin' and It Won't Be Long" declared, "On to Mississippi with speed we go, Freedom's comin' and it won't be long" (Carawan and Carawan 41). In Albany, Georgia, protestors sang "Come and Go with Me to That Land" and "Ain't Gonna Let Nobody Turn Me Around." In Birmingham, a turning point for the movement and the nation, they sang "Guide My Feet While I Run This Race," "Hard Travelin'," and "Ballad for Bill Moore," the last of which was based on the same tune used in "You've Got to Walk That Lonesome Valley." The adapted "Ballad" was sung in honor of Moore, a native Mississippian who had been journeying on Highway 11 to present his personal plea for civil rights to Governor Ross Barnett, when he was gunned down. Other freedom road songs included "Traveling Shoes," "Freedom Train A-comin'," and "Murder on the Road in Alabama." In perhaps the most prominent anthem of the civil rights movement, "We

Shall Overcome," the protestors sang, "We'll walk hand in hand" (Carawan and Carawan 8-9).

As Selby argues, the language of the biblical exodus pervaded the movement's music, providing a framework of meaning for the movement's primary modes of collective action, the march:

> Complementing this use of the journey motif to frame events in the protest was the music that played a central role in the campaign's daily mass meetings. The "freedom songs," as they were called, powerfully heightened participants' sense of emotional involvement in the movement's symbolic world of ideas, participation reinforced by the interactive character of traditional African American preaching and worship. (Selby 153)

What each of these songs reveals is not only the central importance of the march and the freedom songs but also, more importantly, how the theme of the road, actual and anagogical, rhetorical and mythical, was its ultimate inspiration. Put differently, and in more theoretical language, just as the Hebrews turned to the "Songs of Ascents" while they moved, quite literally, upward toward Jerusalem (the Upward Way, where their encounter with the divine Other inspired the mythic ideal beyond ideas), so too the people of the civil rights movement turned to freedom songs on their own Upward Way toward the Promised Land.

Making a Way Out of No Way

As I conclude my metaphorical journey through the history of the African American civil rights experience, I turn our attention to other roots of King's civic and sermonic discourse, which will occupy my attention for the remainder of this essay. I conclude this section by focusing on how the road functioned rhetorically in King's civil rights orality, particularly in his speeches and sermons. The themes of the freedom songs typify the themes of the marches, particularly the road motif. Here, I focus on how orality worked in conjunction with song, spirituals, and freedom songs, for instance, and the rhetorical significance of road imagery in and to both.

One challenge we face as rhetorical critics is how we account for oral discourse, a challenge Walter Ong elucidates in *Orality and Literacy*:

> Formulas help implement rhythmic discourse . . . as set expressions circulating through the mouths and ears of all. . . . Fixed, often rhythmically balanced, expressions of this sort and of other sorts can be found occasionally in print, indeed can be "looked up" in books of sayings, but in oral cultures they are not occasional. They are incessant. They form the substance of thought itself. (35)

African American orality, for instance, is often defined by its communal nature in call-and-response exchanges. Robert and Linda Harrison argue that a failure to recognize the importance of call-and-response results in a "failure to account fully for the way in which King's presence as an orator animated his listeners to participate in his message as active performers and thus to become one with the message he presented." They note that in some traditional African American religious services, the

> power of music is enhanced by interaction between group members and the audience. A lead singer provides the calls, while the group members' responses are repetitive and supportive, often reflecting the tone and intensity of the lead singer. The power or impact of the communication is affected by this interchange. (163-65)

The congregants, then, both physically and emotionally, are prepared through song, making the congregation more cohesive. The preacher sets the process in motion and directs its progress, while the congregation provides the energy to sustain the process. This tradition had a significant impact on the style of Martin Luther King Jr. within the tradition of Southern Baptist ministers. He knew the timing and cadences of the call-and-response method, which he learned from his father and other ministers. Coretta Scott King writes that the "feeling [the congregants] had of oneness and unity was complete" (240). They experienced it in their churches. They sang songs together while marching together in the streets.

They used call-and-response in everyday communication. The congregants were creating *with* King. "The [call-and-response] occasion marked a kind of cultural sharing with people from other cultures participating in the experience" (Harrison and Harrison 177). In other words, call-and-response required a give-and-take language that united the rhetor and the audience as one (Mieder 6). In *The Land Where the Blues Began,* Alan Lomax writes:

> During the last two hundred years, . . . black ministers created a highly dramatic order of service and a style of oratory of unmatched eloquence. Its beauty sheltered and consoled its hearers. Their orally composed folk sermons, which far outdo those of Reverend King, likened their oppressed congregations to the children of Israel and to the heroes of the Old Testament, thus thrilling and heartening their listeners, particularly the women. The art of the black sermon flourished especially during revival services. (103)

Call-and-Response, Proverbs, and King's Use of Road Imagery

To illustrate the relationship between call-and-response orality and the songs of the movement, Keith D. Miller argues that King, like other folk preachers, traditionally ended his oral sermons (and almost every major speech) by merging his voice with the lyrics of a spiritual, hymn, or gospel song (121). One of the most persistent themes in these songs is the road. For instance, consider how each of the following speeches concludes by using the underlying imagery of the road. In King's "Our God is Marching On!" and "I See the Promised Land," he quotes from "The Battle Hymn of the Republic," a marching song (see Washington, 230, 286). In King's "If the Negro Wins, Labor Wins," "The American Dream," and "I Have a Dream," he punctuates the address with the spiritual "Free at Last" (see Washington 207, 216, 220). In "Give Us the Ballot—We Will Transform the South," King recites James Weldon Johnson's poem: "Though who has brought us thus far on the way; ... Keep us forever in the path, we pray" (see Washington 200). And in "Where Do We Go From Here?" King ends by alluding to "We Shall Overcome" (see Washington 252).

As Mieder argues, this blending of song and sermon helps give discursive power to King's discourse. When we consider that by 1957 King had delivered more than two hundred speeches and sermons a year, and then delivered even more as the movement progressed, it is no wonder that King's sermonic discourse was preeminently concerned with the archetype of the road: he himself was constantly, and quite literally, on the road and on the move, and his speeches and sermons were filled with references to the road. He used these references rhetorically to persuade, but he also used them, more importantly, *psychagogically,* to lead souls toward a more just society along the Upward Way.

To demonstrate this claim, I look to Wolfgang Mieder's *Making a Way Out of No Way*, which examines King's proverbial rhetoric and aptly frames the central theme of the movement's discourse—*making a way out of no way.* (Likewise, one can also see King's concern with road imagery in some of the titles he gave to his own works, such as *Stride Toward Freedom* and *Where Do We Go from Here*). Mieder, in his analysis of six thousand pages of King's published texts, finds that proverbs about the road are quite common, including "have a long way to go" (which appears 14 times), "have come a long way" (14 times), "on the move" (8 times), "making a way out of no way" (5 times), and "to go down the line" (3 times), not to mention various other examples. Although King draws upon the past in many of his images, he is often explicitly focused on the future. As Mieder puts it, "Realizing that the end of the road towards racial justice is still far off, King exhibits an incredible faith in the future, with his strong belief in a benevolent God giving him the strength to continue on the long and treacherous way that lies ahead" (174). As he once told his followers, "We have come a long, long way in the struggle to make justice and freedom a reality in our nation, but we still have a long, long way to go. And it is this realistic position that I would like to use as a basis for our thinking together" (qtd. in Mieder 528). Imagery of the road appeared often in his works, whether he was citing such imagery from proverbs, using it in titles, speeches, or sermons, or singing about it as he led both a literal and metaphorical movement.

Works Cited

Arsenault, Raymond. *Freedom Riders: 1961 and the Struggle for Racial Justice*. Oxford UP, 2011.

Bertelsen, Phil. "Rise!" *The African Americans: Many Rivers to Cross*. Inkwell Films, 2013.

Brinkley, Douglas. *Rosa Parks*. Thorndike, 2000.

Burke, Kenneth. "Revolutionary Symbolism in America." In *American Writers' Congress*. Edited by Henry Hart, Martin Lawrence, 1935, pp. 87-94.

Carawan, Guy, and Candie Carawan. *Sing for Freedom: The Story of the Civil Rights Movement Through Its Songs*. New South, 2007.

Gregory, James. *The Southern Diaspora: How the Great Migrations of Black and White Southerners Transformed America*. U of North Carolina P, 2005.

Harrison, Robert, and Linda Harrison. "The Call from the Mountaintop: Call Response and the Oratory of Martin Luther King, Jr." In *Martin Luther King Jr. and the Sermonic Power of Public Discourse*. Edited by Carolyn Calloway-Thomas and John Louis Lucaites, U of Alabama P, 1993.

King, Coretta Scott. *My Life with Martin Luther King, Jr.* Holt, Rinehart and Winston, 1969.

King, Martin Luther, Jr. "Address at Public Meeting of the Southern Christian Ministers Conference of Mississippi." In *The Papers of Martin Luther King, Jr.: Volume V: Threshold of A New Decade, January 1959-December 1960*. Edited by Clayborne Carson, U of California P, 2005.

——————. "Address at the Fourth Annual Institute on Nonviolence and Social Change at Bethel Baptist Church." In *The Papers of Martin Luther King, Jr.: Volume V: Threshold of A New Decade, January 1959-December 1960*. Edited by Clayborne Carson, U of California P, 2005.

——————. "Address to MIA Mass Meeting at Holt Street Baptist Church." In *The Papers of Martin Luther King, Jr. Volume II: Rediscovering Precious Values, July 1951-November 1955*. Edited by Clayborne Carson et al, U of California P, 1994.

——————. "The American Dream." In Washington, pp. 208-16.

——————. "I Have a Dream." In Washington, pp. 217-20.

_____. "If the Negro Wins, Labor Wins." In Washington, pp. 201-07.

_____. "Keep Moving from this Mountain." In *The Papers of Martin Luther King, Jr.: Volume V: Threshold of A New Decade, January 1959-December 1960*. Edited by Clayborne Carson, U of California P, 2005.

_____. "Our God is Marching On!" In Washington, pp. 227-30.

_____. "*Playboy* Interview." In Washington, pp. 340-77.

_____. *Where Do We Go from Here: Chaos or Community?* In Washington, pp. 555-631.

Lomax, Alan. *The Land Where the Blues Began*. Pantheon, 1993.

Mieder, Wolfgang. *"Making a Way Out of No Way": Martin Luther King's Sermonic Proverbial Rhetoric*. Peter Lang, 2010.

Miller, Keith D. "Martin Luther King, Jr. and the Black Folk Pulpit." *Journal of American History*, vol. 78, no. 1, June 1991, pp. 120-23.

Morris, Aldon D. *Origins of the Civil Rights Movements*. Simon & Schuster, 1986.

Ong, Walter. *Orality and Literacy: The Technologizing of the Word*. Routledge, 1982.

Selby, Gary S. *Martin Luther King and the Rhetoric of Freedom: The Exodus Narrative in America's Struggle for Civil Rights*. Baylor UP, 2008.

Washington, James M., editor. *A Testament of Hope: The Essential Writings and Speeches of Martin Luther King, Jr.* HarperOne, 1986.

The Traits and Impact of Martin Luther King's Speeches and Sermons: A Review of Reactions

Robert C. Evans

Martin Luther King was a famously effective speaker and preacher, and in fact his "I Have a Dream" address of 1963 has often been called the most important speech of the twentieth century. King delivered many orations and sermons, and numerous people who heard them or who have read them have testified to their immense power and persuasiveness. What kind of impact, precisely, did his speeches and sermons have? How and why, exactly, were they so effective? Answering these kinds of questions is the main purpose of this essay. I will open, first, by reporting various reactions to King's speaking and preaching by many people who actually heard him speak or preach. Then, during the rest of the essay, I will survey some of the scholarly literature dealing with the stylistic, rhetorical, and structural traits that made his speeches and sermons so memorable as pieces of writing.

Reactions by Persons Who Knew and Heard King

One of the most valuable but least known and most obscure books about King was compiled by Russel Moldovan. It is entitled *Martin Luther King, Jr.: An Oral History of His Religious Witness and His Life*. As this title suggests, Moldovan interviewed numerous people who personally knew King. He recorded and transcribed their responses to his questions about various aspects of King's achievements, including his accomplishments as a speaker. Especially interesting is the book's fourth chapter, "Nine Components of the Preaching of Martin Luther King, Jr." These nine components are specified as follows: "1. Incarnating the Word with Truth through Personality" (79); 2. "Protestant Christianity with an African American Religious Experience" (93); 3. "Social Crisis Preaching" (102); 4. "A Time for American Reformation" (107); "5. The Bible and American Civil

Religion" (109); "6. Belief and Conviction" (112); "7. Charisma" (118); "8. Ecumenical and Inclusive" (121); and "9. A Twentieth Century Prophet" (125). Inevitably, comments assigned to each of these categories sometimes overlap, but the list just cited gives some sense of the way Moldovan structured his fourth chapter.

Early in that chapter, Moldovan quotes Calvin S. Morris, who joined King's Southern Christian Leadership Conference a year before King's assassination. In comments similar to many other remarks included in Moldovan's book, Morris said of King that

> there was an integration of his acting and being and his doing and his verbalizing. That was what was so powerful to me. And then of course he was able to blend the rhetoric of a kind of Protestant Christianity which was deeply flavored by the black religious experience and tie that to some of the great ideas and issues of the Western world. So that he had a facility with language. There was a poetry about his speech—a biblical poetry and imagery while he spoke also to a kind of American civil religion because of his understanding of the Constitution, Declaration of Independence, the kind of ideal of the American dream, obviously which had not been fulfilled. And he wed that with a passion, you sensed, particularly when he was overwhelmed or felt heavy his responsibility or the pressure and the demands of his leadership were palpable. You could hear it in his voice. (qtd. in Moldovan 77)

Many of Morris's individual observations were also made by others who knew King or heard him speak, but Morris seems worth quoting at length because he packs so many relevant comments into a relatively short space. Morris's comments are also fairly specific. Whereas other people Moldovan interviewed could sometimes be rather vague or general in trying to explain the impact of King's words, Morris was fairly precise.

Numerous persons interviewed by Moldovan stressed that King could speak effectively, and simultaneously, to different kinds of people, including the educated and the uneducated, prominent people and common persons, the religious and the secular, and the religious of all different kinds (see, for instance, 78, 94, 98, 114, 122,

124). Especially interesting, however, are Lornell M. McCullough's comments about King's demeanor:

> [H]e was so calm. And he was so cool, whether it was a disaster, whether it was death, whether it was something to be joyful about, whatever. He was never that person who . . . overdid anything whether it was for sorrow, or whether it was for joy. (qtd. in Moldovan 80)

King's calm, cool, rational persona certainly helped him inspire African Americans who appreciated his sense of confidence and self-control and probably also helped allay the worries of various white Americans who might have feared, and opposed, a more consistently fiery, threatening, or potentially violent speaker. This was one more way in which King managed to appeal to an unusually diverse set of listeners and readers.

In comments similar to those by many people Moldovan interviewed, C. T. Vivian praised not only the ways King could make his words seem powerfully relevant to real, everyday life (81) but also the way his words seemed validated by his own way of living: "You knew that you were listening to someone who had already done it" (82)—that is, the ways his words matched (and grew out of) his own conduct; the ways he himself "practiced what he preached" (Fred Shuttlesworth in Moldovan 84; see also 85-86, 88, 89, 90, 113). Many admired how he spoke in ways directly relevant to contemporary problems (see also 82, 84, 103). King himself, said Bernard Lafayette, seemed committed, "heart and soul," to the meaning and truth of his words (83). But Christian listeners and readers were especially impressed by the fact that King's words were clearly tied to the biblical Word itself. As Bobby Hill put it, "he just jumped out of the scripture every time. He started with Scripture. He wouldn't get too far from it" and could easily find scriptural parables—and parallels—appropriate to any contemporary situation and any individual's life (83; see also 118, 120). But various people interviewed by Moldovan stressed that King was not a hellfire and brimstone preacher. In other words, he did not stress the rewards of heaven or the fear of hell so much as he emphasized the practical, real-world consequences of love and ideal laws—the need not simply to grow spiritually but to ensure the growth of justice (88; see also 98, 104, 107, 109, 110, 113, 114, 119).

Lornell McCullough admired King's ability to combine "serious and practical" concerns with a good sense of humor (qtd. in Moldovan 90) as well as the sheer modesty of his physical appearance: "He never tried to wear fine, fine clothes. He dressed ordinary. . . . He was so down to earth" (90). This is an important matter, since it contributed to the ethical impact (the *ethos*) of King's public speaking; his sensible appearance lent credibility to the good sense of his arguments. The way he dressed reflected his entire sensibility—the feeling that he lacked pride and was genuinely approachable and sincerely concerned about others. As Martha Hemmans put it, "even though he was eloquent when he spoke, he could still get down to the human touch of people. . . . Some ministers you put on a pedestal. You feel that you've got to be so religious. Now he was a religious person but he was just so humanizing. I get right back to that human touch" (90; see also 91, 93). Paradoxically, it may have been part of King's "human touch" that made his moments of greatest religious eloquence so powerful. According to many witnesses, it was partly his ability to move from the ordinary to the exalted, from the commonplace to the sublime, that gave his rhetoric its greatest impact. When King was at his finest, rhetorically and spiritually, he could move even the nonreligious. As Julian Bond put it,

> I have to tell you that I'm not a very religious person, but I cannot hear those remarks [in one of King's sermons] without being just so incredibly moved and without thinking that there's got to be some power greater than we are. It's just amazing. I've never had anyone else . . . I've been in churches all my life; I've never had anybody else give me that feeling. I can't play it [the sermon] in my class without choking up. I can't repeat it to you now without choking up. (92)

Lornell McCullough similarly commented about a particular example of King's preaching by saying, "When he would preach that sermon, it would just tear you up" (92).

Additional Reactions from King's Contemporaries

Another example of King's ability to bridge rhetorical and cultural divides is mentioned by James Shannon in Moldovan's book. He said that because King had been

> educated in [a] white seminary he was able to touch a number of worlds with his preaching and with his style of delivery. . . . [He was] rooted and grounded in the genre of the black community, but he was also able to articulate the things that the white world understood as far as the biblical language. (94)

This point was also made, at valuable length, by Dorothy Cotton, who described King's reliance on African American styles of preaching (including call-and-response) as well as his simultaneous abilities to draw on white traditions and to adapt black traditions to white audiences. King, she said, drew on African American conventions for "a particular kind of cadence, a particular kind of rhythm." Some African Americans, she said, "think that preaching has not been good preaching if it doesn't have those cultural patterns in terms of the rhythm and the sequence and the style." She continued: "In his earlier years, he was preaching in the African American context, and people just loved that, because it was them; it was their style. It was artistry right out of their life experience" (98). Later, however, King would often speak before largely white audiences in very large and prestigious churches and he "was able to adapt such that if the full cultural expressions didn't seem appropriate, say if in a London Cathedral, he could adapt it so that if you didn't get the full flavor, . . . there was some resemblance or some coloring from the African American experience which I think people enjoy in any setting" (98; see also 124; but, for a different view, see 123). Cotton (like many others) additionally admired King's ability to invent or use memorable phrasing: "he was really a kind of poet in terms of the way he put words together, the way he could coin a phrase, and deeply touch people" (98; see also Ruth Greene and G. Murray Branch [99]). He used repetition effectively, often engaging in a kind of "roll call" (in the words of Elise Gilham) of human achievements and accomplishments, whether modern or biblical (99). And, as has already been mentioned, often his sermons and speeches would eventually build to a kind of crescendo. As Jethro English put it,

> He would get to a kind of point where he had that dynamic, and he just got into it, he exploded when he wanted to get his point over.... I mean it wasn't a show, it was for real for him. When he gets into what we call his "high road preaching," where his voice carries, he just exploded like that. (qtd. in Moldovan 100)

Bernard Lafayette described the effect of King's preaching as both a call to conscience and a kind of affirmation: "He challenged you, and you went away uplifted with the determination to do more" (106).

King's preaching, according to several of Moldovan's interviewees, was always clear and broadly accessible; even children could understand it (114, 122) although his words never seemed patronizing (122). In addition, in the words of L. Henry Welchel, "he had the unique ability of bringing together intellectualism and emotionalism. He did it in a way that the intellectual would not frown upon it, and the emotional person would receive more than just an emotional catharsis, but it would give them some depth of meaning as well" (qtd. in Moldovan 114-15; see also 121). He could draw on a capacious memory, not only of phrases but of faces (119-20), and he could preach repeatedly on the same themes and still bring something new to each new statement of his ideas (120). Listeners rarely lost interest in what he was saying; they did not tune him out (120). King, of course, was also blessed with what Julian Bond called "a strong voice—a voice that caught you" (122). It was ultimately his power of delivery, as much as his words themselves, that impressed so many listeners (126).

Scholarly Reactions: Keith D. Miller

If Moldovan's valuable book quotes from the responses of people who actually knew and heard King, Keith D. Miller takes a more scholarly approach. Miller's important 1992 book—*Voice of Deliverance: The Language of Martin Luther King, Jr. and Its Sources*—offers an equally valuable assessment of the topics mentioned in its subtitle. One of Miller's especially intriguing claims is that

> King's magnificent rhetorical triumphs do *not* reflect his tutelage from white professors. Nor does his persuasiveness result from his study of any of the Great White Thinkers whose works he examined in graduate school. Instead, King succeeded largely because he resisted numerous ideas proffered by his professors and the Great White Thinkers and instead drew on two powerful and popular rhetorical traditions. The first is a veritable torrent of sermons delivered and published by Harry Emerson Fosdick, [J. Wallace] Hamilton, [Harold] Bosley, and other prominent (and mainly white) preachers. The second, underlying, and more significant influence was the black folk pulpit of King's grandfather, father, Rev. [J. H.] Edwards, and several generations of anonymous, often illiterate folk preachers. (7)

Miller's book clearly and carefully provides much evidence to support these claims, including many side-by-side comparisons of King's language with language, often identical, taken from unacknowledged sources. Miller emphasizes, however, that such unacknowledged borrowing was very common among white and black preachers of King's time and was often seen as a compliment rather than as plagiarism. According to Miller, King managed to adapt the traditions of the black folk pulpit into "the idiom of Hamilton and Fosdick—an idiom most suited to persuade white listeners" (11; see also 70). These were the listeners he often *needed* to persuade in order to raise funds and support, especially in the North and particularly among white liberals. According to Miller, as

> he adapted sermonic boilerplate and refined and retested his best original material, King skillfully inserted his arguments against segregation into a web of ideas and phrases that moderate and liberal white Protestants had already approved. Undoubtedly, many of King's Northern white supporters who annually poured money into his organization had listened for years to Fosdick's nationally broadcast radio sermons. . . . By incorporating into virtually all of his mainline sermons the old-fashioned, yet radical black demand for equality, King accomplished a feat that no one else had ever achieved.

> He reached white audiences and thereby turned the traditional black demand into something it had never been before—a mainstream American idea. (85)

Interestingly, Miller's book provides much evidence that King, when adapting the sermons of white preachers, often improved upon the original language, making it more vivid, more personal, and more compelling. For example, Miller at one point quotes from a sermon by Fosdick to which King was clearly indebted. Here are Fosdick's words:

> FOSDICK: Professor Seelye Bixler . . . has lately made some shrewd comments on our new psychological talk about the well-adjusted life. At its finest, the well-adjusted life is so beautiful. . . . But in much of our popular rendition the well-adjusted life settles down into contentment with the status quo. . . . The sacredest obligation of the Christian is to be maladjusted—to the war system, to the inequities of an acquisitive economic order, to the wrongs of race prejudice, to the vulgarities of popular morals, to the crude sectarianisms of the churches. . . . The deepest obligation of a Christian, I should suppose, is to be maladjusted to the status quo. (106-07)

King, in the following passage, clearly borrowed from Fosdick, but he also breathed real life and passion into Fosdick's rather abstract phrasing. In the following quotation, I have placed in literal bold type the kind of phrasing that seems, in my opinion, to make King's words so much persuasively bolder than Fosdick's

> KING: Some years ago Professor Bixler reminded us of the **danger of over-stressing** the well-adjusted life. We must, of course, be well-adjusted to **avoid neurotic and schizophrenic personalities**, but there are some things in our world to which **men of good will** must be maladjusted. **I confess that I never intend** to become adjusted to **the evils of segregation** and the **crippling effects of discrimination**, to the **moral degeneracy of religious bigotry** and the **corroding effects of narrow** sectarianism, to economic conditions that **deprive men of work and food**, and to the **insanities of militarism** and the

self-defeating effects of physical violence. **Human salvation lies in the hands of the creatively maladjusted.** (107)

Miller's valuable book provides plenty of evidence that although King often simply echoed his sources, literally word for word (see, for instance, 3-4, 5, 6-7, 16, 59-60, 78, 79-80, 89, 100-01, 101, 106, 164-65), he also often vastly improved upon them (see, for instance, 15, 56, 90, 90-91, 107-08, 120-21, 165-66, 166).

But Miller also offers many other arguments to help explain the sheer effectiveness of King as a preacher, orator, and writer. He notes, for example, that "King concentrated on oral communication, devoting far more time to his thousands of addresses than to his writing" (118). Miller also explains that like "all other good preachers, King delighted in narrative," drawing especially on stories from the Bible in general and on New Testament parables in particular (118). He frequently used "deductive-then-inductive persuasion" rather than the reverse method often favored in seminaries (122). Like most "African-American folk sermons," King's preaching and speaking were often "loosely organized in associational clusters" involving related "images, phrases, and ideas" (122). King knew how to respond spontaneously to the spontaneous reactions of his listeners (122) and often repeated earlier sermons partly because he simply did not have the time (or even the inclination) to write brand new sermons each week (122). Instead, he relied on variations of tried-and-true, frequently tested phrasing that had already proven to be successful.

Later, Miller explains how King (and many other, similar preachers) compared present-day figures and events with similar people and happenings in the Bible. "King's interpretation of the Bible," Miller writes, "recapitulates and reenacts the archetypal, typological view of slave religion and the folk pulpit" (132)—the same kind of typological thinking that soon led many people to see King himself as a kind of latter-day Moses figure. All in all, Miller's book provides one of the most comprehensive, thorough, and persuasive studies of the kind of rhetoric that made King so effective in the pulpit, at the rostrum, and on the printed page. First published in 1992, Miller's study remains one of the very best ever undertaken of King's language, and it is now supplemented and updated by his two contributions to the present collection.

Scholarly Reactions: Essays Edited by Carolyn Calloway-Thomas and John Louis Lucaites

Shortly after Keith Miller's book was published, a collection of essays edited by Carolyn Calloway-Thomas and John Louis Lucaites also explored King's phrasing and rhetorical methods. *Martin Luther King Jr. and the Sermonic Power of Public Discourse* (1993) opened with a lengthy introduction that surveyed the volume's contents. Calloway-Thomas and Lucaites noted, for instance, that the collection began with an essay by Miller himself, who highlighted King's familiarity with black theology (especially its emphasis on the biblical Book of Exodus, its tendency to recycle language, and its stress on sacred, cyclical, nonlinear views of time). Reporting Miller's "controversial" claim that King was indebted more to previous preachers than to the white intellectuals he had studied at seminary, the editors concluded that he had made "a compelling case for examining the black religious underpinnings of all King's public discourse" (11).

Next describing an essay by E. Culpepper Clark on King's famous "Letter from Birmingham Jail," the editors paraphrased Clark's argument that the letter sought to "appeal to the white, liberal conscience, at once implying the values consistent with . . . peaceful and progressive goals . . . and simultaneously altering the underlying conservative assumptions upon which [those goals] rested" (12). Calloway-Thomas and Lucaites then paraphrased an essay by Judith D. Hoover also examining the "Letter." They said that Hoover looked at this text "in order to discern the rhetorical situation that it produced for those who would be affected by it" (12). They then observed that an essay by Martha Solomon saw the power of King's famous "I Have a Dream" speech as partly a "function of its vivid imagery, thematic unity, and philosophical substance, all of which King integrates through the metaphor of the 'covenant'" (13). Further paraphrasing Solomon, Calloway-Thomas and Lucaites said she argued that King

> legitimized the incorporation and integration of sacred and secular allusions, archetypal metaphors, and aphorisms, all of which combined to lend cultural authority and authenticity to both the speech's vision of a beloved community and its demands for public moral action. (13)

Turning next to an essay by John Louis Lucaites and Celeste Michelle Condit, the editors reported that this piece emphasized King's "sermonic (re)vision of America's ideological creed" and saw his "intertextualization of America's prevailing secular and spiritual narratives in 'I Have a Dream' as a timely and culturally appropriate universalization of the commitment to equality" (14). Finally, the editors summarized one more essay on the "I Have a Dream" speech—this one by John H. Patton—by paraphrasing its claim that the famous refrain "satisfies a mnemonic function for both the immediate audience hearing the speech and the nation's long-term cultural memory" and "adds presence and vitality" to the speech's "specific images" (14).

Summarizing an essay by Frederick Antczak on King's famous speech against the Vietnam war ("A Time to Break Silence"), Calloway-Thomas and Lucaites asserted that Antczak's analysis of that speech "offers an important insight into the general power of King's lifelong persuasion, for it demonstrates" how "King was a loving critic of America's social and political institutions" while also showing how "his leadership rhetorically performed the same critical demands that he would have the members of his beloved community enact, whatever the cost to himself" (15-16). Calloway-Thomas and Lucaites next paraphrased an essay by Michael Osborn, who was actually present to hear King's very final speech ("I've Been to the Mountaintop"), which was delivered not long before his assassination. They reported that in Osborn's opinion the "key to understanding King . . . is to recognize that in the final analysis he was not a political orator but a preacher, 'a converter of souls'" (16). Finally, the editors noted that their "volume concludes with

Robert D. Harrison and Linda K. Harrison's Afrocentric perspective on the performative dimensions of King's oratory and the sermonic function" of the famous call-and-response method often used in African American preaching (17). The nine essays included in the Calloway-Thomas and Lucaites collection offered a range of responses to King's rhetorical talents while also paying close attention to some of his most notable speeches, especially the famous "I Have a Dream" address delivered in 1963.

Scholarly Reactions: Drew D. Hansen

That address—one of the most famous in American history and perhaps the most important speech of the twentieth century—is the subject of Drew D. Hansen's 2003 book *The Dream: Martin Luther King, Jr., and the Speech That Inspired a Nation*. Hansen set the speech in its historical context, described how and why it was composed and revised, discussed it as a kind of sermon and example of prophecy, and explored its initial impact and long-term reception. He also analyzed it almost sentence-by-sentence, showing how it developed and especially how it depended, crucially, on King's decision to depart from his prepared script in the final, most famous part (featuring the repeated "I have a dream" sequence). King had actually used the dream metaphor in many previous speeches, but his sudden decision to include it in perhaps the most significant speech he would ever give proved to be inspired. In an especially interesting section of his book, Hansen sets, side by side, the speech King had planned to deliver with the speech he actually did deliver. Hansen notes all the subtle (and sometimes not so subtle) differences between the prepared script and the words King actually uttered before a huge crowd and a nationwide TV audience. At one point, Hansen observes that the "text King prepared the night before the march resembles only about half the speech King actually delivered" (94). It is, Hansen wrote,

> a measure of King's compositional ability that even though he had spent four days thinking about his speech for the march, and nearly all night writing it by hand, he was able to compose a far better address at the podium, taking the best passages from his prepared

text and combining them with a conclusion that he improvised as he spoke. (98)

Later, Hansen discusses the biblical allusions embedded in King's language; the ways the King James Bible affected the substance, style, structure, syntax, and rhythms of his speech; and the oratorical skill with which King actually delivered the address (including such matters as pauses, emphasis, meter, rhythms, variations in pitch, and so on). Hansen provides what is, perhaps, the most thorough discussion imaginable of King's most famous speech.

Scholarly Reactions: Eric J. Sundquist
As its title suggests, *King's Dream* (2009), by Eric J. Sundquist, focuses mainly on King's most famous speech—the "I Have a Dream" address of 1963. It acknowledges the value of previous work, especially Miller's, while also making valuable points of its own. Although Sundquist is interested in the speech more as a historical document than as a piece of rhetoric per se, he does discuss its roots in previous writings, speeches, and songs. Interestingly, he reports that by

> the late 1980s, according to a study by the National Endowment for the Humanities, high school seniors more often correctly identified the source of "I have a dream" (88.1 percent) than the opening words of the Gettysburg Address (73.9 percent) or the Declaration of Independence (65.7 percent); by 2008 recognition of King's words among American teenagers had reached 97 percent. (2)

Commenting on the possible inspirations and sources of King's speech as a whole and/or its various parts (especially the phrase "I have a dream"), Sundquist reviewed such possibilities as pre-Civil War writings and speeches (22, 72), a black woman King heard praying in 1962 (22), a white woman who had spoken similar words at around that same time (22), the Bible (23), the words of a speaker who preceded him in addressing the 1963 rally (a speaker who had also mentioned the word "dream" [27]), a speech given at the 1952 Republican National Convention (96), the song "America" (dating from 1853 [174]), and the writings and speeches of Abraham Lincoln, Frederick Douglass, and others. Sundquist explores many potential sources and parallels while also setting the speech within the contexts of the developing civil rights movement. He also shows how the speech was received at the time of its delivery and the varied ways it has been used for political purposes and even in judicial rulings in the years since then.

Scholarly Reactions: Wolfgang Mieder and Gary Younge

Among more recent studies of King's general rhetoric, Wolfgang Mieder's work is especially noteworthy, particularly his massive book from 2010 entitled *"Making a Way Out of No Way": Martin Luther King's Sermonic Proverbial Rhetoric*. As this title suggests, Mieder is mainly concerned with King's use of proverbs, but he also at one point offers a very useful survey of scholarship on King's language in general. He mentions, for instance, a "promising early dissertation by Mervyn A. Warren," *A Rhetorical Study of the Preaching of Doctor Martin Luther King, Jr.*, from 1966, which "deals with the 'vividness and imagery' as well as the 'figures of speech'" present in King's style and which also discusses his employment of such devices as "alliteration, anaphora, comparison, metaphor, repetition, and simile" (5). Mieder reports that work from 1969 by Marcus H. Boulware discusses some of these same issues as well as King's use of allegory and personification (5). Noting that Hortense J. Spillers in 1971 commented on King's intense interest in metaphors, Mieder also observes that Birgit Ensslin in 1990 explored King's "stylistic preoccupation with metaphors, repetition, parallelism, and antithesis" (5). Mieder praises a brief reference to King's rhetoric in a 1991 book by Lewis V. Baldwin, *There is a Balm in Gilead: The Cultural Roots of Martin Luther King, Jr.*, and he also recommends an "insightful book" from 2008 written by Jonathan Rieder, *The Word of the Lord Is upon Me: The Righteous Performance of Martin Luther King, Jr.* (6). He additionally commends a 1995 dissertation by David Fleer, *Martin Luther King, Jr.'s Reformation of Sources: A Close Rhetorical Reading of His Compositional Strategies and*

Arrangement (8-9). And, of course, Mieder pays strong tribute to the pioneering work of Keith D. Miller already cited.

At more than 550 pages, Mieder's book is certainly the longest of the texts surveyed here. It consists of sixteen separate chapters— chapters focusing, respectively, on King's use of proverbs in general, in his first five books, in letters, in sermons, and in writings offering practical advice. In other chapters, Mieder explores King's use of various *kinds* of proverbs, including biblical and folk proverbs; proverbs rooted in language of the body and economics; proverbs involving tension, hope, progress, and dreams; and proverbs involving quotations. It is difficult to imagine a more thorough book ever being written on King's use of proverbs, especially since more than half the volume consists of an index of proverbs and proverbial phrases employed by King, with many extended quotations from his writings, sermons, and speeches. In a typically clear and detailed passage, Mieder reports that he examined 436 different texts by King, that he examined 1092 distinct proverbs (or "fixed phrases"), that the total number of pages of the texts he examined amounted to roughly 6000, and that these pages contain "on average one proverbial statement for every 5.5 pages" (19).

Mieder notes that some of King's longer texts did have ghost writers, whose contributions King often freely acknowledged (21), although King of course would have approved anything written for him and the proverbial style of his works is consistent throughout. He used proverbs in his letters but not as often in his interviews (49); often used proverbs as the starting points, foundations, and titles of sermons (61, 66); showed less interest in folk proverbs than in ones drawn from the Bible (87); sometimes repeated a proverb in adjacent paragraphs (123); sometimes strung proverbs together (127); and saw some of his own use of language widely quoted to the extent that in a sense it became proverbial (132). Clearly a labor of love, Mieder's book is just one of the latest in the developing tradition of scholarly studies devoted not simply to King as a political and spiritual leader but also to King as a master of the English language.

Also worth mentioning is Gary Younge's 2013 volume titled *The Speech: The Story behind Dr. Martin Luther King Jr.'s Dream.*

Younge sets the "dream" address in a variety of historical contexts before then examining the speech itself as well as its legacy. Younge discusses such issues as King's decision to trust his gut rather than rely entirely on his prepared script (93), the ways his family background and education had prepared him to compose and deliver this speech (94), the process of composing it (95-97), the potential sources of some of its phrasing (97-98), his hopes for the address (100), and many other matters, including much of King's specific phrasing. Younge's book indicates once more the enduring impact of "The Speech," a text and a moment which have probably never been equaled by any other public address of the last sixty years.

Works Cited

Calloway-Thomas, Carolyn, and John Louis Lucaites. *Martin Luther King Jr. and the Sermonic Power of Public Discourse.* U of Alabama P, 1993.

Hansen, Drew D. *The Dream: Martin Luther King, Jr., and the Speech That Inspired a Nation.* HarperCollins, 2005.

Mieder, Wolfgang. *"Making a Way Out of No Way": Martin Luther King's Sermonic Proverbial Rhetoric.* Peter Lang, 2010.

Miller, Keith D. *Voice of Deliverance: The Language of Martin Luther King, Jr., and Its Sources.* Free, 1992.

Moldovan, Russel. *Martin Luther King, Jr.: An Oral History of His Religious Witness and His Life.* International Scholars, 1999.

Sundquist, Eric. *King's Dream: The Legacy of Martin Luther King's "I Have a Dream" Speech.* Yale UP, 2009.

Younge, Gary. *The Speech: The Story behind Dr. Martin Luther King Jr.'s Dream.* Haymarket, 2013.

Martin Luther King's "I Have a Dream" Speech: A Pluralist Analysis

Jordan Bailey

Pluralism is less an individual approach to literary criticism than a way of dealing with all other approaches. It suggests that different kinds of literary theory are like different kinds of tools: a hammer differs from a screwdriver, a wrench differs from a saw, a drill differs from a pair of pliers. No single tool is superior to another; instead, each is designed to do a different job. And each tool must be used competently if the job is to be done well. Here's another analogy: a microscope differs from a telescope, which differs from a pair of glasses, which differs from a pair of binoculars. Again: no single way of looking at things is superior to any other; each way is appropriate to a particular task. If this basic pluralistic assumption were constantly kept in mind, much useless fighting about which approach to literary criticism is better could be avoided.

In the following pages, various students from a course in literary criticism (whose names are listed at the end) analyze Martin Luther King's "I Have a Dream" speech by using many different critical approaches. Each approach makes a particular basic assumption. Criticism inspired by **Plato** emphasizes the need for logic and universal moral standards. Criticism inspired by **Aristotle** stresses highly skilled craftsmanship. Criticism influenced by **Horace** highlights any text's need to be clear and broadly appealing. Criticism indebted to **Longinus** applauds texts that are uplifting and ennobling. All four of these theories associated with ancient thinkers are relevant to King's famous speech.

Also relevant are more modern theories. For example, **traditional historical critics** stress the need to see texts in light of their historical eras. **Thematic** critics explore key ideas or central motifs. **Formalists**, like Aristotle, admire beautiful, well-written, and complexly unified works. **Psychoanalytic** critics scrutinize the individual psychologies of authors, characters, readers, and listeners.

Archetypal critics emphasize typical psychological traits, such as common desires and fears. **Marxist** critics examine how texts are rooted in conflicts between different economic classes. **Feminists** study how texts reflect women's interests and the oppression women have endured.

Among more recent theories, **structuralists** examine how humans make sense of reality by using binary codes to divide experience into opposites (black/white, male/female, right/wrong, etc.). **Deconstructors** argue that such codes are inherently simplistic and unstable and self-contradictory (for example, any simple opposition of black and white ignores various shades of gray). **Reader-response** critics think different audience members will interpret any text in different ways. **Dialogical** critics emphasize the different voices any text contains and must anticipate, including the voices of other past or present texts. **New historicists** argue that traditional historical criticism tended to simplify history by deemphasizing conflicts, power struggles, and the fact that cultures are sites of constant renegotiation. **Muliticultural** critics (like many other recent theorists) emphasize the sheer diversity of possible influences on, and reactions to, a text, including any kind of distinct identity or combination of identities, such as racial, ethnic, national, sexual, linguistic, physical, and so on. **Postmodernism**, like deconstruction, assumes that reality is far too complex to be understood simply and that diversity, rather than uniformity, should be not only tolerated but celebrated and embraced. **Ecocritics** explore how texts reflect and affect humans' complex interactions with the environment, including other living things. And **Darwinian** critics, like archetypal thinkers, stress the common traits most humans share—traits that have evolved through "natural selections" over millions of years.[1]

The following pages suggest how all these various theories can be used to analyze practically any text, including Martin Luther King's famous "I Have a Dream" speech.

The "I Have a Dream" Speech

I am happy to join with you today in what will go down in history as the greatest demonstration for freedom in the history of our nation.

Thematic critics see "freedom" as a central unifying theme of this entire speech [AM; KC; KS; SK]. **Traditional historical** critics would say King was almost certainly right about this gathering: it was attended by roughly 250,000 people and had an enormous historical impact [MG].

Five score years ago, a great American, in whose symbolic shadow we stand today, signed the Emancipation Proclamation. This momentous decree came as a great beacon light of hope to millions of Negro slaves who had been seared in the flames of withering injustice. It came as a joyous daybreak to end the long night of their captivity.

Dialogical critics would note that King alludes to two major American texts: the Gettysburg Address (in the words "Five score years") and the Emancipation Proclamation [SK; MB; MDB]. **Formalist** critics are most interested in how ideas are expressed. King could have said, "Black people were so relieved when the Emancipation Proclamation was signed. Slaves had been treated very badly and looked forward to improving their lives." But those words completely lack the power and depth of King's phrasing [AW; also KC, MB, and MDB]. A **traditional historical** would explain that the "great American" was Abraham Lincoln and that King was speaking from the steps of the Lincoln Memorial, with its massive statue of the slain "Emancipator" [JC; also KC; JL]. Such a critic might also (1) say that any historically accurate statement King made would add to his credibility [JL] and (2) establish a clear timeline from 1863 to 1963 and beyond to show the history of African American rights in the United States and the impact of King's own address [KT]. A critic influenced by **Plato** would applaud King's pervasive emphasis on the moral ideal of justice and would admire King's effort to deal with a serious subject in a logical, rational manner [RCE], although such a critic might be suspicious of any passages in which King's language seems excessively emotional [LB].

But one hundred years later, the Negro still is not free. One hundred years later, the life of the Negro is still sadly crippled by the manacles of segregation and the chains of discrimination. One hundred years later, the Negro lives on a lonely island of poverty in the midst of a vast ocean of material prosperity. One hundred years later, the Negro is still languished in the corners of American society and finds himself an exile in his own land. And so we've come here today to dramatize a shameful condition.

> **Traditional historical** critics would note how King effectively compares the distant past with the present [CL; JR] and would also note that *Negro*, a word commonly used by both blacks and whites in King's day, has long since fallen out of favor [ER]. **Structuralist** critics might note that segregation was an especially clear example of the ways humans make sense of reality by perceiving "binary opposites." Segregationists divided people into literal black and white, and that basic division led to a whole cultural code and social structure rooted in these perceived opposites [AM; also DK; PH]. **Formalist** critics might admire the vivid metaphor of a "lonely island of poverty" surrounded by an ocean of wealth [MB; MDB], but the word *ocean* might remind **historical** critics of the so-called Middle Passage—the trade triangle across the Atlantic Ocean that made whites rich and blacks slaves. Moreover, formalists would appreciate the use of epimone in the repetition of the phrase "one hundred years later" [MDB]. **Marxist** critics might note that economic and racial inequality went hand in hand: the poverty of most blacks and the relative wealth of most whites made it easy for whites to treat blacks as inferiors. White wealth, Marxists would argue, had been weaponized and used to make and keep blacks inferior economically, socially, and culturally [JC; also JL; ER].

In a sense we've come to our nation's capital to cash a check. When the architects of our republic wrote the magnificent words of the Constitution and the Declaration of Independence, they were signing a promissory note to which every American was to fall heir. This note was a promise that all men, yes, black men as well as white men, would be guaranteed the "unalienable Rights" of "Life, Liberty and the pursuit of Happiness." It is obvious today that America has defaulted on this promissory note, insofar as her citizens of color are concerned. Instead of honoring this sacred obligation, America has given the Negro people a bad check, a check which has come back marked "insufficient funds."

Dialogical critics would note King's explicit reference to the Declaration of Independence (a text known by almost all Americans), with which his own speech is in a kind of open dialogue [MB; MDB; YY; DK]. He does not merely echo the Declaration silently or allude to it in some subtle or understated way; instead, he brings it directly into a kind of public conversation [RCE]. **Horace** might see the second sentence here as an attempt to appeal to a very broad audience who believed that the Declaration and the Constitution were guarantees of human rights for all [MG]. However, a **deconstructor** might particularly focus on the contradictions embedded in the first, unamended version of the Constitution. Each black American was counted there as only three-fifths of a person. This stipulation, ironically, was designed by nonslave states so that populous slave states could not use their numerous slaves to justify greater federal power. For example, the size of a state's Congressional delegation depended on the number of persons living in each state. If blacks had been counted as full persons, their sheer numbers would have meant that the slave states' whites (who alone had the power to vote) would benefit from large numbers of residents, many of whom had no right to vote. In fact, under the original Constitution, in many states (but not all), even free blacks could not vote, and in all states the right to vote was reserved to white male property owners. Poor men, along with women of any color, were excluded. For all sorts of complicated reasons, then, the Constitution itself destabilized what would seem, at first glance, to be a very simple concept—the concept of one individual person. In the original Constitution, there was no single, simple, consistent definition even of such a straightforward concept as an individual human being. There were, instead, numerous categories of persons, and even single, distinct persons were sometimes (as in the case of slaves) not counted as complete individuals. And then, to make matters even more complicated, one reason for treating each black slave as three-fifths of a person (as already noted) was to prevent white slave owners from enjoying too *much* power! Counting each slave as three-fifths of a person— which might seem an utterly racist idea—was actually intended, in part, to restrict the power of white slave owners. Deconstructors search for the instabilities within any apparently simple concept (such as the concept of *individual human being*) and call attention to all the complexities and contradictions such concepts contain.

Deconstuctors also search out the ways simple oppositions (such as the opposition between *black* and *white*) are rarely if ever simple at all [JC]. **Multicuralist** critics might note that the promises King mentions were not made to all people living in America, even at the time those promises were made [MG]. **Formalist** critics would be interested in this passage's complexity as well as in how the phrasing comes together to eloquently communicate the text's purpose. King's use of the metaphors of a promissory note, check, and bank are phrases any reader can relate to [YY; also DK; PH]—a point **Horace** might also appreciate [RCE]. **Feminists** might note that King, here and throughout, refers to humans as "men," thus (probably without intending to) neglecting to explicitly include women (AM; KC; MG; SK; JL; ER). Noting that he refers to the nation as "her," they might find this reference disturbing [AW], although **historical** critics might note that both of these references—to humans as men and to a nation as female—were conventions of the time [RCE; MG]. **New historicist** critics might note that African Americans would actually have had great trouble trying to cash an out-of-town check during this period of time [MDB].

But we refuse to believe that the bank of justice is bankrupt. We refuse to believe that there are insufficient funds in the great vaults of opportunity of this nation. And so, we've come to cash this check, a check that will give us upon demand the riches of freedom and the security of justice.

Not only would **formalist** critics applaud the drawn-out analogy that spans paragraphs and grows from a simple illustration to a rallying cry, but they would also enjoy the double meaning of "the riches of freedom and the security of justice." *Riches* and *security* are banking terms related to stashing wealth and allowing it to mature and develop. Similarly, these terms also relate to the opportunities black people would enjoy if what is already theirs were properly granted: the opportunity to prosper and the opportunity to find protection in a hostile society. Formalists might also admire how King hides the emotional struggle of racial injustice behind the lacquer of business logic. A discourse of dollars and cents, credits and debits, is easier for his audience to engage with than one of overt blame [JB]. **Structuralist** critics might note that this entire passage draws on codes widely understood in American culture that might not be immediately comprehensible to people from different cultures.

For example, in the United States bad checks—marked with an insufficient funds stamp in bold red ink—indicate shameful poverty, irresponsibility, and downright thievery. So King turns the tables and uses those very same code words while pointing at the metaphorical (white) bank of American justice. Further, he employs the code word *bankrupt*. If a check comes back marked "insufficient funds" and the issuer is not in fact out of currency, then there must be foul play. King suggests that the bank of American values is not at all bereft of currency, yet some checks just won't clear. In order to understand the message, the code must also be understood [MDB]. **Thematic** critics might suggest that by linking a key idea not only to a vivid metaphor but also to the very common practice of using a bank, King helps ensure that his idea will be remembered. They might argue that from now on, whenever his listeners used a bank, they might be inclined to remember a crucial theme of his speech [LB].

We have also come to this hallowed spot to remind America of the fierce urgency of Now. This is no time to engage in the luxury of cooling off or to take the tranquilizing drug of gradualism. Now is the time to make real the promises of democracy. Now is the time to rise from the dark and desolate valley of segregation to the sunlit path of racial justice. Now is the time to lift our nation from the quicksands of racial injustice to the solid rock of brotherhood. Now is the time to make justice a reality for all of God's children.

A **Formalist** critic would be interested in this passage's images, such as "the dark and desolate valley," "sunlit path," and "solid rock," as well as how their juxtaposition supports King's metaphors. [MG; KT; CL; DK]. Formalists would also admire the balanced, parallel phrases [MG]. **Structuralists** would note the dichotomies that structure the thinking here, such as segregation versus racial justice and racial injustice versus brotherhood [KT]. **Archetypal** critics might argue that the desire for justice is fundamental to just about all "normal" human beings as well as to many other animals, such as monkeys, dogs, and others. It is deeply rooted in the nature of many creatures [JC]. A **Darwinian** critic might suggest that humans and other animals are hardwired by evolution to seek their fair share since animals and humans who failed to do so in the past were less likely to survive [RCE]. An **archetypal** critic would find King's speech comparable to literary expressions involving seeking justice found in other cultures, whether it be in the form of the Akan tales of Anansi the Spider or the French novel *Les Misérables*. Any trait that transcends particular cultures would interest both archetypal and Darwinian critics [JC].

It would be fatal for the nation to overlook the urgency of the moment. This sweltering summer of the Negro's legitimate discontent will not pass until there is an invigorating autumn of freedom and equality. Nineteen sixty-three is not an end, but a beginning. And those who hope that the Negro needed to blow off steam and will now be content will have a rude awakening if the nation returns to business as usual. And there will be neither rest nor tranquility in America until the Negro is granted his citizenship rights. The whirlwinds of revolt will continue to shake the foundations of our nation until the bright day of justice emerges.

Dialogical critics might comment on King's allusion, in his reference to a "sweltering summer of … discontent" to Shakespeare's *Richard II*, which famously uses the phrase "winter of our discontent." This allusion would have implied King's education and would have been especially appealing to his educated listeners [AW]. **Archetypal** critics would appreciate King's appeal to the universal experience of seasons. While the nature of summer and autumn vary depending on geographical location, the basic concept of different seasons is familiar to all humans across demographics, time, and space. Archetypal critics might also point out that freedom and equality are desires all humans share [KT]. **Traditional historical** critics might note that King specifies a particular year—1963—and that his speech would make most sense to people who knew about events of that year and preceding years [AW]. From the January inauguration of George Wallace as governor of Alabama to King's arrest in April and the assassination of Medgar Evers in Mississippi in June, 1963 had been fraught with racial tension [YY]. **Structuralists** might note that King's distinction between an "end" and a "beginning" exemplifies the common human tendency to perceive life in terms of opposites [SK]. Thus, all throughout the rest of this paragraph, King implies a pair of opposites even when he mentions only one half of the pair. For example, blowing off steam is the opposite of staying below the boiling point. A rude awakening is the opposite of a sound sleep. The "whirlwinds of revolt" are the opposite of a calm, gentle breeze or of no wind at all. The "bright day of justice" is the opposite of the dark night of injustice. All the positive phrases imply their opposites, and vice versa [RCE]. A **reader-response** critic might note this passage's potential to be received differently by different audiences, especially its initial audience, which included black activists and white racists, among others. While a black activist might feel emboldened and encouraged by this passage, a white racist would likely feel threatened or angered (something a **multicultural** critic would also be interested in) [KT; also KS;MB; MDB; PH; ER]. **Formalists** might focus on all the passage's vivid figurative imagery, such as "sweltering summer," "invigorating autumn," "whirlwinds of revolt," and so on [SK]. **Reader-response** critics might especially focus on the warning implied in the final sentence: some readers or listeners might have been comforted and inspired by the warning; others might have heard it as an implied threat; still others might have interpreted it as simply an accurate prediction [KM]. **New historicist** critics, who emphasize the ways cultures involve power struggles, might be especially interested in these final sentences. King is arguably involved in a kind of negotiation here by implying that unless power is freely shared it may be fought for [JC; KM; KS]. New Historicist critics might argue that King's speech illustrates that few if any cultures are ever really settled and peaceful; struggles for power are always occurring on various levels and in various ways [JC]. Such critics might argue that King's speech did not merely reflect its historical moment but helped to shape it [MDB]. **Deconstructors** love the close, very close, word-by-word reading of a text. This passage provides enough material for pages of deconstructive criticism. Consider, for instance, words such as *fierce, rise, lift, fatal, sweltering, discontent, whirlwind,* and *revolt*. Those are fighting words; however, none of them can actually be defined as overt threats or acts of physical violence. Their full meaning is left quite unsaid [MDB].

But there is something that I must say to my people, who stand on the warm threshold which leads into the palace of justice: In the process of gaining our rightful place, we must not be guilty of wrongful deeds. Let us not seek to satisfy our thirst for freedom by drinking from the cup of bitterness and hatred. We must forever conduct our struggle on the high plane of dignity and discipline. We must not allow our creative protest to degenerate into physical violence. Again and again, we must rise to the majestic heights of meeting physical force with soul force.

Archetypal critics might note that the impulse to commit violence is extremely common, especially when people feel mistreated.

King urges his audience to restrain that natural impulse [MG]. **Psychoanalytic** critics might argue that violent impulses are rooted in the emotional id but can sometimes be controlled by the rational ego and the morally rooted superego [YY]. They might suggest that King's strong faith in God reflects the influence of his superego, the seat of morality and conscience [LB]. **Plato** might admire this emphasis on controlling emotions, especially violent ones [JL].

The marvelous new militancy which has engulfed the Negro community must not lead us to a distrust of all white people, for many of our white brothers, as evidenced by their presence here today, have come to realize that their destiny is tied up with our destiny. And they have come to realize that their freedom is inextricably bound to our freedom.

Multiculturalist critics might suggest that King's position as a black man influenced both his speech and the speech's reception. This speech, if delivered by a white, might seem more abstract and less personal [KT]. Some multiculturalist critics might question King's emphasis on similarities between whites and blacks; they might argue that the differences were more significant and that even sympathetic whites still benefit from white privilege [CL]. Some multiculturalists might wonder why King never mentions other oppressed minority groups, such as Native Americans, LGBTQ people, ethnic or religious minorities, and so on [AM]. Still other multiculturalists might argue that oppressed people can advance most quickly by winning allies from other groups and building coalitions. They might also argue that it was (and is) strategically valuable to whites to ally themselves with people of color [RCE]. **Horace** might admire King's desire to appeal to as broad an audience as possible in simple, clear language [KS; LB]. **Feminist critics** might dislike the word *brother* as opposed to a more inclusive term. They might also point out how King links "brother" and "people," which implies that "people" refers specifically to men ("brothers"). Feminists might note how the civil rights movement in the sixties provided a model for the feminist movement of the seventies. They might also emphasize the numerous women involved in the civil rights movement [KT; also JL]. **Structuralist** critics might note how King opposes society's tendency to divide people into distinct and opposite groupings of white and black. They might say that King recognizes that this division is part of an artificial, arbitrary code, with no root in reality per se. Instead, it is a code that some humans have *imposed* on reality [JR]. **Archetypal** critics might focus on the desire of all people to feel part of a larger community or brotherhood [MB; MDB; PH; JL; LB].

We cannot walk alone.

And as we walk, we must make the pledge that we shall always march ahead.

We cannot turn back.

There are those who are asking the devotees of civil rights, "When will you be satisfied?" We can never be satisfied as long as the Negro is the victim of the unspeakable horrors of police brutality. We can never be satisfied as long as our bodies, heavy with the fatigue of travel, cannot gain lodging in the motels of the highways and the hotels of the cities. We cannot be satisfied as long as the Negro's basic mobility is from a smaller ghetto to a larger one. We can never be satisfied as long as our children are stripped of their self-hood and robbed of their dignity by signs stating: "For Whites Only." We cannot be satisfied as long as a Negro in Mississippi cannot vote and a Negro in New York believes he has nothing for which to vote. No, no, we are not satisfied, and we will not be satisfied until "justice rolls down like waters, and righteousness like a mighty stream."

Dialogical critics might be interested in King's inclusion of dissident voices. Rather than ignoring people who disagree with them, he engages them in a kind of dialog [JR]. **Formalist** critics might say that King's technique of repeatedly beginning sentences with "we can never be satisfied," alternated with "we cannot be satisfied," creates a list of inequalities that, as he continues, seems to gain momentum in the same way as the accumulating waters of the "mighty stream." The anaphora builds upon itself, creating a sense of tension that continues to increase until he introduces the idea that one day the dam will burst, allowing the release that comes with "justice" and "righteousness" [AW]. **Multicultural** critics would be interested in King's general emphasis on racial discrimination [JR; also MB; ER]. **Traditional historical** critics would want to find as much evidence as possible to substantiate King's claims here [LB], while **new historicist** critics, with their interest in conflicts within cultures, might be especially interested in the reference to "police brutality" [RCE] and might see this paragraph, in particular, as evidence that conflicts almost always exist within cultures [MG].

Some new historicists might note that some African Americans, of a higher economic class than other blacks, actually worried that King might be proceeding too quickly in his push for civil rights; they advised a more moderate, gradual approach. New historicists might note that this conflict between gradualism and radicalism existed in the black community from at least the time of Booker T. Washington, who was a gradualist [RCE]. **Marxist** critics would emphasize King's interest in the economic oppression blacks suffered: by being considered inferior, they were consigned and confined to a lower economic class [SK; KC; KS; MG; YY; DK]. Marxists might also be interested in whether King had much personal familiarity with economic inequality [KT]. **Structuralist** critics, with their interest in codes, might find it interesting that King mentions a now-obsolete code in the United States: signs that allowed and barred entry based on race. Because this code no longer formally dictates human interactions, a structuralist might analyze the effectiveness of King's speech, since this code *has* been abolished. Knowing both that King was a prominent figure during the civil rights movement in 1963 and that the Civil Rights Act (which banned racial discrimination) came into effect in 1964, a structuralist critic might conclude that this speech—and King's work as a whole—helped eliminate some discriminatory codes. Structuralists might also be interested in this portion of King's speech because although the formal code changed, the informal code held by millions of individuals continued for many years beyond 1964. Structuralists might wonder how long it was before the formal denouncement of this code was accepted throughout society [MDB].

I am not unmindful that some of you have come here out of great trials and tribulations. Some of you have come fresh from narrow jail cells. And some of you have come from areas where your quest— quest for freedom left you battered by the storms of persecution and staggered by the winds of police brutality. You have been the veterans of creative suffering. Continue to work with the faith that unearned suffering is redemptive. Go back to Mississippi, go back to Alabama, go back to South Carolina, go back to Georgia, go back to Louisiana, go back to the slums and ghettos of our northern cities, knowing that somehow this situation can and will be changed.

Structuralist critics might note that the phrase "trials and tribulations" is a very common expression and is thus part of the code of speaking or writing English. People familiar with English would immediately recognize this phrase, while someone unfamiliar with English might not realize that it is a commonly used phrase [MG]. **Formalist** critics would admire the phrase's alliteration and emphatic repetition and even the fact that the shorter word comes first [RCE]. **Archetypal** critics might note that all people, everywhere, have probably experienced literal storms and would thus be able to relate to King's storm imagery [YY], which a **formalist** would also admire [RCE]. **New historicist** critics might be interested in King's emphasis here on power struggles within a larger culture [KT]. **Reader-response** critics might note that people's responses to King's words might differ depending on whether they had or had not suffered from police brutality. Similarly such critics might argue that people who have more recently suffered from such brutality would especially be able to relate to King's words, even though those words were spoken many years ago [CL; also JL]. **Marxist** critics might think the reference to "slums and ghettos" indicates King's realization that segregation is just one of many ways to oppress poor people, especially poor blacks [PH].

Let us not wallow in the valley of despair, I say to you today, my friends.

And so even though we face the difficulties of today and tomorrow, I still have a dream. It is a dream deeply rooted in the American dream.

Thematic critics might argue that this and subsequent paragraphs stress a key theme of the entire speech—the dream of a better future. Rather than implying the theme, King makes it as explicit and emphatic as possible [CL; also MB; PH]. **Archetypal** critics might argue that King's dream is "deeply rooted" not only in the American dream but in an even more basic, more widely shared human dream for liberty, respect, and self-respect [AM; KM].

I have a dream that one day this nation will rise up and live out the true meaning of its creed: "We hold these truths to be self-evident, that all men are created equal."

I have a dream that one day on the red hills of Georgia, the sons of former slaves and the sons of former slave owners will be able to sit down together at the table of brotherhood.

Postmodernist critics, as well as **deconstructors**, might argue that "self-evident," indisputable, and objective "truths" do not exist, at least in matters of politics, morality, and culture. The very fact that the signers of the Declaration of Independence were able to proclaim the "self-evident" truth that all persons are created equal at the same time that they countenanced and even in some cases practiced slavery shows how complex reality can be and how difficult it can be to state, let alone practice, "self-evident" truths [JC]. **Feminist** critics might note King's habit of referring to all humans as males [CL; YY; DK]. **Multicultural** critics might note that even if King had referred to women, he would not have been referring to all the possible "gender categories" that exist, especially those involving LGBTQIA people [YY]. **Historical** critics might note that King's phrasing was conventional, and **new historicist** critics might note that this convention changed, in part, because of political changes. Therefore, this sort of phrasing is used far less often today than it once was [RCE]. **Reader-response** critics would note that different persons might respond differently to this appeal because of their different personal backgrounds and experiences [MG]. **Traditional historical** critics might note that in 1963, King's imagery of blacks and whites "sit[ting] down together at [a] table" was, at least in many places in the South, not just a metaphor but a literal impossibility. That fact would interest and trouble **multicultural** critics [PH].

I have a dream that one day even the state of Mississippi, a state sweltering with the heat of injustice, sweltering with the heat of oppression, will be transformed into an oasis of freedom and justice.

Formalists and **Aristotle** would admire not only the metaphors used here but also the ways opposite metaphors are juxtaposed. Both the metaphors and the juxtapositions imply the writer's skill [JR]. **Marxists** would focus less on King's phrasing than on the injustice and oppression he attacks [JR; also MB].

I have a dream that my four little children will one day live in a nation where they will not be judged by the color of their skin but by the content of their character.

I have a *dream* today!

I have a dream that one day, down in Alabama, with its vicious racists, with its governor having his lips dripping with the words of "interposition" and "nullification"—one day right there in Alabama little black boys and black girls will be able to join hands with little white boys and white girls as sisters and brothers.

Historical critics would be especially interested in the reference to the governor of Alabama (George C. Wallace) and the doctrines of "interposition" and "nullification." They would argue that understanding this passage depends on understanding not only these doctrines but also Wallace's motivations and behavior [SK]. Wallace strongly supported segregation and made many racist remarks. In January 1963 he proclaimed his endorsement of "segregation now, segregation tomorrow, segregation forever." Just a little over a month before King's speech, Wallace had stood in front of the doors of the University of Alabama to oppose integrating the university [AM; also ER]. **New historicists** would definitely be interested in the social tensions and conflicts King mentions [YY]. **Feminist** critics might note that King's only explicit reference to human females is a reference to girls rather than adult women. They might suggest that in this respect King reflects a patriarchal culture, in which men typically had more power, whether they were white or black [JC]. **Psychoanalytic** critics might find the mental states of the vicious racists and "interposing" governor particularly interesting. They might conclude that these unsavory characters allowed themselves to be controlled by their ids instead of maintaining control of themselves and acting with the decency associated with the superego. But they might also suggest that given the commonness of racism in the United States in 1963, "giving in" to one's id through racism was temporarily accepted as a social norm. The contrast between King and the racist Alabamians would also interest psychoanalytic critics. In spite of the racists choosing to indulge their ids, King's response is tempered by his superego and is a call not for retribution or punishment but for brotherhood. King rises above his tormentors and chooses the higher mental path rather than giving in to base desires of the id—desires that satisfy only for a moment while prolonging the problems he and his followers face [JC].

I have a *dream* today!

I have a dream that one day every valley shall be exalted, and every hill and mountain shall be made low, the rough places will be made plain, and the crooked places will be made straight; "and the glory of the Lord shall be revealed and all flesh shall see it together."

> **Longinus**, with his emphasis on loftiness, exaltation, inspiration, and morality, would probably find this passage especially inspiring [AW; also JL]. **Dialogical** critics would note how King, here and throughout his speech, is in dialogue with perhaps the most influential text of his culture: the Bible [KM; MB].

This is our hope, and this is the faith that I go back to the South with. With this faith, we will be able to hew out of the mountain of despair a stone of hope. With this faith, we will be able to transform the jangling discords of our nation into a beautiful symphony of brotherhood. With this faith, we will be able to work together, to pray together, to struggle together, to go to jail together, to stand up for freedom together, knowing that we will be free one day.

> **Aristotle** believed that powerful metaphors were a sure sign of a true poet [KS]. **Horace** believed that writers should speak to broad audiences and that their messages should teach by pleasing. King, here, is not speaking just to blacks or whites or even just to those assembled to hear his speech. Using memorable, pleasing language, he is addressing the whole country, "all of God's children," and espousing concerted action for collective advancement [AW]. **Longinus** believed morally elevated people, like King, should use lofty language to communicate sublime ideals, as King does here [KT; also JR; LB].

And this will be the day—this will be the day when all of God's children will be able to sing with new meaning:

My country 'tis of thee, sweet land of liberty, of thee I sing. Land where my fathers died, land of the Pilgrims' pride, From every mountainside, let freedom ring!

> **Dialogical** critics would note this allusion to another famous text [AM; CL; KT; DK; PH]. **Traditional historical** critics might report that this song had been around since the 1830s and was widely used to celebrate America before "The Star-Spangled Banner" was adopted in 1931 as the national anthem. Therefore, most if not all of King's audience would have known this song [AM]. **Thematic** critics might note that King was also able to use the lyrics of the song to reinforce his basic message [AM].

And if America is to be a great nation, this must become true.

And so let freedom ring from the prodigious hilltops of New Hampshire.

Let freedom ring from the mighty mountains of New York.

Let freedom ring from the heightening Alleghenies of Pennsylvania.

Let freedom ring from the snow-capped Rockies of Colorado.

Let freedom ring from the curvaceous slopes of California.

But not only that:

Let freedom ring from Stone Mountain of Georgia.

Let freedom ring from Lookout Mountain of Tennessee.

Let freedom ring from every hill and molehill of Mississippi.

From every mountainside, let freedom ring.

And when this happens, and when we allow freedom to ring, when we let it ring from every village and every hamlet, from every state and every city, we will be able to speed up that day when *all* of God's children, black men and white men, Jews and Gentiles, Protestants and Catholics, will be able to join hands and sing in the words of the old Negro spiritual:

Formalist critics would note King's effective use of emphatic repetition [JL]. **Multicultural** critics would note King's allusion here to various subgroups within the general population, while **archetypal** critics might be interested in his focus on the desire of all people, whatever their backgrounds, for freedom and dignity [AW; KS; JL]. **Multiculturalists** might note not only the religious and ethnic groups King mentions [YY] but also the sheer number of other kinds of groups or subcultures he implies [MG], even involving potential differences between thousands of villages, cities, and states [RCE]. **Feminist** critics might note the reference to "black *men* and white *men*" (emphasis added) and suggest that such phrasing, perhaps unintentionally, diminished the importance of women [KS]. **Ecocritics** might be interested in the ways King relates the real and present physical beauty of the United States to the ideal and potential social beauty that might be achieved if racism could be eliminated [RCE]. **Traditional historical** critics might comment on the reference to Stone Mountain, which was not simply a stunning piece of geography but a highly controversial site. To many, it symbolized the Ku Klux Klan, the Confederacy, and white racism. In 1963, Stone Mountain was (and had been) in the news for all these reasons [PH].

Free at last! Free at last!

Thank God Almighty, we are free at last!

Thematic critics might note that the very last words of the speech emphasize its key theme of freedom [YY]. **Formalist** critics might admire the way in which the final three words bring the speech to an effective and tightly unified conclusion [LB].

Contributors

Anna Meadows [AM]; Ashley Warren [AW]; Chloe Langston [CL]; Deiondre Kinard [DK]; Erin Rembert [ER]; Jordan Chapman (= Jordan Bailey) [JC]; Johnathon Lawrence [JL]; Jaila Rhodes [JR]; Katelyn Martin [KM]; Kelly Snyder [KS]; Keyonté Croom [KC]; Keri Tankersley [KT]; Laura Bowden [LB]; Molly Belew [MB]; Marshall D. Buford [MDB]; Marcus Goodbee [MG]; Pamela Harris [PH]; Robert C. Evans [RCE]; Simran Kumari [SK]; Yolanda York [YY].

Note

1. For much more information about these theories, including many applications of them, see Evans, Little, and Wiedemann.

Work Cited

Evans, Robert C., Anne C. Little, and Barbara Wiedemann. *Short Fiction: A Critical Companion.* Locust Hill, 1997.

Contraries and Progression in Martin Luther King

Nicolas Tredell

Much of Martin's Luther King's prose is structured around contraries, binary oppositions such as conformity/nonconformity, courage/cowardice, divine/human, joy/sorrow, optimism/pessimism, realism/idealism, and violence/nonviolence. His texts sometimes state these explicitly and at other times assume or imply them. Those texts also make use of contrasts, juxtaposing different qualities that are not exactly opposites but that may come into conflict, such as expedient/ethical: expedient and ethical courses of action may sometimes happily, or suspiciously, coincide, but they may also diverge and clash and when they do it is necessary to make a judgement, which may or may not be consciously formulated, as to whether expediency or ethics—and what kind of expediency or ethics—should prevail.

Even when King's texts express such contraries and contrasts, they do not enumerate them explicitly but embed them in continuous prose and present, amplify, and complement them through a range of rhetorical devices involving sound and sense—for example, alliteration, grammatical parallelism, adjectival elaboration, and a variety of imagery (such as simile, metaphor, and metonymy). To speak of "rhetorical devices" may seem to imply an element of contrivance, mechanicalness, even insincerity, in King's written and spoken utterances, but this is in itself to posit a dubious though undoubtedly durable binary opposition between rhetoric and sincerity; the impression of sincerity is itself a rhetorical effect. In the first sonnet in Sir Philip Sidney's poetic sequence *Astrophil and Stella*, for instance, the poet, "fain [eager] in verse my love to show" struggles to find suitable words, studying the work of other writers that could serve him as models, but only achieves fluency when he obeys his muse's exhortation to "look in thy heart and write." In his preface to the 1800 edition of *Lyrical Ballads*, William Wordsworth declares that "all good poetry is the spontaneous overflow of powerful feelings" (Wordsworth and Coleridge 246) to justify the disruption, in the poems themselves, of conventional eighteenth-century poetic diction. But in the case of both Sidney's sonnet and Wordsworth's preface and poems, the evocation of emotion, the sense of spontaneity, are themselves rhetorically produced, created in language and through a range of rhetorical devices. Sincerity, without rhetorical shaping, can result in language that is clumsy, inexpressive, or banal. King's texts do indeed read and sound as if, like the speaker of Sidney's sonnet, he had looked in his heart to speak and write, and as if they were "the spontaneous overflow of powerful feelings"; but they do so because of the rhetorical skills that this son and grandson of preachers, steeped in African American religious discourse and educated in a Western canonical tradition of literature and philosophy, employs, skills that are not divorced from, but married to feelings, marshalling both head and heart.

This essay explores these oppositions in light of the assertion, in William Blake's *Marriage of Heaven and Hell*, that "[w]ithout Contraries is no progression" (Blake 149). Blake has been deliberately chosen here as a writer who does *not* feature in King's texts; for King, Blake would have been, at least in one important strand in his work as represented in *The Marriage*, too antinomian in a Romantic way; whereas traditional antinomianism believed that grace allowed exemption from moral law, *The Marriage*, and other elements in Blake's work, presented energy as the exempting factor; King, although willing, as we shall discuss further, to break secular law in certain circumstances, affirmed the existence of a God-given moral law. Blake may also have been too mystical for a person geared, as King was, to social activism (the repressive and reactionary results of the French Revolution stifled Blake's own activist impulses). King's preference is not for a Blakean language of contraries but for one of thesis, antithesis, and synthesis, an approach that is both more idealist, in the manner of the German philosopher Hegel, whose work he encountered as a student (see King 32), and more pragmatic, in the manner of the American philosopher William James. But Blake offers insights into the intensities that inform King's work and power its rhetoric, with its contrary drives toward conflict and consensus, resistance and reconciliation, while William James encompasses both the practical functions of faith (which are irrespective of its ultimate "truth") and the intensities of religious experience in ways that both partly complement and partly complicate King's worldview.

As well as the Blakean language of "contraries," the Hegelian one of "thesis/antithesis/synthesis," and the Jamesean one of the pragmatic uses and experiential force of religion, two further interconnected ways of talking about oppositions are relevant to our exploration here: one is structuralism, an influential mid-twentieth-century intellectual movement that sought to interpret not only language but the whole of human culture in terms of binary oppositions such as good/evil, male/female and—an opposition with evident racial implications—black/white; the second, developing in the later twentieth century from and to some extent against structuralism (in what might itself seem like a binary movement) is deconstruction, which argued that binary oppositions were interdependent and that their implicit hierarchy was inevitably self-subverting: the superiority of white in the white/black hierarchy, for example, depended on its supposedly inferior term and was undermined by it so that it was possible to switch them around and, finally, to arrive at a situation in which neither term was privileged, a state of undecidability, an aporia or impasse that might seem baffling or, in a utopian perspective, liberating. Had King lived to encounter deconstruction, he would have rejected it since he did believe in a hierarchy in which God, truth, and moral law were, however obscured, unshakably privileged terms; and in a postdeconstructive era it is evident that binary oppositions, in theological, political, social, and ethical discourse, continue to have a strong hold; but it remains an interesting perspective to apply to King's use of such oppositions.

Contraries

Contraries, oppositions, are especially evident in the sermons collected in *A Gift of Love*; given their nature as sermons, these were originally delivered orally, for the ear and for the "inward eye" (Wordsworth) rather than for the outward eye, and although, as King tells us in his preface, they have undergone some revision to accommodate them to the reading eye and mind, they retain key characteristics of their original mode of delivery that function to give them impact and memorability—and the use of contraries is perhaps their most prominent characteristic. The first sermon, for instance, is entitled "A Tough Mind and a Tender Heart" and takes as its New Testament text "Be ye therefore wise as serpents, and harmless as doves" (Matt. 10:16; King, *Gift* 1), an imperative that itself offers, not exact opposites, but two contrasting qualities—wisdom/harmlessness—which are given specificity by similes drawn from both from the natural world and from a biblical bestiary—serpents/doves. In adapting this text, King turns a contrast into a contrary by replacing "wisdom" with "toughness" and "harmless" with "tender"—but urging their combination rather than conflict: "We must combine the toughness of the serpent and the softness of the dove, a tough mind and a tender heart" (2).

King's opposition both echoes and revises, not necessarily in a conscious way, the distinction William James made between the "tough-minded" and the "tender-minded," keeping the tough/tender binary opposition but substituting "heart" for "mind." In *Pragmatism*, James offered, in tabular form, an outline of what he saw as the respective characteristics of the two kinds of mind (12):

The tender-minded
Rationalistic (going by "principles")
Intellectualistic
Idealistic
Optimistic
Religious
Free-willist [*sic*]
Monistic
Dogmatical

The tough-minded
Empiricist (going by "facts")
Sensationalistic
Materialistic
Pessimistic
Irreligious
Fatalistic
Pluralistic
Sceptical [*sic*]

For King, the characteristics of the two states, extracted from his continuous prose on pages 1-4 of *A Gift of Love*, and set out in tabular form here for the purpose of comparison with James, are as follows:

Tough-minded
Incisive thinking
Realistic appraisal
Decisive judgment
Sharp and penetrating
Sifting the true from the false
Astute and discerning
Strong austere quality
Firmness of purpose
Solidness of commitment
Postjudges

Tender [or "soft"]-minded
Gullibility
Prone to embrace all kinds of superstitions
Irrational fears

Fears change
Prejudges (5)

We can see some similarities between the qualities King and James attribute to each category: for example, "empiricist," a characteristic of tough-mindedness for James, might overlap to some extent with "realistic appraisal" (2) and "sifting the true from the false" (2) in King's tough-minded inventory; "dogmatical" in James's tender-minded list might map to some degree onto "fears change" (3) and "prejudges" (4) in King's tender-minded category.

James's attribution of "religion" to the tender-minded category, however, links uncomfortably with King's consignment to that category of "prone to embrace all kinds of superstitions" (3) and even perhaps "irrational fears" (3); despite James's interest in, positive pragmatic evaluation of, and respect for religion, his assignment of it to the tender-minded category might suggest, when linked with King's categorizations, that "religion," "superstition," and "irrational fears" were on a continuum that could cast religion in a pejorative light. This highlights the fact that whereas James's tender-minded category embraces elements that could seem positive, King's encompasses elements that have largely negative connotations.

We might say that James anticipates a deconstructive perspective in which "tough-minded" and "tender-minded" are not in a fixed hierarchy in which one term is superior to another but in a more shifting, uncertain relationship; it is King who presents a fixed hierarchy here, a put-down of tender-mindedness. This could appear to concur with a widespread cultural bias in favor of toughness, associated with strength, and deprecatory of tenderness, associated with weakness. Such a concurrence comes close to contradicting the combination of toughness and tenderness King has proposed earlier; he tried to retain a sense of the value of the latter by, as we have seen, assigning it to the emotions (the heart) rather than the intellect.

It is also evident that King from this comparison often uses an adjective (occasionally two) and a noun, or two nouns joined by a conjunction (*and*) or a preposition (*of*), in contrast to James's use of one noun. This is partly due to the fact that he is employing continuous prose, which permits expansiveness, rather than the tabular form James adopts, which conduces to brevity: but adjectival elaboration is a more general feature of King's work and evinces his search for nuanced meaning and fuller definition. Consider, for instance, the question in his first sermon: "What is more tragic than to see a person who has risen to the disciplined heights of toughmindedness but has at the same time sunk to the passionless depths of hardheartedness?" (6). Here we have a heights/depths binary opposition but the adjectives "disciplined" and "passionless" further define and implicitly evaluate the two opposed elements: the first adjective is positive, the second negative, its suffix "-less" marking a lack. It is also notable here that the oppositions are combined in the same (hypothetical but possible) person—and while combination is often fruitful in King, here it is diminishing, subtracting from a discipline that might otherwise be admirable. We can also see in this quotation how King's oppositions are figured in imagery and it is worth exploring this important aspect of his texts.

Imagery in King's texts

The last quotation we considered deploys a culturally familiar binary image: heights/depths. But "heights" and "depths" are themselves relatively abstract qualities that can apply to a variety of specific phenomena; topographical imagery, however, can make them more concrete—as a notable example, imagery of hills and valleys. Concluding his thirteenth sermon in *A Gift of Love*, King's version of the Letter he thinks St. Paul might have written to twentieth-century American Christians, he speaks of God as able to "lift us from the dark valley of despair to the bright mountain of hope" (148). He sometimes adds other topographical elements: his first sermon, for example, advocating a balanced combination of science and religion, contends: "Science keeps religion from sinking into the valley of crippling irrationalism and paralyzing obscurantism. Religion prevents science from falling into the marsh of obsolete materialism and moral nihilism" (4). "Marsh" joins "valley" here as a metaphor for the hazards on the terrain the pilgrim traverses to truth.

Meteorological imagery, often of a seasonal kind, also figures significantly, for instance, when King develops the tough mind/tender heart binary distinction we considered earlier: "Toughmindedness without tenderheartedness is cold and detached, leaving one's life in a perpetual winter devoid of the warmth of spring and the gentle heat of summer" (5). Seasonal alterations also provide images for the changes in life. "Like the rhythmic alternation in the natural order, life has the glittering sunlight of its summers and the piercing chill of its winters" (109). Here King draws on a familiar and potent strand of analogies between the seasons and their changes, and life experiences and emotions and their metamorphoses, which stretches back to early modern, medieval, and ancient literature.

King's texts also employ imagery invoking specific meteorological phenomena rather than the seasons, again as images of existential experiences: for example, "Adversity assails us with hurricane force" (108); or the feeling that God is especially needed "on the day when the storms of disappointment rage, the winds of disaster blow, and the tidal waves of grief beat against our lives" (109); or, in a combination of topographical and meteorological imagery with the light/dark imagery discussed below: "we can transform bleak and desolate valleys into sunlit paths of joy and bring new light into the dark caverns of pessimism" (110); or, mixing meteorological with the light/dark imagery and the diurnal/nocturnal imagery also discussed below: "Glowing sunrises are transformed into darkest nights" (108).

Light/dark imagery occurs in, for example, King's eighth sermon in *The Gift of Love*: "When the lamp of hope flickers and the candle of faith runs low, he restoreth our souls" (88-89). Here, the imagery is of artificially produced light—from lamp or candle—but at other times the light/dark imagery takes the form of invocations of the natural rhythms of day and night, of earth's diurnal and nocturnal course: for instance, in that same sermon, God "is with us not only in the noontime of fulfillment, but also in the midnight of despair" (89). The plural pronoun—*us* rather than *me*—is significant here: for King, salvation is both an individual and a collective goal and takes the shape of actual material freedoms and fulfilments; light/dark imagery is also applied to the collective endurance and struggle of African Americans under slavery: "Their bottomless vitality transformed the darkness of frustration into the light of hope" (99). Also notable is the stress here on active, inexhaustible, transformative agency on the part of those suffering. We can see as well—and hear, with the inward ear, or the outward ear if read aloud—the rhythmic strength of King's sentences and the way in which grammatical parallelism—as in the noun/preposition/noun structure common to the contraries "darkness of frustration"/"light of hope"—helps to bring home the meaning. This is a further key element of his treatment of contraries and contrasts that we can explore.

Contraries, Sound, and Wordplay

Links between sounds, and plays on words, often enhance the pleasure and power of King's texts and reinforce his contraries and contrasts. His plays on words do not serve the jocular purpose of puns but contribute to memorability and impact and to an underlying sense of the ultimate interdependency of apparent opposites and alternatives. In the second sermon in *A Gift of Love*, for instance, we find: "Christianity has always insisted that the cross we bear precedes the crown we wear" (20). Here a single fourteen-word sentence brings together the contrasting terms *cross* and *crown*, metonymies that encapsulate the Christian story with its pilgrim's progress through excruciating agony to eternal glory and stresses their linkage not only semantically but also aurally by the alliteration of *Chr*istianity/*cr*oss/*cr*own, and by the internal rhyme bear/wear.

The seventh sermon in the same volume includes the short, pithy sentence: "We have guided missiles and misguided man" (77). Within its seven words, this plays on sound and meaning, with its first adjective *guided* turning, after the conjunction *and*, into the suffix of its second adjective—*misguided*—and the order of its homophones reversed—guided *miss*- becomes *mis*guided. This is one of those Kingian sentences that takes on an aphoristic, quotable force, one that could function as powerfully, perhaps in a sense more powerfully because of its compactness and isolation, if taken out of context and presented as a freestanding quote (which is not to deny or diminish its importance as part of the argument of the sermon within which it is embedded).

Almost immediately afterward in the same sermon, an even shorter sentence, only five words long, occurs: "We have absorbed life in livelihood" (77). This plays on the similar sounds, separated only by a consonant, of *life* and *live*[…] and also on the contrasting meanings of *life* and *livelihood*, where the latter is seen as material and the former as vital—though King is fully aware of the importance of material things. As he says a little earlier in the sermon, "[w]e have both a privilege and a duty to seek the basic material necessities of life" (70). Livelihood makes life possible, but the two are not, and should not be, synonymous. Nonetheless, this is one of those plays on words that suggest the likeness, as well as the difference, of contraries and contrasts and it is an index of two important desires King's prose enacts: it wants to address contraries and contrasts, not to ignore them or pretend they do not exist; but it also wants to negotiate between them and to bring them together. We shall now explore this desire for negotiation and convergence.

Neither/Nor, Both/And

King has two main strategies for negotiating between and bringing together contraries and contrasts. One is the neither/nor approach. *Enten-Eller—Either/Or* (1843) was the first published book by the nineteenth-century Danish philosopher and theologian Søren Kierkegaard, an early exponent of the Christian existentialism with which King, especially through his study of Paul Tillich, partly allied himself. At significant points, King's texts offer a counterformulation to the demanding alternatives of Kierkegaard's title: neither/nor. For example, in *A Gift of Love*, "God is neither hardhearted nor softminded" (9); "man is neither totally depraved, nor is God an almighty dictator" (134); "the truth about man is found neither in liberalism nor in neo-orthodoxy" (151). This recurrence of the neither/nor pattern suggests that, to some extent and in certain instances, King seeks a *via media*, a middle way between contraries. But he does not stop at either pragmatic compromise in the William James sense or undecidable aporiae in the deconstructive sense: he claims that "the contradictions of life are neither final nor ultimate" (67) —that; for example, "[a]n adequate understanding of man is found neither in the thesis of liberalism nor in the antithesis of neo-orthodoxy, but in a synthesis which reconciles the truths of both" (151). In King's texts, neither/nor can progress to both/and, not in easy coexistence but in a higher synthesis that is different from the two contraries, the thesis and antithesis, which fed into it.

King sees opposites, or apparent opposites, and contrasts, as capable of creative combination; and creativity, in its form as noun, verb, or adjective, is a favorite term in his texts. Near the start of his first sermon he says: "life at its best is a creative synthesis of opposites in fruitful harmony" (1), and this idea of "a creative synthesis of opposites" features strongly in his work. In King's perspective, achieving "a creative synthesis" is, ultimately, following the divine example, according with the divine substance, as we see from an affirmation in the last sentence of the first sermon, which repeats the phrase "creative synthesis" from its opening paragraph: "our God combines in his nature a creative synthesis of love and justice" (9).

Apparently negative experiences can also promote creative responses: "Fear," for instance, "is a powerfully creative force. Every great invention and intellectual advance represents a desire to escape from some dreaded circumstance or condition" (115). It is possible to respond creatively to suffering as well, as King illustrates through personal testimony: "As my sufferings mounted I soon realized that there were two ways in which I could respond to my situation—either to react with bitterness or seek to transform the suffering into a creative force" (157). A key example of such a transformation is the famous "Letter from Birmingham Jail" (16 April 1963) he wrote while in prison and which we shall now consider.

Binaries in Birmingham
King's "Letter from Birmingham Jail" is a polemic, an intervention in an ongoing and immediate struggle, that takes a clear side but

that also aims, through argument, to assimilate to some extent, and eventually to surpass, the contrary side that it challenges, as expressed in a statement published in a newspaper from eight fellow clergymen from Alabama criticizing the direct-action demonstrations in Birmingham in which King had been involved. King's response challenges and creates a series of oppositions that his opponents and he himself raise.

The first of these is insider/outsider. His opponents deployed the latter in an attempt to disqualify those who supposedly come from outside a community from advocating and actualizing agitation. King replies on two levels. One is factual: he claims that he and some of his staff were invited to Birmingham rather than intruding on their own initiative and that he has "organizational ties" with the city (King 188). In effect, he blurs the boundary between *insider* and *outsider* by suggesting that, in a sense, he is not wholly an outsider. But this is a fragile response insofar as it implies that if he had *not* been invited to Birmingham or had organizational ties there, he could have been categorized as an outsider: the insider/outsider boundary, even if blurred, stays intact. But he then takes the argument to another level by a bold universalization: he posits "the interrelatedness of all communities and states" (189). This perspective dissolves the insider/outsider opposition: in a sense, no man, woman, or child is an outsider anywhere because existing links bind all together, wherever they may be.

King goes on to bring another binary opposition into play: "Injustice anywhere is a threat to justice everywhere" (189). Here we have two clearly contrary nouns – injustice/justice—and two contrasting but complementary adverbs: *anywhere* and *everywhere*, the first meaning *in any place* and the second *in all places*; thus, for example, "it happens anywhere" does not entail that "it happens everywhere" but that its possible occurrence is not restricted to any one particular location; the two terms can be conjoined, however, to reinforce a sense of ubiquity and universality, as in the phrase "it happens anywhere and everywhere." In King's locution here, the joining of the two terms dissolves the outsider/insider opposition by removing the opposition between the global and the local, not by effacing the identity of either or absorbing one into the other but by presenting them as complementary rather than contradictory, interactive rather than inimical.

The "Letter" goes on to challenge the opposition between "direct action" and "negotiation." These are not contrary alternatives, King contends, but codependent activities: when negotiation has apparently failed (and, in any given instance, whether it has in fact failed is disputable), "Nonviolent direct action seeks to create such a crisis and foster such a tension that a community which has constantly refused to negotiate is forced to confront the issue" (190). The initial adjective in this sentence invokes an implicit binary opposition that is absolutely crucial to King's conceptual framework, rhetoric, and advocated action: nonviolence/violence.

It could be argued, however, that this too is not quite such a binary opposition as King makes it seem: that *forcing* a community to confront an issue is a form of violence, albeit of a psychological rather than physical kind. King does not address this objection directly, but he does acknowledge that the idea of creating tension "may sound rather shocking"(190) and then introduces another binary opposition by adjectival means: instead of using two opposed nouns he employs the same noun, *tension*, but differentiates its two uses by adjectives that invoke the violence/nonviolence binary opposition: "violent tension" and "constructive nonviolent tension" (191). Moreover, he adds to the latter contrary a further adjective, "constructive," which implicitly invokes its most obvious opposite, "destructive," and links with a favorite King term we have already considered: "creative."

In elaborating the function of "constructive nonviolent tension," King draws on the heights/depths and dark/light binary oppositions familiar from his sermons (though *light* is only implicit here): such tension "will help men rise from the *dark depths* of prejudice and racism to the majestic *heights* of understanding and brotherhood" (191, italics added). He concludes this part of his argument with a further binary opposition: for too long the American South has stagnated "in a tragic effort to live in monologue rather than dialogue" (191). Given King's implied preference for dialogue, a possible objection arises here to the very form in which he is indicating that preference: for is not the "Letter" a polemic, a kind of monologue in which we hear only King's voice? The response to this objection would be that the "Letter" is dialogic insofar as it aims to incorporate and represent fairly the views of his opponents and then rebut them in a measured way: the "Letter" is polemic but not propaganda: it offers its readers the chance to disagree and even suggests grounds on which they might base their disagreement.

The "Letter" then moves on to address another binary opposition, timely/untimely, tackling the objection that it is not the right time in Birmingham for the kind of nonviolent direct action King has advocated. King challenges this opposition by arguing that "timeliness" depends on your location in relation to particular circumstances: that time—the time of experience, the time for action—is not homogeneous and universal: "Frankly, I have yet to engage in a direct-action campaign that was 'well timed' in the view of those who have not suffered unduly from the disease of segregation" (191). Timeliness and untimeliness are contraries that clash when different ideas of what is timely and untimely, held by different individuals and groups, clash; those clashes bring confrontations that may lead to violence but can produce positive progression.

One way in which direct action may seem untimely is when it breaks existing laws, instead of waiting and working legally for a change in those laws, in the fullness of time, which would remove the grievances that prompted direct action. Given the perceived importance of law in holding a society together and King's nonantinomian belief that Christianity entails obedience to the moral law and God's law, the advocacy of lawbreaking presents a particular problem, as King recognizes. His response is to introduce a binary opposition and, as in the case of "tension" discussed above, he does so adjectivally, by using the same noun but prefacing it with contrary adjectives: in this instance, just/unjust. He asserts that "there are two types of laws: just and unjust" and continues: "One has not only a legal but a moral responsibility to obey just laws. Conversely, one has a moral responsibility to disobey unjust laws" (193). Here a further binary opposition appears—"obedience"/"disobedience"—and a further contrast—"legal"/"moral", two terms that, in King's perspective, coincide when a law is just but clash when it is unjust.

It could be argued, however—and this is one of those many moments in the "Letter" when King, rather than stating his case in a dogmatic, monologic fashion, allows for dialogue and disagreement on the reader's part—that there is both a legal and a moral responsibility to obey the law whether or not it is perceived as "just" in order to uphold the authority of the law and the whole framework of justice: after all, any person, and any group, could claim that a particular law—one that forbids theft, for instance—is "unjust" because it discriminates against those with less or no property and can therefore be broken; it may even be claimed that one has a moral responsibility to break it. If one does accept the adjectivally produced just/unjust law binary opposition, the problem is then: how to determine which laws are just or unjust.

The "Letter" acknowledges this issue and proposes a way to distinguish between just and unjust laws: "A just law is a man-made code that squares with the moral law or the law of God. An unjust law is a code that is out of harmony with the moral law" (193). King seems aware, however, that this criterion of correspondence is not enough; it raises the same sort of question in different terms: how to determine what the moral law and/or the law of God are, since both ethics and theology have not produced universally or even widely accepted answers—and, of course, the "law of God" will not have much traction upon those who reject the existence of God. As if in tacit recognition of this latter problem, King's second sentence drops the phrase "the law of God" and speaks only of "the moral law."

King then offers another definition of a just and an unjust law, in a binary opposition encapsulated in two grammatically parallel eight-word sentences: "Any law that uplifts human personality is just. Any law that degrades human personality is unjust" (193). This couples the two contraries of just/unjust and uplifting/degrading (the latter contrary also employs a height/depth metaphor of a familiar Kingian kind). The two sentences are another example of an instantly isolable, eminently quotable formulation but, especially within the context of his overall argument, its terms seem to need further definition: what is human personality? How do we determine what uplifts or degrades it (not least in a Christian perspective where, as King himself has already stated, and as we saw earlier, an earthly cross may lead to a heavenly crown, and degradation may prove ultimately uplifting).

The "Letter" then introduces three more coupled contraries: segregator/segregated, superiority/inferiority, and true/false. Segregation "gives the segregator a false sense of superiority and the segregated a false sense of inferiority" (193). He also offers what he calls "a more concrete example of just and unjust laws" (193) that turns on an opposition between *sameness* and *difference*:

> An unjust law is a code that a numerical or power majority group compels a minority to obey but does not make binding on itself. This is *difference* made legal. By the same token, a just law is a code that a majority compels a minority to follow that it is willing to follow itself. This is *sameness* made legal. (193, italics in original)

Sameness as a criterion of a just law is questionable, however, since it may discriminate against those who are different; for example, if a majority passed a law compelling a minority to abandon a particular set of religious practices that did not infringe any other law, and even if that majority itself obeyed such a law, it could still be argued that it was unjust to the minority that wished to engage in those practices.

In the "Letter," King does not resolve the question of what constitutes a just and unjust law and one would not expect him to—it is a question that philosophers, jurists, and lay people have debated through the centuries and it remains unsettled and perhaps unsettleable. King does, however, show remarkable assiduousness in addressing the issue in a polemic composed in the heat of struggle and displays vibrant creativity in his generation of contraries to progress discussion of it. If the issue leads, on one level, to an undecidable impasse, an aporia, it provides, on another level, and even in potentially embittering or enervating circumstances, the energy for action; and, as Blake's *Marriage of Heaven and Hell* affirmed: "Energy is Eternal Delight" (149).

Conclusion: Politics, Ethics, Aesthetics

King's concern with contraries and their synthesis is, then, not merely a matter of rhetorical technique; rather it carries a politics, an ethics, and even an aesthetics. The politics and ethics themselves emerge from a contrary that pervades King's work and life: action/inaction. King comes firmly down on the side of action and is particularly hard on those who counsel quietism in the face of injustice; but he does, nonetheless, assimilate a kind of inaction into this advocacy of action: the kind of inaction that entails eschewing violence. So it is not that King entirely excludes inaction; rather he recognizes that inaction, in the form of nonviolence, can marry with and inform action. He fuses contraries to make things progress, bringing action and inaction together in a higher, and vital, synthesis.

There is also an implicit aesthetics in King's texts. We may make a link here with the dominant form of literary criticism in mid-twentieth-century North America: the New Criticism. New Criticism especially valued those literary texts, particularly short poems, that held tensions and oppositions in a vibrant equilibrium, avoiding the crudities of didacticism; but this could also be seen as an alibi for inaction: contemplating the well-wrought urn of the literary text might be a refuge from the political tumults of the era, a retreat into quiescence: a charge that gathered force as the conformities of the 1950s gave way to the confrontations of the 1960s. King's texts do, in a sense, achieve a kind of vibrant equilibrium, through the rhetorical devices we have outlined above, which bring contraries and contrasts into the same textual space and counterpoise and conjoin them in that space through grammatical, aural, imagistic, and semantic resonances. It is possible to imagine, in some future utopia from which racial and other forms of injustice have vanished, reading King's texts as the New Critics might have read the kinds of texts they favored, as a pulsing holding-in-tension of opposites with no road through into action. But in the world in which King was writing, they constituted a calling out, a call to action, which could not be sealed off in some aesthetic zone—and which still reverberate today.

Works Cited

Blake, William. *The Marriage of Heaven and Hell.* In *Complete Writings.* Edited by Geoffrey Keynes, Oxford UP, 1974.

James, William. *Pragmatism: A New Name for Some Old Ways of Thinking: Popular Lectures on Philosophy.* Longmans, Green, 1907. archive.org/details/157unkngoog/page/n8.

King, Martin Luther, Jr. *A Gift of Love: Sermons from Strength to Love.* Penguin Kindle Edition, 2017.

_____, *The Autobiography of Martin Luther King, Jr.* Edited by Clayborne Carson, Little, Brown, 1999.

Sidney, Sir Philip. *Astrophil and Stella* (1591), Sonnet 1. www.poetryfoundation.org/poems/45152/astrophil-and-stella-1-loving-in-truth-and-fain-in-verse-my-love-to-show.

Wordsworth, William, "I wandered lonely as a cloud" (1815). www.poetryfoundation.org/poems/45521/i-wandered-lonely-as-a-cloud.

_____, "Preface [to 1800 edition]." In Wordsworth, William, and Samuel Taylor Coleridge, *Lyrical Ballads.* Edited by R. L. Brett and A. R. Jones, Methuen, 1968, pp. 241-72.

CRITICAL READINGS

Martin Luther King: The Uses of Intertextuality

Nicolas Tredell

Martin Luther King's published sermons, speeches, public letters, and articles are packed with intertextual references in the form of direct quotations from, allusions to, or echoes of classical, biblical, early modern, and nineteenth and twentieth-century literary, political, philosophical, and theological writings—for example, those of Plato, Aristotle, and Epictetus; the Old and New Testaments; Shakespeare and Donne; Tennyson and Arnold; James Russell Lowell, Emerson and Thoreau; Frederick Douglass and Paul Dunbar; and T. S. Eliot. This essay will examine a selection of significant intertextual references in key King texts.

The term *intertextuality*, rather than the older term *influence*, has been preferred here for two main reasons. One is that intertextual references need not have been intended, consciously or unconsciously, by the named author of the texts in which they occur; where that author gave a direct quote and attributed it, as King often does, it is reasonable to infer that they did so consciously, but apparent allusions in a text to other texts can result from the *reader* making an intertextual connection—this is the case with the "No man is an island" link discussed below, where King may indeed have been aware of Donne's phrase, but need not have been for the connection to be legitimately made.

The second reason for preferring the term intertextuality, particularly in relation to King, is that it emerged from a moment in late twentieth-century critical theory when the concepts of the "author" and of "originality" came under challenge. As Roland Barthes put it in a seminal essay "The Death of the Author":

> a text is not a line of words releasing a single "theological" meaning (the "message" of the Author-God) but a multi-dimensional space in which a variety of writings, none of them original, blend and clash.

> The text is a tissue of quotations drawn from the innumerable centres of culture. (146)

In this perspective, every text is an intertext, a melting pot of other textual fragments.

We need not go all the way with this idea to see that it continues to cast a searching light on concepts of the author and text, in a twenty-first century where it is still or perhaps even more the case that, as Barthes put it in that essay, the "image of literature to be found in ordinary culture is tyrannically centred on the author, [their] person, [their] life, [their] tastes, [their] passions" (143). It is particularly interesting to shine this light on King, both because he has an iconic status and historical importance that is not primarily dependent on his identity as an author of written texts, and because, as Peter Ling puts it at the start of his online *Literary Encyclopedia* entry: "If a literary encyclopaedia should confine itself to writers, then Dr. Martin Luther King, Jnr., would be a contentious choice" (Ling) because of the now-acknowledged plagiarism in his 1954 PhD thesis for Boston University and because some of the books that appeared under his name were written at least partly by others—Ling instances *Why We Can't Wait* (1964), "largely crafted by professional ghost writer Alfred Duckett" and *Where Do We Go From Here: Chaos or Community?* (1967), to which Stanley Levison, Clarence Jones, and Bayard Rustin made a large contribution. But it could be argued that these attributions only matter in a culture that is, in Barthes's words, "tyrannically centred on the author"; if we see these texts as intertexts that assemble quotations, actual and paraphrased, from a variety of sources, the fact that they are not wholly by King but the fruits of collective effort becomes less important.

Given, however, that twenty-first-century culture is, possibly more than ever, "tyrannically centred on the author," this essay will focus on texts that are more definitely attributable to King—the sermons collected in *A Gift of Love* and the "Letter from Birmingham Jail"—and will examine the functions of those intertextual references within these texts that are, for the most part, definitely identified and attributed as quotations from others. For the purposes of analysis, we shall consider them chronologically, from classical times to the twentieth century, but it is important to bear in mind that King's texts do not necessarily present them in chronological order.

Classical References

There are relatively few references to classical authors in King's texts. In his eleventh sermon in *A Gift of Love*, "Antidotes for Fear," he does, in examining the nature of "one of the supreme virtues known to man," courage, invoke Plato, to whom he attributes the idea, in the form of a paraphrase rather than a direct quotation, that "courage" is "an element of the soul which bridges the cleavage between reason and desire"; Aristotle, who "thought of courage as the affirmation of man's essential nature"; and the first- to second-century Greek stoic philosopher Epictetus (55 CE-c 135 CE), as transcribed by his pupil Arrian in the *Discourses*—King quotes from Book 1, Chapter 2 of the Oldfather translation: "For it is not death or hardship that is a fearful thing, but the fear of hardship and death." (qtd. in King, *Gift* 117; the original has "hardship or death"). The religious element in the teachings of Epictetus appealed to early Christian thinkers and thus entered into theological tradition, even though his observations on the fear of death have also been cited approvingly by agnostics and atheists.

As the above examples indicate, King's classical references are mainly to philosophers. He does, however, make a general reference, not giving any titles, to ancient Greek drama in his ninth sermon in *A Gift of Love*, "Shattered Dreams," when he considers those who fatalistically accept their lot: "They never actively seek to change their circumstances, for they believe that all circumstances, *as in the Greek tragedies*, are controlled by irresistible and foreordained forces" (95, italics added). King vigorously opposes this view, even though he acknowledges that some deeply religious people hold it.

While classical references are sparing in King's texts, biblical references are copious and crucial.

Old Testament References

The Old Testament story of the Hebrew exodus from Egypt was especially important to African Americans and could also serve as a more general image of the difficulties of escaping from any kind of bondage. In "A Tough Mind and a Tender Heart," King's first sermon in *A Gift of Love*, he challenges (as in the ninth sermon discussed in the previous section and elsewhere in his work) resignation to one's lot—in this case, segregation—and uses an Old Testament analogy: "When Moses led the children of Israel from the slavery of Egypt to the freedom of the Promised Land, he discovered that slaves do not always welcome their deliverers" (6-7). The title of his eighth sermon in *A Gift of Love*, "The Death of Evil Upon the Seashore," is itself an Old Testament reference to the verse from Exodus (14:30) that provides the sermon's epigraph: "and Israel saw the Egyptians dead upon the sea shore." That sermon makes extensive use of the Exodus analogy, comparing it, for instance, to the anticolonial struggles that gathered strength in the midtwentieth century and that could seem, at that time, to offer freedom to subject peoples: the "oppressed masses in Asia and Africa have won their freedom from the Egypt of colonialism and now move toward the promised land of economic and cultural stability" (83-84). King likens those who, in the United States, worked to maintain segregation to the rulers of ancient Egypt: "the pharaohs have employed legal maneuvers, economic reprisals, and even physical violence to hold the Negro in the Egypt of segregation. Despite the patient cry of many a Moses, they refused to let the Negro people go" (86). Here Moses becomes a type, in the sense of a forerunner, of a multitude of African American leaders calling for freedom.

Marking the progress made in the struggle against segregation, King continues the Old Testament metaphor, once again invoking, as he did with the Asian and African anticolonial struggles, the journey to the promised land: "at least we have left Egypt, and with patient yet firm determination we shall reach the promised land. [...] A Red Sea passage in history ultimately brings the forces of goodness to victory, and the closing of the same waters marks the doom and destruction of the forces of evil" (86). Near the end of the same sermon, he generalizes the intertextual metaphor, arguing that Christian faith "will sustain us in our struggle to escape from the bondage of every evil Egypt" (90); here the alliteration of the phrase "every evil Egypt" combines with its meaning to reinforce and make more memorable its universalization of a specific, though central, biblical event. It may be said that the evocation of dead Egyptians, albeit in ancient times, contradicts, or at least troubles, King's stress on nonviolence; the Old Testament can be a very violent text, conveying relish in the physical destruction of one's enemies. But King is using this event as a metaphor of the destruction of evil rather than of individuals who may, sometimes inadvertently or temporarily, embody evil (even if, in practice, that distinction is hard to make).

The Old Testament Psalms, with their rich poetry, are a major source of quotations and allusions for King. In his second sermon in *A Gift of Love*, "Transformed Nonconformist," King makes an intertextual reference to perhaps the best-known verse from that book: "Yea, though I walk through the valley of the shadow of death, I will fear no evil: for thou *art* with me; thy rod and thy staff they comfort me" (Psalms 23:4; italics in original). King adapts this by substituting "suffering" for "death" to produce the phrase "the valley of the shadow of suffering" (19)—an adaptation that both widens the application of the original to include miseries that fall short of mortality and improves on it aurally insofar as it creates an alliterative link between "shadow" and "suffering."

In "The Man Who Was a Fool," his seventh sermon in *A Gift of Love*, King, contending that science is not enough, affirms: "We must lift up our minds and eyes unto the hills from whence cometh our true help" (75). This echoes and adapts another famous Psalm: "I will lift up mine eyes unto the hills, from whence cometh my help" (Psalms 121:1). King alters this so as to stress the role of the intellect and imagination ("mind") as well as the visual sense ("eye") and to reinforce a sense of the authenticity of the "help" that comes from thence by adding the adjective "true."

In his tenth sermon in *A Gift of Love*, "Our God is Able," he says, speaking of the inevitable ultimate defeat of tyrants: "The

Hitlers and the Mussolinis have their day, and for a period they may wield great power, spreading themselves like a green bay tree, but soon they are cut down like the grass and wither as the green herb" (106). This combines, within one sentence, references to two notorious dictators in twentieth-century history with allusions to two verses from Psalms, though reversing the order in which they occur in the biblical text: "I have seen the wicked in great power, and spreading himself like a green bay tree." (Psalms 37:35) and "For they [evildoers and workers of iniquity] shall soon be cut down like the grass, and wither as the green herb" (Psalms 37:2).

The Old Testament book of Jeremiah was especially important for King as an endorsement of Christian activism. As he said in an extract, included in the *Autobiography*, from a course paper written at Crozier College in November 1948: "Jeremiah is a shining example of the truth that religion should never sanction the status quo" (22). King felt the modern church should follow this example: "Religion, in a sense, through men like Jeremiah, provides for its own advancement and carries within it the promise of progress and renewed power" (22). For King, Jeremiah embodied the powerful urge to speak the holy word. In the first sermon King delivered as minister of Dexter Avenue Baptist Church in Montgomery, Alabama, he quoted and slightly adapted a passage from the Book of Jeremiah that reads, in the King James Bible (20:9) "But *his word* was in mine heart as a burning fire shut up in my bones" (italics in original). King rendered this as: "The word of God is in my heart like burning fire shut up in my bones" (46). (Although King does not cite William Blake in his writings and speeches, this sentence, with its intensity of frustrated feeling, would not be out of place in Blake's Prophetic Books.) Jeremiah also provided an image of endurance in suffering: in King's ninth sermon in *A Gift of Love*, "Shattered Dreams," which is about coping with disappointment, he quotes, and again slightly adapts Jeremiah (10:19): "Truly this *is* a grief, and I must bear it" (italics in original)—King drops "Truly" so it reads: "This is a grief and I must bear it" (96). King felt that Jeremiah's fate—tradition says he was stoned to death—was characteristic of those who spoke against the status quo: society "destroys such men.

Jeremiah died a martyr" (22). (This of course anticipates King's own fate and was perhaps chosen for inclusion in the *Autobiography* at this point, and set apart in a separate boxed section to give it emphasis, not only because of its chronological position in the story of King's life but also because it foreshadowed that fate.) Jeremiah's importance as an example for King was enhanced because, in the prophet's challenge to the status quo and his violent and premature death, biblical interpreters could see him as a type of Christ—*type* in the theological sense of a person or event in the Old Testament that anticipates a person or event in the New Testament—another major source of intertextual references for King, to which we shall now turn.

New Testament References
In the seventh sermon in *A Gift of Love*, "The Man Who Was A Fool," King, arguing against an overvaluation of science, technology, and material goods, weaves words from Luke's Gospel into a sentence of his own: "We will not find peace in our generation until we learn anew that 'a man's life consisteth not in the abundance of the things which he possesseth'[Luke 12:15], but in those inner treasuries of the spirit which 'no thief approacheth, neither moth corrupteth'" [Luke 12:33] (77-8). He also draws on light/dark biblical imagery— for example, Christ's words in John (8:12): "I am the light of the world; he that followeth me shall not walk in darkness, but shall have the light of life." In his thirteenth sermon in *A Gift of Love*, "Paul's Letter to American Christians" [as imagined and written by King], he tells the audience invoked in his title: "You are to be the light of the world" (141), an interesting transference of Christ's luminary quality to his followers.

King's ninth sermon in *A Gift of Love* takes as its text a sentence from Paul's Letter to the Romans (15:24): "Whensoever I take my journey into Spain, I will come to you" (qtd. 91). The text fits the sermon's title, "Shattered Dreams," because Paul never reached Spain to spread the holy word; and he only got to Rome, where he had originally planned to disseminate it, as a prisoner, not as a preacher, and the city proved to be his place of execution. "Paul's life is a tragic story of a shattered dream" (91-92). King turns this intertextual reference into a metaphor with wide, perhaps universal application, in which the specific country and city that give the image a local habitation and a name are replaceable by any other location appropriate to the experience of a given hearer or reader: "Who has not set out toward some distant Spain" only to be disappointed? "We never walk as free men through the streets of our Rome" (92).

After outlining a range of possible negative responses to disappointment—bitterness, withdrawal, fatalism (we have already mentioned his objection to this last attitude)—King argues for a positive, transformative response, again using Paul's story as a general metaphor applicable to any individual's disappointment: "How may I, confined in some narrow Roman cell and unable to reach life's Spain, transmute this dungeon of shame into a haven of redemptive suffering?" (96-97).

Many other biblical references occur in King's texts, and these and the ones we have discussed serve four main functions: they give authority of a theological and (for non-Christians and nonbelievers) cultural kind, by drawing on a text that has proved so influential in shaping individual and collective consciousness, even if any or all particular beliefs and dogmas associated with it are rejected; they provide poetry, a rich corpus of sound, sense, and imagery, especially in the King James version of the Bible from which King usually quotes, a translation produced in that same rich flowering of the English language in which Shakespeare and the other Elizabethan and Jacobean dramatists flourished; they offer, through their poetry and poetic prose, memorability, feeding into oral as well as print culture; and they supply advice, anecdotes, characters, consolations, cues for action, examples, exhortations, guidelines, illustrations, metaphors, and words of wisdom—all, as it happens, elements of King's oratory as well, which linked the Bible with his own tumultuous time as preachers in seventeenth-century England had linked the Bible to the ferments of the English Civil War, and as William Blake, in the later eighteenth and early nineteenth century would link the Bible with the French and industrial revolutions. But King was a man of the twentieth century, aware of key literary, philosophical, and theological texts that came after the Bible, and he often interweaves his biblical references with references to later texts and events.

Shakespeare and Donne

We have mentioned that the King James version of the Bible, the 1611 translation favored by King as a source of biblical quotations, appeared in the same era as Shakespeare and other prominent Elizabethan dramatists; and Shakespeare sometimes features, though much less often than the Bible, in King's texts. In his first sermon in *A Gift of Love*, considering the unwillingness of some oppressed people to revolt against their lot, he alludes to and partly assimilates, without giving their source, Hamlet's lines from the "To be or not to be" soliloquy: "they [slaves] would rather bear those ills they have, as Shakespeare pointed out, than flee to others that they know not of" (7; *Hamlet* 287; 3.1.80-1). In his eighth sermon, he again quotes Hamlet, as one of several quotations from other sources, in support of his argument that there is a principle that assists good in its struggle against evil:

> Something in this universe justifies Shakespeare in saying:
> There's a divinity that shapes our ends,
> Rough-hew them how we will. (qtd. 82; *Hamlet* 434; 5.2.10-11)

A literary critic would point out that it is not Shakespeare who says this but one of his main characters, Hamlet. But King is making a familiar move here in attributing an important statement in a fictional text, especially one that seems to encapsulate, with pith and poetry, some general truth about life, to its author. In his eleventh sermon in *A Gift of Love*, "Antidotes for Fear," he does attribute the saying to the character in the striking sentence: "The terrifying spectacle of nuclear warfare has put Hamlet's words, 'To be or not to be,' on millions of trembling lips" (114; see *Hamlet* 284; 3.1.55). Here King takes the first six words of what is probably Shakespeare's best-known line, virtually a cliché, and renovates it by linking it with nuclear war and by adding the phrase "millions of trembling lips," making it both widely collective and intimately physical, so that it is no longer, as it has usually tended to be, especially since the Romantic era, an isolated, individual, perhaps incipiently narcissistic expression of existential angst.

King does, however, identify the character, and separate it from its author, when, in his sixth sermon, "A Knock at Midnight," he points to those who "cried out with Shakespeare's Macbeth that life

> is a tale
> Told by an idiot, full of sound and fury
> Signifying nothing. (qtd. 61; *Macbeth* 76-77; 5.5.27-8).

This is, of course, a view King strongly rejects, but he does not assume (as some literary commentators have done) that it is Shakespeare's own view.

Hamlet and *Macbeth* are frequent and familiar sources of Shakespeare quotes, but "Love in Action," King's fourth sermon in *A Gift of Love*, plumbs a slightly less usual source, Sonnet 94, which starts "They that have power to hurt, and will do none" (*Sonnets* 299). To support his statement that "Nothing in all the world is more dangerous than sincere ignorance and conscientious stupidity" (41), King quotes the concluding couplet of the sonnet:

> For sweetest things turn sourest by their deeds;
> Lilies that fester smell far worse than weeds. (qtd. 41)

It should be said that there is something of a mismatch here between the quote and King's own words: do Shakespeare's lines primarily illustrate "sincere ignorance" and "conscientious stupidity"? The verb *fester*, combined with the verb *smell*, evokes a kind and level of corruption that the qualities King identifies do not possess. Readers who know the whole sonnet are likely to feel this mismatch more strongly. It is also worth noting an effect that can sometimes occur when a text quotes such powerful passages of poetry or prose—they seem stronger, verbally, than the text they are supposed to reinforce and thus risk undermining it, especially when the quotation is from the King James Bible or from Shakespeare. But, even if such quotes can threaten to undermine a text in which they are included, they enhance the overall prestige of that text. While Shakespeare's phrasing does not have the religious authority of the King James Bible, it undoubtedly has immense cultural authority, and, like that Bible, it has poetry and poetic prose, memorability, and a cornucopia of materials that can fit so many different experiences and events.

In considering King's intertextual references chronologically, we find that, after Shakespeare, there is something of a hiatus until the nineteenth century. But there is one seventeenth-century inclusion that is worthy of mention. King's first sermon in *A Gift of Love*, outlining the characteristics of the hardhearted person, says: "He is an isolated island. No outpouring of love links him with the mainland of humanity" (8-9). This is an example of an intertextual reference that takes the form of an allusion rather than a direct quotation. King's island/mainland metaphor here calls to mind the famous sentences in *Meditation XVII* [17] in *Devotions upon Emergent Occasions* (1624), a prose work by the seventeenth-century English poet and clergyman John Donne: "No man is an island, entire of itself; every man is a piece of the continent, a part of the main." Bringing this to bear upon King's statement, we see that, in Donne's perspective, it is impossible for a man—and in the twenty-first century, we would discard the gendered exclusivity of that noun—impossible for anyone to be an island. So the hardhearts who think of themselves as islands are laboring under an illusion of insularity. This is a perspective that King would share.

Nineteenth-Century Intertexts

We can now move on to the nineteenth century. Most of King's quotations come from its mid-to-late decades. In his first sermon in *A Gift of Love*, which advocates a combination of "a tough mind and a tender heart," he quotes from Tennyson's early poem "The Palace of Art," which is about aesthetic detachment from the world, to reject the idea that God takes a similarly detached view of human affairs: "If God were only toughminded, he would be a cold, passionless despot, sitting in some far-off heaven 'contemplating all,' as Tennyson puts it in 'The Palace of Art'" (9; "Palace" 45).

In his seventh sermon, where King wrestles with the question of the existence of evil and aims to affirm its ultimate defeat, he quotes, soon after the *Hamlet* lines about "a divinity that shapes our ends" mentioned above, from the fourth stanza of Canto 54 of "In Memoriam," a much more famous poem than "The Palace of Art" and one central to the Victorian religious crisis, which works through personal bereavement and wavering belief to offer a tentative affirmation of faith:

I can but trust that good shall fall,
At last—far off—at last, to all,
And every winter change to spring. (243)

Another Victorian writer who, like Tennyson, wrestled with the receding authority of Christian belief in the nineteenth century was Matthew Arnold. King does not cite Arnold's poems but does quote from his prose book *Literature & Dogma*, with its affirmation of the existence of "an enduring power, not ourselves, which makes for righteousness" (qtd. 88; original in Arnold 61), a form of words that proved controversial in the nineteenth century because it could seem to be eliminating God; but the context in which King uses the quote strongly implies the "enduring power" is God.

So far, we have cited only British texts (insofar as the King James Bible can be regarded as such) and it is indeed the case that King's repertoire of quotations is biased toward English literature, an index of a more general cultural deference toward the former colonial power that continued even into twentieth-century America. But among the nineteenth-century American authors whom King quotes in *A Gift of Love* are James Russell Lowell, Paul Dunbar, Ralph Waldo Emerson, Henry David Thoreau, and Frederick Douglass. King quotes Lowell's poetry three times, first to endorse the importance of nonconformity— "They are slaves who dare not be / In the right with two or three" (qtd. 17)—then, from "The Present Crisis" (1845), to assert the ultimate victory of Truth— "Though the cause of Evil prosper / Yet 'tis Truth alone is strong" (qtd. 82)—and finally, from the same poem, to affirm the ultimate power of God even in a world that shows "Truth forever on the scaffold / Wrong forever on the throne" (qtd. 108).

King quotes Emerson twice: once in his second sermon stressing the importance of nonconformity, where he uses a dictum from *Self-Reliance*: "Whoso would be a man must be a nonconformist" (qtd. 17); and once in his eleventh sermon on combating fear, where he quotes from Emerson's essay "Courage" in *Society and Solitude*: "He has not learned the lesson of life who does not every day surmount a fear" (qtd. 114). Later in the same sermon, he quotes from Thoreau's *Journal* (7 September 1851): "Nothing is so much to be feared as fear" (qtd 17; Thoreau 1906, 468). Interestingly, King does not directly quote Thoreau elsewhere in the sermons or in his *Autobiography*, though in the latter he mentions reading Thoreau's essay "On the Duty of Civil Disobedience" and stresses Thoreau's eloquence, passion, and commitment and his influence on, and significance to, the struggle against segregation: "The teachings of Thoreau came alive in our civil rights movement" (14).

King quotes only two nineteenth-century nonwhite American writers: Frederick Douglass and Paul Laurence Dunbar. In his eighth sermon, he observes that "the significance of the Emancipation Proclamation was colorfully described by a great American, Frederick Douglass" and quotes a passage from *Douglass' Monthly* that opens "It [the Proclamation] recognizes and declares the real nature of the contest and places the North on the side of justice and civilization" and concludes that it "concerns the national life and character and is to determine whether that life and character shall be radiantly glorious with high and noble virtues, or infamously blackened, forevermore" (qtd. 85; Douglass 114). The adverb *colorfully* in King's preamble sounds slightly patronizing—was there still, at the time of the first publication of King's sermons, a sense that Douglass was not quite intellectually respectable, not a canonical author? *Colorfully* also carries a certain irony, and perhaps betrays a certain deliberate or unconscious defensiveness, in that it was probably directed at the concluding words of the quoted passage, where Douglass's dramatic rhetoric, with its dazzling, vertiginous contraries of light and dark, of height and (implicitly) depth, sounds rather like King's own.

Paul Laurence Dunbar offers the opposite of exalted rhetoric in "Life," from *Lyrics of Lowly Life*, which King quotes in his tenth sermon, as one instance of the power of life's travails that, in King's perspective, God gives us the strength to overcome:

> A crust of bread and a corner to sleep in,
> A minute to smile and an hour to weep in,
> A pint of joy to a peck of trouble,
> And never a laugh but the moans come double;
> And that is life! (qtd. in *Gift* 109)

This is accomplished and accessible verse, in its spare diction, its grammatical parallelism, its rhythm, and its rhyme. From a literary perspective, we might also say that it is premodernist poetry, like most of the other poetry—and prose—King quotes. There is one significant occasion, however, on which King does quote from the most famous modernist poet of the twentieth century.

Conclusion: Absences

The poet in question is T. S. Eliot, although, perhaps significantly, King cites a verse play that Eliot deliberately intended to reach a wider audience, rather than a poem. In his "Letter from Birmingham Jail," when challenging the use of "the moral means of nonviolence to maintain the immoral end of racial injustice" (203), King quotes from Eliot's *Murder in the Cathedral*, a play about a twelfth-century "turbulent priest": "The last temptation is the greatest treason: / To do the right deed for the wrong reason" (qtd. 203; Eliot 258), lines that succeed in being impactful, memorable, and ethically, philosophically, and theologically profound and that reinforce King's point.

Eliot apart, however, twentieth-century literary texts are largely absent from King's work. He does discuss a range of twentieth-century thinkers—most prominently, Mahatma Gandhi, Reinhold Niebuhr, and Paul Tillich—but hardly refers to twentieth-century fiction, poetry, and drama. It is perhaps most significant that he typically does not quote from, or even mention the names of, twentieth-century African American and mixed race writers, such as the poet Countee Cullen and the novelist Nella Larsen, both linked with the Harlem Renaissance of the 1920s, the novelists Zora Neale Hurston and Richard Wright from the 1930s, Ralph Ellison in the 1950s, or his near contemporary and, for a time, friend, with a similar religious formation, James Baldwin.

To mention the names of Larsen and Hurston indicates a further absence in King's range of intertextual references that stands out today: that of women writers. King's canon, as it emerges from his texts, is mainly male and white. To highlight this is not to censure King; he was not a literary critic or historian and had other pressing matters on his mind; and mainstream literary critics of his own era hardly registered writers like Larsen or Hurston. But these absences do mark out the limits of his intertextuality, which were not merely his own but those of a culture; and to highlight them is to be true to the spirit of King, who himself challenged, changed, and widened culture, setting an example for those who come after and seek to continue that creative process of expansion and emancipation.

Works Cited

Arnold, Matthew. *Literature & Dogma: An Essay Towards a Better Apprehension of the Bible*. Smith, Elder, 1873. openlibrary.org/books/OL14005134M/Literature_dogma. Accessed 7 Oct. 2018.

Barthes, Roland. "The Death of the Author." 1967. In *Image Music Text*. Translated by Stephen Heath, Fontana, 1977, pp. 142-48.

Donne, John. "Meditation XVII [17]: Nunc lento sonitu dicunt, morieris. Now this bell tolling softly for another says to me, Thou must die." From *Devotions Upon Emergent Occasions*. In *The Works of John Donne*, vol. 3. Edited by Henry Alford, John W. Parker, 1839, pp. 574-75. www.luminarium.org/sevenlit/donne/meditation17.php. Accessed 7 Oct. 2018.

Douglass, Frederick. "January First, 1863. *Douglass' Monthly* (January 1863). In *"... the real war will never get in the books": Selections from Writers During the Civil War*. Edited by Louis P. Masur, Oxford UP, 1993, pp. 114-15. books.google.co.uk/books/about/the_real_war_will_never_get_in_the_books.html?id=hylFrjAN94AC&redir_esc=y. Accessed 7 Oct. 2018.

Dunbar, Paul Laurence. "Life." 1895. www.poemhunter.com/poem/life-1152/. Accessed 7 Oct. 2018.

Eliot, T. S. *Murder in the Cathedral*. 1935. In *The Complete Poems and Plays*. Book Club Associates by arrangement with Faber and Faber, 1977.

Emerson, Ralph Waldo. "Courage." 1870. In *The Complete Works* (1904), vol. 7, *Society and Solitude*. www.bartleby.com/90/0710.html. Accessed 7 Oct. 2018.

_____. "Self-Reliance." In *Essays*. 1841. Edited by Edna H. L. Turpin, Charles E. Merrill, 1907, pp. 79-116. www.gutenberg.org/files/16643/16643-h/16643-h.htm. Accessed 7 Oct. 2018.

Epictetus. *The Discourses as Reported by Arrian, The Manual, and Fragments*. 2 vols. Vol. 1: *Discourses Books 1 and 2*. Translated by W. A. Oldfather, Loeb Classical Library: Harvard UP and William Heinemann, 1925, pp. 209-436. en.wikisource.org/wiki/Epictetus,_the_Discourses_as_reported_by_Arrian,_the_Manual,_and_Fragments/Book_2/Chapter_1. Accessed 7 Oct. 2018.

King, Martin Luther, Jr. *A Gift of Love: Sermons from Strength to Love*. 1962. Penguin Kindle Edition, 2017.

_____. "Letter from Birmingham Jail" (16 April 1963). [In King 1969 (see below), pp. 188-204. In the originally published version, which was, as King wryly remarked, "composed under somewhat constricting circumstances" (King 1969, 188), the Eliot lines are telescoped and paraphrased rather than quoted directly and in full: "T. S. Eliot has said that there is no greater treason than to do the right deed for the wrong reason": see www.thekingcenter.org/archive/document/letter-birmingham-city-jail-0#. Accessed 7 Oct. 2018.]

_____. *The Autobiography of Martin Luther King, Jr.* Edited by Clayborne Carson, Little, Brown, 1999.

Ling, Peter. "Martin Luther King." The Literary Encyclopedia. First published 9 February 2010. www.litencyc.com/php/speople.php?rec=true&UID=5603. Accessed 29 Sep. 2018.

Lowell, James Russell. "The Present Crisis" (1845): www.bartleby.com/102/128.html. Accessed 7 Oct. 2018.

_____. "They Are Slaves Who Dare Not Be." www.poemhunter.com/poem/slaves-13/. Accessed 7 Oct. 2018.

Shakespeare, William. *Hamlet*. Edited by Ann Thompson and Neil Taylor, Bloomsbury, 2006.

_____. *Macbeth*. Edited by Robert S. Miola, Norton, 2004.

_____. *Shakespeare's Sonnets*. Edited by Katherine Duncan-Jones, Thomson Learning, 2007.

Tennyson, Alfred, Lord. "The Palace of Art." 1832/1842. In *Poems and Plays*. Edited by Herbert T. Warren. Revised and enlarged by Frederick Page, Oxford UP, 1975, pp. 42-46.

_____. "In Memoriam A. H. H." 1850. In Tennyson, pp. 230-66.

Thoreau, Henry David. On the Duty of Civil Disobedience." 1849. In *Journal: The Writings of Henry David Thoreau*. Vol. 7. Edited by Bradford Torrey, Houghton Mifflin, 1906.

Balanced Thinking and Balanced Phrasing in Martin Luther King's "Facing the Challenge" Speech

Robert C. Evans

Anyone who reads the writings, speeches, and sermons of Martin Luther King will probably be impressed by them not simply as pleas for racial justice but as pieces of effective prose. King wrote in ways that were intelligent and thoughtful but also simple and accessible. It is hard to imagine a person who might read King and *not* admire his command not only of rhetoric but of the English language. Practically every sentence King wrote illustrates all the standard advice typically given about good writing. His prose is unusually clear, is full of memorable images and striking phrasing, and is rhythmic without seeming contrived or gimmicky. (In this latter respect, for instance, he differs from Al Sharpton and Jesse Jackson, two other civil rights leaders who can often seem to overdo things when speaking, as if wanting to call attention more to their own verbal cleverness than to the deeper significance of their words.) In King's prose, the focus is always on the message, not on the writer or speaker. In almost every way imaginable, King achieves a kind of verbal and intellectual balance that makes him sound like an eminently rational man, even when he is addressing topics that inspired great and sometimes violent emotions on both sides.

In this essay, I want to examine, very closely, one of King's earliest public addresses. I want to explore this speech not only to discuss the kinds of rhetorical devices King uses but also to assess his measured, moderate, reasonable, and therefore persuasive tone and manner. King, in some ways, was the ideal leader of the American civil rights movement. Far more than some other potential leaders, he was able to command respect both for the substance of his message and for the style of his writing and delivery. With his baritone voice, his unhurried pace, his complete sense of self-control, and his almost entirely serious manner (although occasionally leavened with humor), King came across to many white Americans as the perfect example of the kind of person who had been treated unfairly. He was obviously a man of enormous gifts (mental, moral, and spiritual) who had been denied the opportunity to use his gifts in ways whites could take for granted. He was a man whom it was difficult to ignore or disrespect. And, for all the reasons just mentioned, he was also an inspiration to many African Americans. All the traits just discussed are fully on display in one of the earliest of King's speeches, a 1957 address entitled "Facing the Challenge of a New Age."

"Facing the Challenge of a New Age"

King's early speech is partly worth examining precisely because it *is* an early work. It was written before he had become a major national figure—or at least while he was in the process of becoming one. It was, presumably, written entirely by King himself, without the help of any ghost writers who might have become necessary later in his career, when he had so much to do besides write his own works. But even in this early text, King shows his skill in using words as well as the measured, balanced nature of his thinking. That sense of balance already appears in the speech's opening paragraph. King there expresses gratitude for living in a period of momentous social change. Blacks, he says, "stand today between two worlds—the dying old and the emerging new" (135). This pattern of balancing phrases not only typifies the way King writes but also, apparently, exemplifies his habits of thought—the way his mind fundamentally worked. Balance is a trait that runs all throughout this speech and, in fact, all throughout many of King's other writings, especially his speeches and sermons.

But King's phrasing is balanced in many more ways than one. The opening of the very next sentence, for instance, exemplifies his tendency always to imagine counterarguments to his own. King rarely just states his own ideas; he often explicitly engages in a kind of dialogue with opposing views. Thus he mentions that he is "aware of the fact that there are those who would contend that we live in the most ghastly period of human history. They would argue . . ." (135). Of course, King mentions these opinions only to try to refute them, but the key point is that he *does* mention them. And he does this sort of thing throughout this speech and throughout many other works. King thus comes across as a person willing to consider others' ideas, even if he strongly disagrees. In speeches and sermons like this, he does not write or speak dogmatically—as a kind of propagandist or even as a kind of inspired prophet who is sure that he knows what God commands. Instead, King writes and speaks as a reasonable human being open to the viewpoints of other people. And the fact that his language is so simple and transparent makes him sound modest rather than pretentious, accessible rather than intimidating.

Interestingly enough, King next lays out a possible rationale for his typical way of thinking, writing, and speaking:

> Long ago the Greek philosopher Heraclitus argued that justice emerges from the strife of opposites, and Hegel, in modern philosophy, preached a doctrine of growth through struggle. It is both historically and biologically true that there can be no birth and growth without birth and growing pains. Whenever there is the emergence of the new we confront the recalcitrance of the old. (135)

The final two sentences here exemplify, once more, King's reliance on balanced thinking and phrasing, especially balance involving opposites. But the earlier sentence suggests the common philosophical idea of the dialectic: that from the conflict between thesis and antithesis, a synthesis can be born. Dialog between opposed ideas, in other words, can result in a new and better idea. The opening sentence of the quoted passage implies that King had actually given this matter some real philosophical thought rather than simply operating by instinct. Notice, however, how even King's references to Heraclitus and Hegel sound modest and unpretentious. For listeners who may be unfamiliar with the names of these men, he briefly and simply explains who they were. And he doesn't actually quote them (which might have sounded pompous and intimidating); instead, he translates their ideas into language anyone could understand. Although King was a learned man, he rarely paraded his learning. He wrote and spoke in ways that gave him a common touch—that made him seem down-to-earth.

In the next two sentences of the speech, King uses repetition in an intriguing way. Often he repeats words or phrases, frequently at the beginning of a sentence or clause. Here, however, he uses words at the end of one paragraph which he then repeats at the beginning of a new paragraph, thereby achieving especially strong emphasis:

> Whenever there is *the emergence of the new* we confront *the recalcitrance of the old.* So the tensions which we witness in the world today are indicative of the fact that *a new world order is being born* and *an old order is passing away.*
> We are all familiar with *the old order that is passing away.* We have lived with it for many years. (135; italics added to highlight the repetitions)

King, of course, is not a flawless writer (almost no one is): "are indicative of the fact that" could have been shortened to "indicate." But King almost always seems to know what he is doing; he was skilled not only as a leader but as a writer and speaker. In fact, the latter two skills were central to his successes in leadership.

In the speech's ensuing sentences, King uses one of his favorite rhetorical devices—*anaphora*, or the repetition of a key word or phrase at the beginning of a series of clauses or sentences. In this case, the phrase repeated is "We could turn," which King uses four different times to emphasize the sheer variety of ways in which, and places where, some humans are being oppressed ("We could turn our eyes to China"). King often uses anaphora to create a sense of an overwhelming number of relevant facts; the clauses build like rising waters behind a dam. Often the dam bursts, as King unleashes a conclusion that makes sense after all the examples that precede it. In this case, however, the list of repeated phrases results in a *balancing* list of similarly repeated phrases:

> But there comes a time when people get tired. There comes a time when people get tired of being trampled over by the iron feet of oppression. There comes a time when people get tired of being plunged across the abyss of exploitation where they experience the bleakness of nagging despair. There comes a time when people get

"Facing the Challenge" Speech

tired of being pushed out of the glittering sunlight of life's July and left standing in the piercing chill of an Alpine November. (136)

The metaphors here *can* sound somewhat contrived (especially that last one, which may seem a bit too "literary"), but there can be no denying the power of the repeated phrase. It is a phrase to which all humans can relate, and that, indeed, is another key to the effectiveness of King's writing, speaking, and preaching: he addresses the specific problems of American blacks, but those problems are, in one way or another, general or universal problems. *Everyone* gets tired of something; *everyone* can feel pushed to a breaking point by injustice of one sort or another. And so almost *anyone* can relate to the feelings and frustration King describes here. By using language that seems relevant to almost all human lives, King creates not only sympathy but empathy.

In later sentences, King returns to his effective use of balanced phrasing. Commenting on the typical black slave, King remarks that "He was a thing to be used, not a person to be respected" (136). Next he discusses the Supreme Court's infamous *Plessy v. Ferguson* decision, which, he says, "established the doctrine of separate-but-equal as the law of the land" (136). This decision, he explains in his typically balanced phrasing, "led to *a strict enforcement of the 'separate,'* with hardly the *slightest attempt to abide by the 'equal.'* So the Plessy doctrine ended up making for *tragic inequalities* and *ungodly exploitation*" (136-37; italics added to emphasize the rhetorical balance). In another sentence—this one containing balances within balances—King writes that "True peace is not merely the absence of some negative force—tension, confusion, or war; it is the presence of some positive force—justice, good will and brotherhood" (137). It is hard to read King, or listen to him, and not come away with the impression of a man whose mind operated like a set of balanced scales.

As it happens, even when quoting *others*, King seems to listen for balanced phrasing. A bit later in his speech, for instance, he quotes this bit of anonymous poetry (from "The Negro's Complaint," by William Cowper:

> *Fleecy **locks** and **black** complexion*
> *Cannot forfeit nature's claim.*
> *Skin may differ, but affection*
> *Dwells in **black** and **white** the same.*
> ***And were I so tall as to reach the pole***
> ***Or to grasp the ocean at a span,***
> *I must be measured by my soul.*
> *The **mind** is the standard of the **man**.*
> (137; italics in original; bold added to emphasize the balances)

It seems intriguing that King should reach to the work of a great eighteenth-century poet to support his claims. The eighteenth century, after all, was an era when writers prized balance of all sorts—intellectual, stylistic, structural, and rhetorical. Cowper's lines feature many standard traits of eighteenth-century poetry, including a strong emphasis on metrical regularity and pronounced rhyme. The first four lines are exactly alike in terms of their meter and rhythm. The fifth line (which mentions being tall and reaching upwards) is, appropriately, the longest line in the whole stanza, and it is also the line that most obviously violates the rhythm established by the lines that precede it. It, in turn, is balanced by the very next line, which mentions not reaching upwards but reaching outwards. And then, in the final quoted line, the very rhyme of "mind" and "man" stresses, through similar sounds, the very similarity of significance that the poem has been arguing for. (Imagine how much less effective that final line would be if it read this way: "*The brain is the standard of the person.*") Whether by mere chance or sure instinct, King selected a quotation that matched not only his own ways of phrasing but also his own habits of mind.

Ensuing paragraphs of King's speech are full of balanced thinking and balanced phrasing. He says, for example, that blacks now feel "a new sense of dignity and destiny" (where both key nouns not only begin with a "*d*" but also share *i*, *t*, *n*, and *y* sounds; share the same number of syllables; and even share the same rhythms: ***DIG**nity* and ***DES**tiny*; 137). One word emphasizes a present feeling; the other word emphasizes a future condition. Whether King had read or heard this combination used by someone else, or whether the phrase simply occurred to him spontaneously, his use of this pairing indicates his tendency to think, both literally and figuratively, in balanced terms.[1] Later in the same paragraph, King moves from balancing single words to balancing longer phrases: "we could gradually see the old order of segregation and discrimination passing away, and the new order of freedom and justice coming into being." And then, a sentence after the one just quoted, he repeats, in shortened form, the essence of the quoted phrasing: "The old order is passing away, and the new order is coming into being" (138). King was a master of balance as well as of repetition, and sometimes (as here) he combined the two effects for even greater emphasis.

The following paragraph is brimming with similar effects and effectiveness. Kings states that "We must all learn to live together, or we will be forced to die together" (138). He says (using a very memorable metaphor) that humans are now able to "dwarf distance and place time in chains" (138). "And so," he continues, "it is possible today to eat breakfast in New York City and dinner in Paris, France." But King, of course, is not interested in these facts for their own sakes but for what they imply socially and culturally. And he expresses those implications, once more, in his typically balanced phrasing: "our world is geographically one. Now we are faced with the challenge of making it spiritually one." And again: "Through our scientific genius we have made of the world a neighborhood; now through our moral and spiritual genius we must make of it a brotherhood" (138). "Whatever affects one directly," he asserts, "affects all indirectly." King's use of balanced phrasing in this speech is *so* pervasive that one comes almost to expect it. When he begins a phrase that seems likely to exhibit balance, readers can almost fill in the rest of the phrase for themselves. The more that King leads us to expect balance, the more likely we are to assume that it will appear. Reading the speech is almost a cooperative venture: it is as if King gives us enough of a lead that we can fill in the blanks for ourselves. And yet he never emphasizes balance *so* much that his phrasing seems stale or predictable. He is, in other words, balanced and moderate even in his use of balanced and moderate diction.

Sometimes, in fact, his phrasing is balanced in ways that are fairly subtle. For example, the "Facing the Challenge" speech is carefully organized in ways that emphasize the key term "challenge": "First, we are challenged . . ." (138); "A second challenge . . ." (138); "A third challenge . . ." (139). As soon as King introduces the word "First," he has created an expectation about structure that he will then fulfill. If good writing (as is often said) involves creating expectations and then fulfilling them, then King is a master of good writing. At almost every level he leads readers or listeners to anticipate a result, and then he provides it. He uses balance not simply by closely juxtaposing related phrases but also by establishing larger structures. And sometimes he creates a kind of balance that is intellectual, not merely rhetorical. Consider, for instance, the following passage:

> In the new age we will be forced to compete with people of all races and nationalities. Therefore, we cannot aim merely to be good Negro teachers, good Negro doctors, good Negro ministers, good Negro skilled laborers. We must set out to do a good job, irrespective of race, and do it so well that nobody could do it better. (139)

In these sentences, the most obvious kind of balance appears in the repetition of "good." But a subtler kind of balance is implied. King is urging black people to equal whites not only in their freedoms but in their accomplishments. Along with stressing the need for rights, he is stressing the acceptance of responsibilities. He is suggesting, to black readers or listeners, that they are fully *capable* of competing with whites; and he is implying, to white readers or listeners, that blacks want to contribute to the larger "good" of society. Any unsympathetic white who felt that King was merely emphasizing the need for black power would (or at least should) have been reassured by passages such as this, which stress the need for black contributions to the welfare of the nation as a whole. Once again, King reveals the balanced nature of his thought. By doing so, especially in passages like this, he made it difficult for opponents to accuse him of being a dangerous extremist, an unbalanced agitator.

Many whites would also have been reassured by King's open embrace of the best of the Western intellectual and cultural tradition, as in the following passage:

> If it falls to your lot to be a street sweeper, sweep streets like Michelangelo painted pictures, like Shakespeare wrote poetry, like Beethoven composed music; sweep streets so well that all the host of Heaven and earth will have to pause and say, "Here lived a great street sweeper, who did his job well." (139)

Here, as so often in his writings and speeches, King juxtaposes apparent opposites, showing what they have in common and showing an equal appreciation for both. He embraces both the "high" and the "low," both the white and the black, both intellectual achievement and manual labor. He shows respect for both ends of a proverbial spectrum, and he shows any nervous whites that he admires the best elements of the Western tradition even as he seeks to change, in fundamental ways, the then-current power structure of the United States.

King would also have reassured nervous whites by his emphasis on nonviolence—an emphasis he again routinely advocates by using balanced phrasing: "if we retaliate with hate and bitterness, the new age will be nothing but a duplication of the old age" (139). In a sense, by urging nonviolence, King was actually undermining a standard kind of "balanced" thinking—the thinking of "an eye for and eye, a tooth for a tooth." He was urging blacks to take the risk of rejecting violence as an answer to violence. He was endorsing a radical Christian social gospel, and he expressed this gospel in his typically well-balanced phrasing: "Love your enemies, bless them that curse you, pray for them that despitefully use you" (140). These, as we have seen, are the standard ways and rhythms of King's thoughts and words. They imply a kind of extreme self-control, a total commitment to rationality born of a total trust in God's goodness. Far from coming across as an angry, violent radical (an extremely easy position to adopt, but one likely to provoke anger and violence as a response), King chose a far more difficult insistence on love, forgiveness, and self-control. He knew, from both Jesus and

Gandhi, that nonviolence had the potential, at least, to disarm one's opponents, to undercut their reliance on brute force, to make them seem ashamed of themselves or, if nothing else, shameful in the eyes of many (or even most) others. By proposing nonviolence as a response to violence, King presented himself and his followers as almost superhumanly self-controlled. They seemed balanced and restrained to an almost incredible, and very impressive, degree. "It is," King asserted in his typically well-balanced way, "*this type of spirit* and *this type of love* that can transform *opposers* into *friends*. It is this type of understanding good will that will transform *the deep gloom of the old age* into *the exuberant gladness of the new age*" (140; italics added).

In pressing such claims, however, King demonstrated another kind of balance. He was fully willing to concede that he might be wrong. Or at least he was fully willing to consider counterarguments. "Now I realize," he says,

> that in talking so much about love it is very easy to become sentimental. There is the danger that our talk about love will merely be empty words devoid of any practical and true meaning. But when I say love those who oppose you I am not speaking of love in a sentimental or affectionate sense. It would be nonsense to urge men to love their oppressors in an affectionate sense. When I refer to love at this point I mean understanding good will. (140)

In passages such as this, King shows that he is fully aware of possible objections to his ideas. But he also shows that he is capable of answering those objections. And he shows as well that he is capable of distinguishing, in a very balanced and insightful way, between one meaning of "love" and other possible meanings. The kind of love he proposes (he explains) is not *eros* but *agape*. By using such terms, he once again shows his familiarity with, and respect for, Western philosophical and religious traditions—traditions that involved not only *eros* and *agape* but also *philia*. In explaining these terms, King proceeds in his typical methodical, logical fashion: "First, it [the Greek language] speaks of love in terms of *eros*"; "And then the Greek talks about *philia*"; "Then ... it speaks of [love] in terms of *agape*" (140). These three terms, of course, are discussed in their order of importance and loftiness, from lowest to highest, from least important to most important. Once again, then, King demonstrates his commitment to logical thought and expression. If blacks embrace *agape*, King promises, they will be able "to stand amid the radiant glow of the new age with dignity and discipline" (141). Earlier he had mentioned "dignity and destiny" (137); now he balances his own previous phrasing by introducing another crucial *d* word.

Almost everywhere one looks in this speech, balance, moderation, symmetry, and proportion of one sort or another can be seen, heard, and experienced. When he quotes from a poem by Shakespeare to support his arguments, he quotes from a sonnet notable for its balanced phrasing, as in these lines: "***Love* is *not love* / which *alters* when it *alteration* finds, / or bends with the *remover to remove***" (140; italics in original; bold added to emphasize balanced phrasing). In fact, *whenever* King quotes another writer in this speech, he is likely to quote someone as fond of balanced rhetoric as he is:

> *There is something in this universe which justifies* William Cullen Bryant in saying, "Truth *crushed* to earth will *rise* again." *There is something in this universe that justifies* James Russell Lowell in saying: *Truth forever* on the scaffold / *Wrong forever* on the throne. (141 italics added to emphasize the balanced phrasing)

And whenever King uses his own words, he can barely resist (nor should he) the instinct to use balanced phrasing, as here:

> We must continue to struggle through *legalism* and *legislation*. There are those who contend that *integration* can come only through *education*, for no other reason than that morals cannot be legislated. I choose, however, to be dialectical at this point. It is neither *education* nor *legislation*; it is both *legislation* and *education*. (142; italics added to emphasize balanced phrasing)

As always with King, the balance is subtler and more pervasive than it initially appears. Thus when he mentions "those who contend," he balances their views against his own. He pays them the courtesy of taking their ideas seriously and responding with serious thoughts of his own. In using the word "dialectical," he implies the very process of synthesis from conflict that is at the heart of much of his own balanced thinking. And then he not only balances "education" and "legislation" but then, in a nicely balanced way, reverses the order of those words as the sentence concludes.

Additional balanced phrasing appears in the rest of this paragraph:

> The law *does not seek to change* one's internal feelings; *it seeks rather to control* the *external effects* of those *internal feelings*. For instance, the law *cannot make a man love*—religion and education must do that—but it *can control his efforts to lynch*. So in order to control the *external* effects of prejudiced *internal* feelings, we must continue to struggle through legislation. (142; italics added to emphasize balanced phrasing)

As his speech begins to draw to a close, King makes his interest in balance and moderation quite explicit. This time, though, he refers not merely to language but to thought, attitudes, and action: "In this period of transition and growing social change, there is a dire need for leaders who are *calm* and yet *positive*, leaders who *avoid the extremes* of "*hot-headedness*" and "*Uncle Tomism*" (143; italics added). More balanced phrasing ensues when King stresses the need for "leaders not in love with money, but in love with justice; leaders not in love with publicity, but in love with humanity; leaders who can subject their particular egos to the greatness of the cause" (143). Clearly King was just such a leader himself, and Americans of all sorts can feel fortunate that such a leader arose, almost miraculously, just where and when he was most needed. Without leaders like King, the 1950s and 1960s might have been even more violent and vicious than they already were. King was the great moderating influence on the civil rights movement, and, for that very reason, he ironically helped that movement make rapid progress. Violence would have begotten more violence; anger would have provoked an answering rage; bloodshed and killing would have retarded and delayed the arrival of justice.

Yet King's insistence on nonviolence was not evidence of cowardice but of courage. The easiest (and least effective) thing to have done would have been to meet violence with violence. Instead, King counseled his fellow blacks (in his typically balanced language) to be defiant without being destructive:

> I would rather be a free pauper than a rich slave. I would rather die in abject poverty with my convictions than live in inordinate riches with the lack of self-respect. Once more every Negro must be able to cry out with his forefathers: "Before I'll be a slave, I'll be buried in my grave and go home to my Father and be saved." (144)

King, then, was one of a long line of thinkers, writers, and speakers who knew that the rhetoric of moderation was often the most effective kind of rhetoric of all. It is, for instance, the kind of rhetoric emphasized in one of the best recent books about academic argumentation—*They Say / I Say*, by Gerald Graff and Kathy Birkenstein. Presenting oneself as the most balanced, thoughtful, reasonable, open-minded, and moderate thinker has long been one of the most effective of all intellectual stances and rhetorical modes, as numerous studies have made clear.[2] One senses, however, that for King balance and moderation were not a calculated rhetorical ploy but essential aspects of his own personality and habits of mind. Certainly his early "Facing the Challenge" speech exhibits these traits from start to finish and foreshadows much of the best writing and speaking he would do later in his career as well.

Notes

1. A search for the phrase "dignity and destiny" in Google Books, focusing on the period from 1900 to 1955, turned up only seven results, most of them in fairly obscure (rather than famous and widely read) sources. Only six results turned up for the entire nineteenth century and, again, none of these sources was famous or well known.
2. Much has been written about the rhetoric of moderation. Only a few examples can be mentioned here. Thus, Harold Barrett mentions that

"Sophrosyne, a name for self-control and moderation," was "valued by the ancient Greeks" (146). Colleen Shogun reports that George Washington, with "regards to both political factions and foreign policy decisions," believed that "the passions must be subordinated (or 'excluded') to the cooler response of moderation and virtue" (56). Sean Wilentz, in his study of the rise of workers' rights, mentions how some "associations of workers, apart from the unions, emphasized the rhetoric of moderation, social harmony, and self-control" (356). Lois Einhorn contends that "Lincoln's moderation and middle-of-the-road principles helped him get elected to the presidency" (91). Ironically (at least in the present context), David Cunningham notes that "Segregation was a pillar of mainstream North Carolina politics, though one almost always couched in the rhetoric of moderation" (75). By far one of the best studies of balanced thinking and balanced rhetoric, at least in texts of the English Renaissance, is the book by Joshua Scodel.

Works Cited and Consulted

Barrett, Harold. *Rhetoric and Civility: Human Development, Narcissism, and the Good Audience.* SUNY Press, 1991.

Einhorn, Lois J. *Abraham Lincoln, the Orator: Penetrating the Lincoln Legend.* Greenwood, 1992.

Cunningham, David. *Klansville, U.S.A.: The Rise and Fall of the Civil Rights-Era Ku Klux Klan.* Oxford UP, 2012.

Graff, Gerald, and Kathy Birkenstein. *They Say / I Say: The Moves That Matter in Academic Writing.* 4th ed., Norton, 2018.

King, Martin Luther, Jr. *A Testament of Hope: The Essential Writings and Speeches of Martin Luther King, Jr.* Edited by James M. Washington, 1986. HarperOne, 1991.

Scodel, Joshua. *Excess and the Mean in Early Modern English Literature.* Princeton UP, 2002. Shogan, Colleen J. *The Moral Rhetoric of American Presidents.* Texas A&M UP, 2007.

Wilentz, Sean. *Chants Democratic: New York City and the Rise of the American Working Class, 1788-1850.* Oxford UP, 2004.

How Samuel Smith and a Parade of Anthem Lovers Created the Conclusion of "I Have a Dream": Martin Luther King's Refusal to Extemporize_____

Keith D. Miller and Colleen Wilkowski

Robert Cox and Christina Foust assert the importance of studying earlier phases of social movements in order to comprehend the "sources of social transformation" (605). In an analysis of Martin Luther King's first speech during the Montgomery Bus Boycott, Kirt Wilson notes that that oration "interacts with a rich discursive field" (299). More broadly, Wilson argues for the importance of understanding specific speeches within their larger discursive fields. Discursive milieus may include earlier occasions, earlier speeches, and—at times—musical performances. Comprehending these milieus can contribute to understanding how grassroots struggles facilitate social transformation.

Here we argue that understanding King's "I Have a Dream" requires a grasp of the process of composing the speech—a process that unfolded over multiple generations—and the larger political and discursive milieu that shaped that process. In doing so, we seek to correct a misrepresentation of "I Have a Dream." Extracting King's most renowned speech from African American oratory, some people falsely assert that King extemporized its conclusion. This inaccurate idea is so widespread that, in 2018, one author ludicrously declared that King "famously" extemporized the ending.[1] Far from being simply erroneous, this bad idea erases those who actually created that ending—a musical composer and more than a century of African American orators and singers. By erasing these crucial creators, this bad idea wrongly encourages people to think that a unique oratorical genius generated a scintillating conclusion instantaneously. Promoting the national tendency to mythologize and fetishize King and "I Have a Dream," this bad idea also falsifies the social change that the civil rights movement actually fostered. In turn, that falsification can create a wrongheaded desire for a future, solitary oratorical genius who is expected to spark future racial progress. Conversely, if everyone understands who *actually* composed "I Have a Dream"—and how, when, where, and why—then that understanding can inform positive social movements now and in the future.

In tracing the sources of King's conclusion, we seek to correct an erroneous idea that began innocently. When King delivered "I Have a Dream" at the March on Washington on August 28, 1963, he followed much of the typescript of the speech that he held in his hands, copies of which he had handed to reporters earlier that day (Jones and Connelly). But, partway through the address, singer Mahalia Jackson, who was sitting near King, told him, "Tell them about the dream, Martin!" Following Jackson's suggestion, King departed from the typed words and launched into the "I have a dream" portion of the speech (Hansen).

Continuing to depart from his typescript, King reached his conclusion by quoting a portion of "America" ("My country 'tis of thee"). His excerpt from this anthem ended with the phrases, "From every mountainside / Let freedom ring." He then expanded those lyrics by adding a resounding, memorable anaphora in which he began consecutive sentences with the phrase "Let freedom ring. . . ." His decision, partway through the speech, to lift his head away from the typescript—and to depart from its words—prompted some to conclude that he extemporized his conclusion. For example, in his best-selling account of the civil rights movement, *Parting the Waters*, which won the Pulitzer Prize, Taylor Branch portrayed King as averting his eyes from the typescript in order to extemporize.

But Branch was wrong: King was not extemporizing at all. Other people wrote his conclusion long before he arrived at the March on Washington. King used the ending as early as 1957, repeated it enough times to memorize it, and then inserted it into "I Have a Dream." Here we examine who *actually* generated King's conclusion and how that happened.

Sources: Samuel Smith

The most important author of the finale to "I Have a Dream" is Samuel Smith, who penned the lyrics of "America," including these words, which King quoted near the end of his renowned oration:

> My country 'tis of thee,
> Sweet land of liberty,
> Of thee I sing.
> Land where my fathers died,
> Land of the pilgrims' pride,
> From every mountainside
> Let freedom ring.

Here Smith endorses American exceptionalism by deeming the U.S. a "sweet land of liberty" and by identifying contemporary Americans with those who fought in the American Revolution of 1776 and, before that, with pilgrims who sailed the Mayflower to Plymouth Rock in 1620. He also compares freedom to a bell and extends that metaphor by declaring that the bell rings on mountains. He creates this metaphor while composing two specific phrases, "From every mountainside" and "Let freedom ring." Each of these elements of Smith's lyrics formed the conclusion of "I Have a Dream."

Though powerful, the impact of Smith's lyric was gradual. "America" rolled like a snowball, growing slowly while accumulating more and more force as it powered downhill until it eventually struck King.

Here's how that happened. After Smith generated his lyrics in 1831, "America" quickly garnered so much popularity that it became an anthem. As Robert Branham cogently explains, compilers included satirical versions of "America" in two popular abolitionist hymnals—*The Anti-Slavery Harp: A Collection of Songs for Anti-Slavery Meetings* and *The Emancipation Car* (633). Another satirical version, he adds, was written by Harriet Beecher Stowe, author of the enormously influential *Uncle Tom's Cabin* (633). But, far from simply lampooning the song, African Americans also cherished it. Branham continues: "The [African American] soldiers who fought the Civil War were largely drawn from the first generation to have learned 'America' in school and its performance was later hailed 'as indispensable and as common as sunshine all through that bitter contest'" (633). On January 1, 1863—the day the Emancipation Proclamation went into effect—Thomas Wentworth Higginson's African American troops celebrated by spontaneously and proudly singing the lyrics of "America," a song they identified with liberation from slavery (Branham 633). Courageous African American troops helped the North emerge victorious in the hard-fought, closely contested Civil War. For that reason, it is not too much to say that the soldiers' enthusiastic singing of "America"—a song "'as indispensable and common as sunshine'"—contributed to the triumph of the Union.

Public speakers also brandished the anthem. As Branham explains, ". . . 'America' became an important touchstone for black abolitionist orators" and for later speakers who also expounded "the African American jeremiad" (633, 640). The rousing song also fueled morale for participants in suffrage, temperance, and labor movements (Branham 633). In 1893, in the wake of abolitionist oratory, Ida B. Wells, the spectacular anti-lynching crusader, looked for patriotic words that seemed so familiar and so sacrosanct that they would fortify her indictment of lynching. Accordingly, she seized the first few lines of the lyrics of "America," slightly altering the final phrase as she inserted the lines into the conclusion of her most famous address, "Lynch Law in All Its Phases":

> My country 'tis of thee,
> Sweet land of liberty,
> Of thee I sing.
> Land where my fathers died,
> Land of the pilgrim's pride,
> From every mountainside,
> Freedom does ring.

Sources: Marian Anderson

Enter Marian Anderson. Praised by Jean Sibelius, Anderson was blessed with a voice superior to that of other opera divas; yet the bigoted management of the Metropolitan Opera refused to allow her to sing a solo there for decades. Similarly, the Daughters of the American Revolution (DAR) prohibited the nonpareil Anderson from performing in Constitution Hall. First Lady Eleanor Roosevelt and leaders of the NAACP protested the DAR's act of bigotry by scheduling Anderson to sing in the open air, on the National Mall. Mounting the steps of the Lincoln Memorial on Easter Sunday, 1939, Anderson faced seventy-five thousand people and a microphone that would carry her voice across national radio.

Her concert proved vastly important to the cause of racial equality. At the dedication of the Lincoln Memorial in 1922, President Warren Harding and Chief Justice William Howard Taft celebrated Lincoln as the National Unifier who held the U.S. together during the Civil War. On that occasion government officials segregated the audience by seating African Americans on a lonely spot behind the rest of the crowd (Sandage, Arsenault).

As Scott Sandage explains, Anderson's stellar performance at the Lincoln Memorial shifted the national memory of Lincoln from the National Unifier to the Great Emancipator while transforming the memorial into a symbol of racial equality. That happened for several reasons. First, simply by staging a concert at the memorial before a huge throng and a vast radio audience, Anderson contended that she was a worthy singer and that discrimination against African Americans was un-American. Second, by performing on Easter Sunday, she maintained that racial discrimination was un-Christian. Acting in the tradition of Frederick Douglass, other abolitionist orators, and Wells, she assailed white supremacy by appealing to a blend of patriotism and Christianity, a blend that constitutes what has been called American civil religion. She fused the appeals by singing at the Lincoln Memorial (signifying patriotism) on Easter Sunday (signifying Christianity). Third, she strengthened this argument by opening her concert with "America," which is both a patriotic barnburner and a Christian hymn.

Anderson also supplied lovely renditions of songs by renowned composers in the European classical tradition. By performing an aria by Gaetano Donizetti and Franz Schubert's "Ave Maria," she unmistakably demonstrated that African Americans could ably interpret "lofty" European music. By credentialing herself as a worthy exponent of treasured European works, she argued that racial discrimination was unwarranted. Alongside this European music, she sang three spirituals written by slave ancestors—"Gospel Train," "Trampin'," and "Nobody Knows de Trouble I Seen." By placing spirituals by anonymous African American composers on the same plane as canonized music by Donizetti and Schubert, she argued for the importance and beauty of the spirituals, thereby again undercutting white supremacy.

Although the lyrics of "Nobody Knows de Trouble I Seen" do not specify the "trouble" experienced by the song's narrator, it takes little imagination to view the lyrics as the slave composer's cry against the cruelties of bondage, cruelties that create anguish so keen and so deep that only God can grasp it. In Anderson's performance the "I" of that spiritual is the slave composer, and the "I" of the spiritual is also Anderson. By merging her voice and her identity with that of the slave composer, Anderson maintained that spirituals were still appropriate and that the slave's "trouble" persisted into the present. In other words, by performing a racial protest at the Lincoln Memorial and by singing this spiritual, Anderson argued that, despite Lincoln's Emancipation Proclamation and the Civil War, slavery persisted in the form of segregation. She made this argument while *simultaneously* appealing to the memory of Lincoln as the Great Emancipator. In other words, she used "America" and a spiritual to paradoxically claim that Lincoln *both did and did not* free the slaves.

Flash forward five years from Anderson's concert to 1944. Then, at age fifteen, Martin Luther King, Jr., discussed Anderson's landmark performance while participating in an oratory contest:

> Marian Anderson was barred from singing in Constitution Hall, ironically enough by the professional daughters of the very men who founded this nation for liberty and equality. But this tale had a different ending. The nation rose in protest, and gave a stunning rebuke to the Daughters of the American Revolution and a tremendous ovation to the artist, Marian Anderson, who sang in Washington on Easter Sunday and fittingly, before the Lincoln Memorial. ("The Negro")

King added, "She sang as never before with tears in her eyes. When the words of 'America' and 'Nobody Knows de Trouble I Seen' rang out over that great gathering, there was a hush on the sea of uplifted faces, black and white, and a new baptism of liberty, equality, and fraternity." In this speech King correctly observed that Anderson's concert amounted to a racial protest through its appeals to American civil religion. He noted with approval her decision to affirm African American culture by singing a spiritual and her decision to assert patriotism by singing "America." Further, he argued for the extreme effectiveness of her protest by claiming that it offered "a new baptism" to those who heard her ("The Negro").

Anderson's concert spawned further African American demonstrations at the Lincoln Memorial, each of which featured speakers who plumped for racial equality. As Sandage notes,

> A standardized civil rights protest ritual evolved from the elements in Marian Anderson's concert, such as using mass rallies instead of pickets, performing patriotic and spiritual music, choosing a religious format, inviting prominent platform guests, self-policing the crowds to project an orderly image, alluding to Lincoln in publicity and oratory, and insisting on using the memorial rather than another site. (136)

One such demonstration occurred in 1957, when King and the NAACP chose the Lincoln Memorial as the site to stage a racial demonstration called the Prayer Pilgrimage for Freedom. From the steps of the marble monument, King addressed a large crowd of dissenters while wearing his preacher's robe, thereby reinforcing his appeal to American civil religion. King remembered Anderson on other occasions as well, extolling her achievements in orations that he delivered in 1949, 1953, and 1959 ("Facing" 89, "Accepting" 140, "Unfulfilled" 365).

Sources: Archibald Carey

Flash forward to 1988, when Taylor Branch inaccurately suggested that King instantaneously invented his conclusion to "I Have a Dream." Exactly one year after Branch's book appeared, one of us noticed a speech by Archibald Carey (Miller, "Voice"). King and Carey became friends during the 1950s: Carey accepted King's invitation to speak at the Second Annual Institute on Non-Violence and Social Change, held in Montgomery, Alabama, in 1957, not only addressing the institute but also spending the night[2] in King's home (King, "To"). In 1952 Carey ended his "Address to the Republican Convention" with a quotation from "America" followed by a succession of sentences that began with Smith's phrase "Let freedom ring. . . ." Starting in 1957, King began to mirror Carey's conclusion ("Realistic"). Both Carey and King—in 1957 and in "I Have a Dream"—repeatedly extended Smith's phrase "Let freedom ring" by naming one mountain after another.

Consider Carey's "Address to the Republican Convention" from 1952:

> We, Negro Americans, sing with all loyal Americans:
> > My country 'tis of thee,
> > Sweet land of liberty,
> > Of thee I sing.
> > Land where my fathers died,
> > Land of the Pilgrims' pride,
> > From every mountainside
> > Let freedom ring!
>
> That's exactly what we mean,
> From every mountainside,
> Let freedom ring!
> Not only from the Green Mountains and White Mountains
> of Vermont and New Hampshire;
> Not only from the Catskills of New York;
> But from the Ozarks in Arkansas,
> From Stone Mountain in Georgia,
> From the Blue Ridge Mountains in Virginia.
> Let it ring not only for the minorities of the United States,
> But for the disinherited of all the earth.
> May the Republican Party, under God,
> From every mountainside,
> Let freedom ring!

Compare "I Have a Dream" from 1963:

> My country 'tis of thee,
> Sweet land of liberty,
> Of thee I sing.
> Land where my fathers died,
> Land of the Pilgrims' pride,
> From every mountainside
> Let freedom ring!

So let freedom ring from the prodigious hilltops of New Hampshire!
Let freedom ring from the mighty mountains of New York! . . .
Let freedom ring from Stone Mountain in Georgia!
Let freedom ring from Lookout Mountain in Tennessee!
Let freedom ring from every hill and molehill in Mississippi!
From every mountainside,
Let freedom ring!

Note that abolitionist orators, Higginson's troops, Wells, Anderson, Carey, and King all embrace American exceptionalism by repeating Smith's words that deem the U.S. a "sweet land of liberty" and a "country" that "tis" of God. Further, they all constitute the American people by bonding them to colonists[3] from 1776 and 1620. Like Smith, Higginson's soldiers, Wells, Anderson, and Carey all liken freedom to a bell. Carey and King both amplify that metaphor, first, by asserting that the bell rings on mountains, then by reiterating Smith's phrases "From every mountainside" and "Let freedom ring" while listing one mountain after another.

Although King's exact wording is not totally identical to Carey's, *King borrowed and adapted his conclusion directly from Carey*. In addition to discovering this source in 1989, one of us explained that discovery in a book that appeared in 1992 (Miller, *Voice*). This attribution has been widely discussed and accepted by many scholars, including David Garrow (King's best biographer), Clayborne Carson (editor of the Martin Luther King, Jr. Papers Project), Drew Hansen (a Rhodes scholar), and Michael Eric Dyson (a prominent public intellectual). No one has ever challenged the attribution.

Mistakes Made

Yet, despite being widely circulated, this attribution did not dispel Branch's mistaken idea. Rather than attempting to refute this scholarly discovery, some writers simply pretend that it never occurred. They act as though Archibald Carey never existed. While these writers also ignore Smith, Higginson's troops, Wells, and (sometimes) Anderson's concert, their erasure of Carey is particularly egregious and lamentable inasmuch as King directly echoed Carey. One author recently produced an entire book about the March on Washington that erases Smith, Higginson's soldiers, Wells, the teenage King, and Carey. Two additional writers generated books *entirely* focused on "I Have a Dream" that also bypass Smith and the parade of anthem enthusiasts, including Carey.[4] Recently a famous philosopher discussed "I Have a Dream" in no fewer than three books and one essay without ever mentioning Smith, Higginson's troops, Wells, Anderson, Carey, or the teenage King.[5] While overlooking Carey, this philosopher and each of these other authors either actively or tacitly reinforced Branch's erroneous and refuted view that King ended "I Have a Dream" with extemporized words.

The same philosopher also inaccurately contends that King reinvigorated the lyrics of a song that Americans sang "complacently."[6] Actually, African Americans, including Higginson's soldiers and Anderson, never sang "America" complacently, but, rather passionately and enthusiastically. Further, sterling African American orators, such as Wells and Carey, also enunciated the lyrics exuberantly. Beginning at age fifteen, King thoroughly realized that Anderson reignited the anthem in 1939. When he began to replay Carey's conclusion in speeches delivered long before "I Have a Dream," he revealed his understanding that Carey rejuvenated "America" yet again in 1952. King recited "America" at the conclusion of "I Have a Dream" not because it had grown stagnant, but precisely because it already resonated powerfully with African Americans.

Like those who conceived the Prayer Pilgrimage for Freedom in 1957, organizers of the March on Washington in 1963 staged their racial protest at the site of Anderson's landmark concert—

the Lincoln Memorial. By inviting Anderson to return to the steps of the marble monument in 1963, activists linked the March on Washington to Anderson's notable performance on the same steps in 1939. After walking up those steps, she sang a spiritual, thereby reaffirming the value of African American culture. By affirming that all people reside in the "hands" of God, this spiritual, "He's Got the Whole World in His Hands," proclaims the unity of all human beings. It thus strongly implies that racial barriers are unjust. Notably, on this occasion, Anderson failed to perform any music by Donizetti, Schubert, or any other European classical composer, thereby emphasizing not her credentials as a singer, but, rather, racial protest. Shortly after she sang "He's Got the Whole World in His Hands," King delivered "I Have a Dream" from the same spot, to the same audience.

King's "I Have a Dream"
King's debt to Anderson surpassed his repetition of the lyrics of "America" and march organizers' effort in 1963 to usher her to the site of her breakthrough performance in 1939. Near the beginning of "I Have a Dream," King alluded to the statue of Lincoln behind him and saluted the Emancipation Proclamation. Then he pivoted. Despite the joy triggered by Lincoln's decree, he asserted, fully one hundred years later ". . . the Negro is still sadly crippled by the manacles of segregation and the chains of discrimination." Note King's use of "manacles" and "chains" to denote black life under segregation. In this sentence he reasserted Anderson's paradoxical claim that Lincoln both did and did not free the slaves.

Cameras recorded King ignoring his typescript during the last third of his stellar address, and reporters noted that he supplied a conclusion that veered from the text that they held in their hands. Noticing that the conclusion of "I Have a Dream" seems magical, some people innocently, but mistakenly, attributed its greatness to King's spontaneity.

The sublimity of "I Have a Dream," however, stems not from King's spontaneity, but precisely from his *lack* of spontaneity. Smith, abolitionist orators, Higginson's soldiers, Wells, Anderson, the teenage King, Carey, and (starting in 1957) the adult King all created the momentum for King's dazzling crescendo. All these people added an important musical and oratorical strand to a grand movement for human rights, a strand that both spurred and created the conclusion of "I Have a Dream." King wisely embraced and reiterated it.

Instead of isolating, distorting, and mythologizing a single orator, Americans should seek to understand how, over many decades, numerous African Americans seized and repurposed Smith's phrases and metaphors in order to create a vision of racial equality. This vision crystallized in the minds of listeners immediately after King repeated Carey's ending, lowered his arm, and stepped away from the microphone at the memorial that Anderson had reinvented.

Notes

1. See Rosenbloom 108.
2. For more on Carey, see Dickerson.
3. For the function of rhetoric to constitute a people, see Charland.
4. See William Jones, Clarence Jones and Connelly, and Younge.
5. See three books and an essay by Nussbaum.
6. See Nussbaum, *Political Emotions* 238.

Works Cited or Consulted

Arsenault, Raymond. *The Sound of Freedom: Marian Anderson, the Lincoln Memorial, and the Concert that Awakened America.* Bloomsbury, 2010.

Branch, Taylor. *Parting the Waters: America in the King Years 1954-63.* Simon and Schuster, 1987.

Branham, Robert. "'Of Thee I Sing': Contesting America." *American Quarterly*, vol. 48, 1996, pp. 623-652.

Carey, Archibald. "Address to the Republican Convention." *Rhetoric of Racial Revolt.* Edited by Roy Hill. Golden Bell, 1964, pp. 149-154.

Charland, Maurice. "Constitutive Rhetoric: The Case of the *Peuple Quebecois.*" *Quarterly Journal of Speech*, vol. 73, 1987, pp.133-150.

Cox, Robert, and Christina R. Foust. "Social Movement Rhetoric." *The SAGE Handbook of Rhetorical Studies*. Edited by Andrea A. Lunsford, Kirt H. Wilson, and Rosa A. Ederly. Sage, 2009.

Dickerson, Dennis. *African American Preachers and Politics: The Careys of Chicago*. UP of Mississippi, 2010.

Hansen, Drew D. *The Dream: Martin Luther King, Jr., and the Speech That Inspired a Nation*. Ecco, 2003.

Jones, Clarence B., and Stuart Connelly. *Behind the Dream: The Making of the Speech that Transformed a Nation*. St. Martin's, 2011.

Jones, William P. *The March on Washington: Jobs, Freedom, and the Forgotten History of Civil Rights*. Norton, 2013.

King, Martin Luther, Jr. "Accepting Responsibility for Your Actions." *The Papers of Martin Luther King, Jr.: Vol. VI: Advocate of the Social Gospel*. Edited by Clayborne Carson et al. Berkeley: U of California P, 2007, .pp. 139-142.

_____. "Facing Life's Inescapables." *The Papers of Martin Luther King, Jr.: Vol. VI: Advocate of the Social Gospel*. Edited by Clayborne Carson et al. U of California P, 2007, pp. 88-90.

_____. "I Have a Dream." https://kinginstitute.stanford.edu/i-have-dream-address-delivered-march-washington.

_____. "The Negro and the Constitution." *The Papers of Martin Luther King, Jr.: Vol. I: Called to Serve*. Edited by Clayborne Carson et al. U of California P, 1992, pp. 108-111.

_____. "A Realistic Look at the Question of Progress in the Area of Race Relations." *The Papers of Martin Luther King, Jr.: Vol. IV: Symbol of the Movement*. Edited by Clayborne Carson et al. U of California P, 2000, pp. 167-178.

_____. "To Archibald Carey." *The Papers of Martin Luther King, Jr.: Vol. III: Birth of a New Age*. Edited by Clayborne Carson et al. U of California P, 1997, pp. 152-153.

_____. "Unfulfilled Hopes." *The Papers of Martin Luther King, Jr.: Vol. VI: Advocate of the Social Gospe*. Edited by Clayborne Carson et al. Berkeley: U of California P, 2007, pp. 359-367.

Miller, Keith D. "Voice Merging and Self-Making: The Epistemology of 'I Have a Dream.'" *Rhetoric Society Quarterly*, vol. 19, 1989, pp. 23-32.

———. *Voice of Deliverance: The Language of Martin Luther King, Jr., and Its Sources.* U of Georgia P, 1996.

Nussbaum, Martha. *Anger and Forgiveness: Resentment, Generosity, Justice.* Oxford UP, 2016.

———. "From Anger to Love: Self-Purification and Political Resistance." *To Shape a New World: Essays on the Political Philosophy of Martin Luther King, Jr.* Harvard UP, 2018, pp. 104-126.

———. *The Monarchy of Fear: A Philosopher Looks at Our Political Crisis.* Oxford UP, 2018.

———. *Political Emotions.* Cambridge, MA: Harvard UP, 2013.

Rosenbloom, Joseph. *Redemption: Martin Luther King, Jr.'s Last 31 Hours.* Beacon, 2018.

Sandage, Scott. "A Marble House Divided: The Lincoln Memorial, the Civil Rights Movement, and the Politics of Memory, 1939-1963." *Journal of American History*, vol. 80, Jun. 1993, pp. 135-167.

Wells, Ida B. "Lynch Law in All Its Phases." https://awpc.cattcenter.iastate.edu2017/lynch-law-in-all-its-phases-february13,1893.

Wilson, Kirt H. "Interpreting the Discursive Field of the Montgomery Bus Boycott: Martin Luther King Jr.'s Holt Street Address." *Rhetoric & Public Affairs*, vol. 8, no. 2, 2005, 299-326.

Younge, Gary. *Speech: The Story behind Dr. Martin Luther King Jr.'s Dream.* Haymarket, 2013.

Precursors to Martin Luther King's 1963 "I Have a Dream" Speech at the Lincoln Memorial

Wolfgang Mieder

Almost all American citizens, from schoolchildren to the very old, know about Martin Luther King Jr.'s famous "I Have a Dream" speech. Indeed, most Americans, and even many people from elsewhere in the world, have actually seen or at least heard the speech thanks to videotape and audio recordings. King's speech is arguably one of the best-known orations ever delivered, and in fact it has recently been judged the greatest speech of the twentieth century. King's famous address seems so eloquent, so perfectly phrased, and so powerfully persuasive that it is easy to think that the words must have come to King in a moment of sudden inspiration. Instead, however, as I will show in this essay, King had been using many of the same words and phrases in various other speeches that preceded his most famous address in 1963 as he stood before the Lincoln Memorial and spoke to hundreds of thousands of people who had assembled in Washington in perhaps the greatest civil rights demonstration ever staged in the United States. The "I Have a Dream" speech resulted from a long series of previous efforts to articulate many of the same ideas.

King's book *Strength to Love* includes a sermon with the pessimistic title "Shattered Dreams," but while much of its content is summarized in the quotable remark "Shattered dreams are a hallmark of our mortal life" (79), the sermon is actually making the strong argument that a solid faith and an unwavering hope in the struggle for civil and human rights will eventually lead to progress (see Franklin and also Ensslin). King himself adhered to the dream of equality and justice for all during his entire life, and he reiterated it one final time in his essay on "A Testament of Hope" that appeared posthumously in the January 1969 issue of *Playboy*. Citing the frequently employed proverbial triad "Life, liberty and the pursuit of happiness" from the Declaration of Independence, King stresses that it is simply not enough to pay mere lip service to these unalienable rights. Engaged action and constant struggle are necessary to bring about a much-needed socioeconomic change not only for African Americans but for all Americans:

> It is time that we stopped our blithe lip service to the guarantees of life, liberty and pursuit of happiness. These fine sentiments are embodied in the Declaration of Independence, but that document was always a declaration of intent rather than of reality. There were slaves when it was written; there were still slaves when it was adopted; and to this day, black Americans have not life, liberty nor the privilege of pursuing happiness, and millions of poor white Americans are in economic bondage that is scarcely less oppressive. Americans who genuinely treasure our national ideals, who know they are still elusive dreams for all too many, should welcome the stirring of Negro demands. They are shattering the complacency that allowed a multitude of social evils to accumulate. Negro agitation is requiring America to reexamine its comforting myths and may yet catalyze the drastic reforms that will save us from social catastrophe. (Washington 315)

Always willing to give his visionary messages a reality check, King admits that basic human rights "are still elusive dreams for all too many," but unless people followed such dreams the status quo would never change and inequality and injustice would forever prevail. King and the many participants in the civil rights movement fortunately had the audacity to dream of making "a way out of no way," and it should thus not be surprising that dreams of an interconnected new world house for all of humanity are a leitmotif in many of King's sermons and speeches, with the very word "dream" repeatedly appearing in their titles (Hoskins).

Early Versions of "I Have a Dream": 1960-1962

A passage from an NAACP address on "The Negro and the American Dream" that King delivered on September 25, 1960, at Charlotte, North Carolina, shows this very convincingly in the first three paragraphs (Sundquist 27). It begins with yet another quotable statement— "America is essentially a dream—a dream yet unfulfilled"—and almost predictably includes the two proverbial claims from the Declaration of Independence. But as always, dreaming the dream is not enough for King, with the challenge of changing America's dream into reality demanding that all people are willing to pay a high price, as King concludes with yet another one of his favorite proverbial expressions:

> This afternoon I would like to speak from the subject, "The Negro and the American Dream." In a real sense America is essentially a dream—a dream yet unfilfilled [sic]. It is the dream of a land where men of all races, colors and creeds will live together as brothers. The substance of the dream is expressed in these sublime words: "We hold these truths to be self-evident, that all men are created equal, that they are endowed by their creator with certain unalienable rights, that among these are life, liberty and the pursuit of happiness." This is the dream. It is a profound, eloquent and unequivocal expression of the dignity and worth of all human personality.
> But ever since the founding fathers of our nation dreamed this dream, America has manifested a schizophrenic personality. She has been torn between [two] selves—a self in which she has proudly professed democracy and a self in which she has sadly practiced the antithesis of democracy. Slavery and segregation have been strange paradoxes in a nation founded on the principle that all men are created equal.
> Now more than ever before America is challenged to bring her noble dream into reality. The shape of the world today does not permit America the luxury of exploiting the Negro and other minority groups. The price that America must pay for the continued opression [sic] of the Negro is the price of its own destruction. (Armstrong et al. 508-09)

This is indeed a memorable passage, of which there can be found so many in King's oeuvre. But it should once again be noted that while this great orator takes his audience to lofty heights regarding the American ideals of democracy, he is very quick to point out that those goals are still far from having been achieved. Democracy, equality, freedom, and so on demand work and struggle, and the best way to verbalize these demands is by way of proverbial expressions. Thus King continues his remarks in this speech by citing the proverbial phrase "to hand something out on a silver platter" and, to be sure, repeating the slightly modified phrase "to pay the price" for good measure:

> We must be willing to suffer and sacrifice to achieve our freedom. Our freedom will never be handed out on a silver platter. Freedom is not free. It is always purchased with the high price of sacrifice and suffering.
> We must be sure that our struggle is conducted on the highest level of dignity and discipline. Our method must be nonviolent to the core. We must not flirt with retaliatory violence or drink the poisonous wine of hate. Our aim must not be to defeat the white man or pay him back for past injustices heaped upon us. (Armstrong et al. 510)

The urgency of making the dream of true democracy a reality is most impressively expressed in the last paragraph of the speech, albeit this time without any proverbial language. Of course, if I as a paremiologist could have had the incredible honor to suggest a proverb or two to King, I would have given him such proverbs as "Dreaming won't help us accomplish our aims, but work will," "Your dreams won't come true until you wake up," and—recorded in Alabama and Georgia— "Dreams are what you hope for; reality is what you plan for" (Mieder et al., *Dictionary* 167 and also Arthurs).[1] King continued:

> Therefore, those persons who are working courageously to break down the barriers of segregation and discrimination are the real saviors of democracy.
> So many forces in our nation have served to scar the dream of our democracy. The Klu [sic] Klux Klan, the White Citizens Council and other extremists groups have scarred the dream by their fanatical acts and bitter words. But our federal government has also scarred the dream through its apathy and hypocricy [sic], its betrayal of the cause of justice. And even many white people of good-will have scarred the dream through silence and fear. In the midst of this conspiracy of

silence and apathy the Negro must act. It may well be that the Negro is God's instrument to save the soul of America. (Armstrong et al. 509)

Continuing with my personal interference—that is, my audacity of dreaming to suggest fitting proverbs to Martin Luther King—let me now also state that as a professor I wish I could have been present at the so appropriately entitled commencement address "The American Dream" that he delivered on June 6, 1961, at Lincoln University in Pennsylvania. As King spoke to the students, faculty, staff, and family members, he recycled a number of his most effective set pieces of quotations, proverbs, and proverbial expressions, including the beginning paragraph of his address on "The Negro and the American Dream" just mentioned. Do note, however, that while he keeps "America is essentially a dream, a dream as yet unfulfilled" as a quotable statement and the two proverbial claims of the Declaration of Independence, he now remarks that "this dream is an amazing universalism" that includes people "of all races, of all nationalities and of all creeds [who] can live together as brothers [and sisters]." As we teach our students today special courses on race and ethnicity, I can well imagine the excitement of these young standard-bearers of the continued fight for equality and justice as they listened to this emotional plea by a true American hero:

> As you [graduates] go out today to enter the clamorous highways of life, I should like to discuss with you some aspects of the American dream. For in a real sense, America is essentially a dream, a dream as yet unfulfilled. It is a dream of a land where men of all races, of all nationalities and of all creeds can live together as brothers. The substance of the dream is expressed in these sublime words, words lifted to cosmic proportions: "We hold these truths to be self-evident, that all men are created equal, that they are endowed by their Creator with certain unalienable rights, that among these are life, liberty, and the pursuit of happiness." This is the dream.
> One of the first things we notice in this dream is an amazing universalism. It does not say some men, but it says all men. It does not say all white men, but it says all men, which includes black men. It does not say all Gentiles, but it says all men, which includes Jews.

> It does not say all Protestants, but it says all men, which includes Catholics. (Washington 208)

And King continues describing, in a somewhat scholarly way—well aware that he was speaking to eager college graduates—the schizophrenic nature of America and its dilemma of advocating that "All men are created equal" while continuing the practice of segregation. He also reminds the students that the country cannot afford "the luxury of an anemic democracy," that America must be willing to pay the proverbial price for its social sins, and that the proverbial clock is ticking, in other words, that the graduates had better be ready to get to work to turn America's "noble dream into reality" and save democracy:

> Ever since the Founding Fathers of our nation dreamed this noble dream [of a true democracy], America has been something of a schizophrenic personality, tragically divided against herself. On the one hand we have proudly professed the principles of democracy, and on the other hand we have sadly practiced the very antithesis of those principles. Indeed slavery and segregation have been strange paradoxes in a nation founded on the principle that all men are created equal. This is what the Swedish sociologist, Gunnar Myrdal, referred to as the American dilemma.
> But the shape of the world today does not permit us the luxury of an anemic democracy. The price America must pay for the continued exploitation of the Negro and other minority groups is the price of its own destruction. The hour is late; the clock of destiny is ticking out. It is trite, but urgently true, that if America is to remain a first-class nation she can no longer have second-class citizens. Now, more than ever before, America is challenged to bring her noble dream into reality, and those who are working to implement the American dream are the true saviors of democracy. (Washington 208-09)

The statement "If America is to remain a first-class nation she can no longer have second-class citizens" is yet another memorable formulation by King, directed primarily at the African American fate in this country. But, of course, King wants to take the students also to the broader view of the interrelatedness of the modern world, and for this he relies on John Donne's quotation turned proverb "No man is an island" as his ever-ready leitmotif. But it is good for King to also quote the proverbial line "to know for whom the bell tolls; it tolls for thee" from the same Donne poem, thereby reminding the students that it is they who must carry on the fight for democracy worldwide:

> All this is simply to say that all life is interrelated. We are caught in an inescapable network of mutuality; tied in a single garment of destiny. Whatever affects one directly, affects all indirectly. As long as there is poverty in this world, no man can be totally rich even if he has a billion dollars. As long as diseases are rampant and millions of people cannot expect to live more than twenty or thirty years, no man can be totally healthy, even if he just got a clean bill of health from the finest clinic in America. Strangely enough, I can never be what I ought to be until you are what you ought to be. You can never be what you ought to be until I am what I ought to be. This is the way the world is made. I didn't make it that way, but this is the interrelated structure of reality. John Donne caught it a few centuries ago and could cry out, "No man is an island entire of itself; every man is a piece of the continent, a part of the main ... any man's death diminishes me, because I am involved in mankind, and therefore never send to know for whom the bell tolls; it tolls for thee." If we are to realize the American dream we must cultivate this world perspective. (Washington 210)

Exhorting the students to never adjust themselves to injustice but rather to be so maladjusted as to become activists in the cause of civil and human rights, King brings his commencement address to a close by speaking to them as a declared preacher—not that he was not doing this all along in his speech (Calloway-Thomas and Lucaites, Lischer, Warren, Rieder). Relying to a certain degree on yet another linguistic set piece, he employs the two Bible proverbs "Let justice run down like waters and righteousness like a mighty stream" (Amos 5:24, see King 1965) and "Love your enemies" (Matt. 5:44) to place the students on the right path on their walk through a life of steady progress, proverbially but not only metaphorically joining hands with the world and its "inescapable network of mutuality":

If you will allow the preacher in me to come out now, let me say to you that I never did intend to adjust to the evils of segregation and discrimination. I never did intend to adjust myself to religious bigotry. I never did intend to adjust myself to economic conditions that will take necessities from the many to give luxuries to the few. I never did intend to adjust myself to the madness of militarism, and the self-defeating effects of physical violence. And I call upon all men of good will to be maladjusted because it may well be that the salvation of our world lies in the hands of the maladjusted.

So, let us be maladjusted, as maladjusted as the prophet Amos, who in the midst of the injustices of his day could cry out in words that echo across the centuries, "Let justice run down like waters and righteousness like a mighty stream" [Amos 5:24]. Let us be as maladjusted as Abraham Lincoln, who had the vision to see that this nation could not exist half slave and half free. Let us be maladjusted as Jesus of Nazareth, who could look into the eyes of the men and women of his generation and cry out, "Love your enemies. Bless them that curse you. Pray for them that despitefully use you" [Matt. 5:44].

I believe that it is through such maladjustment that we will be able to emerge from the bleak and desolate midnight of man's inhumanity to man into the bright and glittering daybreak of freedom and justice. That will be the day when all of God's children, black men and white men, Jews and Gentiles, Catholics and Protestants, will be able to join hands and sing in the words of the old Negro spiritual, "Free at last! Free at last! Thank God almighty, we are free at last!" (Washington 216)

To a certain degree, these "dream" speeches foreshadow King's famous "I Have a Dream" oration of August 28, 1963 (Carson and Holloran xvi-xvii). But before turning to that address with its unforgettable "I have a dream" anaphora, there are at least two precursors that need to be mentioned. The earliest transcribed version of this "dream" sequence appears in a speech that King delivered on November 27, 1962, at Rocky Mount, North Carolina. Unfortunately I was not able to locate a copy of this text, but the "dream" peroration is printed in Drew D. Hansen's invaluable study

The Dream: Martin Luther King, Jr., and the Speech that Inspired a Nation:

I have a dream tonight.

It is a dream rooted deeply in the American dream.

I have a dream that one day down in Sumter County, Georgia, where they burned two churches down a few days ago because Negroes wanted to register and vote, one day right down there little black boys and little black girls will be able to join hands with little white boys and little white girls and walk the streets as brothers and sisters.

I have a dream that one day right here in Rocky Mount, North Carolina, the sons of former slaves and the sons of former slave-owners will meet at the table of brotherhood, knowing that out of one blood God made all men to dwell upon the face of this earth.

I have a dream that one day all over this nation that men will recognize that all men were created equal and endowed by their creator with certain unalienable rights.

I have a dream tonight. One day the words of Amos will become real. Let justice roll down like waters and righteousness like a mighty stream [Amos 5:24].

I have a dream tonight. One day every valley shall be exalted and every mountain and hill shall be made low. Crooked places will be made straight, the rough places will be made plain, the glory of the Lord will be revealed and all flesh shall see it together.

I have a dream tonight. One day men will do unto others as the would have others do unto them.

I have a dream tonight. One day my little daughter and two sons will grow up in a world not conscious of the color of their skin but only conscious of the fact that they are members of the human race.

I have a dream tonight. Some day we will be free. (Hansen 110-11)

This text is quoted here to illustrate that King had a definite "I have a dream" sequence in his rhetorical repertoire as a set piece almost a year before his famous "dream" speech at the Lincoln Memorial. In fact, the proverbs "All men are created equal" and "Let justice roll down like waters and righteousness like a mighty stream" as well as the proverbial expressions "to join hands with someone" and "to be judged by the content of one's character and not by the color of one's skin" will reappear in somewhat varied contexts. However, if I may say so, I think it is a shame that King did not also maintain the ultimate Bible proverb that has become known as the golden rule in most religions of the world: "Do unto others as you would have them to unto you" (Matt. 7:12; see Hertzler; Mieder, *Not by Bread*; Griffin 67-69; Templeton 8-12). As mentioned previously, King preferred the Bible proverb "Love your enemies" (Matt. 5:44) in any case, but he also did not include it in his most famous speech of August 28, 1963.

Early Versions of "I Have a Dream": 1963

Be that as it may, "in the spring and summer of 1963, 'I have a dream' became one of King's most frequently delivered set pieces" (Hansen 111), bringing us to King's major "Address at the Freedom Rally in Cobo Hall" on June 23, 1963, in Detroit (Sundquist 96). This speech, delivered a mere two months before the one at Washington, D.C., is an excellent example of how King integrates certain rhetorical set pieces with some variations again and again into his speeches. Thus, at the beginning of the address, he retains his former link between the two proverbial expressions of "to pay the price for something" and "the clock is ticking" in regard to not being able any longer to "afford the luxury of an anemic democracy" of unconcern for the well-being of others:

> But now more than ever before, America is forced to grapple with this problem [of freedom], for the shape of the world today does not afford us the luxury of an anemic democracy. And the price that this nation must pay for the continued oppression and exploitation of the Negro or any other minority group is the price of its own destruction. For the hour is late, and the clock of destiny is ticking out, and we must act now before it is too late. [*Yeah*] [*Applause*] (Carson and Shepard 62)

But in this particular "dream" speech, King adds a paragraph that stresses his insistence on nonviolence in the struggle for equality and justice, exemplified by the modern proverb "Love or perish" (perhaps modeled on "Publish or perish"?) and his often-repeated Bible proverb "Love your enemies" (Matt. 5:44):

> We are coming to see now, the psychiatrists are saying to us, that many of the strange things that happen in the subconscience [sic], many of the inner conflicts, are rooted in hate. And so they are saying, "Love or perish." But Jesus told us this long time ago, and I can still hear that voice crying through the vista of time, saying, "Love your enemies, bless them that curse you, pray for them that despitefully use you" [Matt. 5:44]. And there is still a voice saying to every potential Peter, "Put up your sword" [John 18:11]. History is replete with the bleached bones of nations; history is cluttered with the wreckage of communities that failed to follow this command. And isn't it marvelous to have a method of struggle where it is possible to stand up against an unjust system, fight it with all of your might, never accept it, and yet not stoop to violence and hatred in the process? This is what we have. [*Applause*] (Carson and Shepard 67-68)

This version of the "I have a dream" speech also includes such quotations, proverbs, and proverbial expressions as "If a man has not discovered something that he will die for, he isn't fit to live," "Injustice anywhere is a threat to justice everywhere," "Last hired, first fired," "No gain without pain," "to put on the brakes," "to be called names," "to have clean hands," and once again "to pay the price for something." But here is the actual "I have a dream" sequence that includes the proverbs and phrases "to join hands with someone," "to be judged by the content of one's character and not by the color of one's skin," "Let justice roll down like waters, and righteousness like a mighty stream" (Amos 5:24), "All men are created equal," "Life, liberty and the pursuit of happiness," and a repetition of "to join hands with someone. " This is indeed a powerful collage of preformulated language, with the "I have a dream" anaphora adding a contagious rhythm to it, as can be seen (heard) from the almost sermonic testifying by the Detroit audience:

> And so this afternoon, I have a dream. [*Go ahead*] It is a dream deeply rooted in the American dream.

I have a dream that one day, right down in Georgia and Mississippi and Alabama, the sons of former slaves and the sons of former slave owners will be able to live together as brothers.

I have a dream this afternoon [*I have a dream*] that one day [*Applause*], one day little white children and little Negro children will be able to join hands as brothers and sisters.

I have a dream this afternoon [*I have a dream*] that there will be a day that we will no longer face the atrocities that Emmett Till had to face or Medgar Evers had to face, but that all men can live with dignity.

I have a dream this afternoon [*Yeah*] that my four little children, that my four little children will not come up in the same young days that I came up within, but they will be judged on the basis of the content of their character, and not the color of their skin. [*Applause*]

I have a dream this afternoon that one day right here in Detroit, Negroes will be able to buy a house or rent a house anywhere that their money will carry them and they will be able to get a job. [*Applause*] [*That's right*]

Yes, I have a dream this afternoon that one day in this land the words of Amos will become real and justice will roll down like waters, and righteousness like a mighty stream [Amos 5:24].

I have a dream this evening that one day we will recognize the words of Jefferson that "all men are created equal, that they are endowed by their Creator with certain unalienable Rights, that among these are Life, Liberty and the pursuit of Happiness." I have a dream this afternoon. [*Applause*]

I have a dream that one day every valley shall be exalted, and every hill and mountain shall be made low; the rough places will be made plain, and the crooked places will be made straight; and the glory of the Lord shall be revealed, and all flesh shall see it together. [*Applause*]

I have a dream this afternoon that the brotherhood of man will become a reality in this day.

And with this faith I will go out and carve a tunnel of hope through the mountain of despair. With this faith, I will go out with you and transform dark yesterdays into bright tomorrows. With this faith, we will be able to achieve this new day when all of God's children, black men and white men, Jews and Gentiles, Protestants and Catholics, will be able to join hands and sing with the Negroes in the spiritual of old:

Free at last! Free at last!
Thank God Almighty, we are free at last! [*Applause*]. (Carson and Shepard 71-73)

Had this address in Detroit drawn as large a crowd and as much (inter)national attention by the press, it might well have become the most treasured speech by Martin Luther King, giving Detroit (my first home when I arrived in the United States as a German immigrant in August of 1960) a much-needed boost as a city that is struggling to this day with racism, poverty, unemployment, and many other social problems. When soul musician Aretha Franklin and her sister Erma, daughters of the Reverend C. L. Franklin (who had invited King to give this address in Detroit), were asked to write a short introduction to this speech by the editors of *A Call to Conscience: The Landmark Speeches of Dr. Martin Luther King, Jr.*, they were absolutely correct in their comments: "The history books say that Dr. King's speech on that day set the stage for his 'I Have a Dream' speech, at the great March on Washington later that summer. And indeed, Dr. King did explore some of the themes and language he would use at the Lincoln Memorial. But on that magical day, we knew that Detroit had been blessed with a tremendous vision of unity and brother- and sisterhood that had never been so well articulated and organized in America, and that somehow things were going to change for the better" (Carson and Shepard 58).

Conclusion

As this essay has shown, the famous "I Have a Dream" speech that King delivered in Washington, D.C., in the late summer of 1963 had had a long gestation period. Like almost any piece of good writing (and good oratory) it was not invented extemporaneously, "on the spot." Instead, King had tried out not only the ideas but also the words, sentences, and cadences many times, before many previous audiences. When he stepped before the rostrum in front of the Lincoln Memorial and looked out over the massive crowd before him, he was delivering the latest version of a speech that he had delivered in a similar way a few times before. Practice often *does* make perfect, and in this case King felt fully prepared to deliver one of the most perfect and most powerful speeches ever conceived.

Note

1. Other works of mine relevant to the topic of proverbs are cited below.

Works Cited and Consulted

Armstrong, Tenisha, Susan Carson, Adrienne Clay, and Kieran Taylor. *Threshold of a New Decade: January 1959-December 1960*. Volume V. Edited by Clayborne Carson et al., *The Papers of Martin Luther King, Jr.* 6 vols. U of California P, 1992-2007; 2005.

Arthurs, Jeffrey D. "Proverbs in Inspirational Literature: Sanctioning the American Dream." *Journal of Communication and Religion*, vol. 17, pp. 1-15. Also in Wolfgang Mieder, editor. *Cognition, Comprehension, and Communication: A Decade of North American Proverb Studies (1990-2000)*. Schneider Verlag Hohengehren, 2003, pp. 37-52.

Calloway-Thomas, Carolyn, and John Louis Lucaites, editors. *Martin Luther King, Jr., and the Sermonic Power of Public Discourse*. U of Alabama P, 1993.

Carson, Clayborne, et al., editors. *The Papers of Martin Luther King, Jr.* 6 vols. U of California P, 1992-2007.

Carson, Clayborne, and Peter Holloran. *A Knock at Midnight: Inspiration from the Great Sermons of Reverend Martin Luther King, Jr.* Warner Books, 1998.

Carson, Clayborne, and Kris Shepard, editors. *A Call to Conscience: The Landmark Speeches of Dr. Martin Luther King, Jr.* Grand Central, 2001.

Ensslin, Birgit, "'I Have a Dream'—Martin Luther King und die Bürgerrechtsbewegung in den USA. Eine rhetorische Analyse ausgewählter Texte von Martin Luther King."*Lebende Sprachen*, vol. 35, 1990, pp. 118-123.

Franklin, Robert Michael. "An Ethic of Hope: The Moral Thought of Martin Luther King, Jr." *Union Seminary Quarterly Review*, vol. 40, 1986, pp. 41-51.

Griffin, Albert Kirby. *Religious Proverbs: Over 1600 Adages from 18 Faiths Worldwide*. McFarland, 1991.

Hansen, Drew D. *The Dream. Martin Luther King, Jr., and the Speech That Inspired a Nation.* HarperCollins, 2003.

Hertzler, Joyce O. "On Golden Rules." *International Journal of Ethics*, vol. 44, 1933-34, pp. 418-36.

Hoskins, Lotte, editor. *"I Have a Dream": The Quotations of Martin Luther King Jr.* Grosset & Dunlap, 1968.

King, Martin Luther, Jr. *Strength to Love.* Harper & Row, 1963.

Lischer, Richard. *The Preacher King: Martin Luther King, Jr. and the Word that Moved America.* Oxford UP, 1995.

Mieder, Wolfgang. *American Proverbs: A Study of Texts and Contexts.* Peter Lang, 1989.

_____. *Not by Bread Alone: Proverbs of the Bible.* New England, 1990.

_____. *"A House Divided": From Biblical Proverb to Lincoln and Beyond.* U of Vermont, 1998.

_____. *The Proverbial Abraham Lincoln: An Index to Proverbs in the Works of Abraham Lincoln.* Peter Lang, 2000.

_____. *"No Struggle, No Progress": Frederick Douglass and His Proverbial Rhetoric for Civil Rights.* Peter Lang, 2001.

_____. *Proverbs Are the Best Policy: Folk Wisdom and American Politics.* Utah State UP, 2005.

_____. *Sprichwörter sind Goldes wert: Parömiologische Studien zu Kultur, Literatur und Medien.* U of Vermont, 2007.

_____. *Yes We Can": Barack Obama's Proverbial Rhetoric.* Peter Lang, 2009.

_____. *"Making a Way Out of No Way": Martin Luther King's Sermonic Proverbial Rhetoric.* Peter Lang, 2010.

_____, Stewart A. Kinsbury, and Kelsie B. Harder, editors. *A Dictionary of American Proverbs.* Ohio UP, 1992.

Rieder, Jonathan. *The Word of the Lord Is Upon Me: The Righteous Performance of Martin Luther King, Jr.* Harvard UP, 2008.

Sundquist, Eric J., 2009. *King's Dream.* Yale UP, 2009.

Templeton. John Marks, *Worldwide Laws of Life.* Templeton Foundation, 1997.

Warren, Mervyn A. *King Came Preaching: The Pulpit Power of Dr. Martin Luther King Jr.* InterVarsity, 2001.

Washington, James M., editor. *A Testament of Hope: The Essential Writings of Martin Luther King, Jr.* Harper & Row, 1986.

The Use of Proverbs in Martin Luther King's 1963 "I Have a Dream" Speech at the Lincoln Memorial_____

Wolfgang Mieder

By the time Martin Luther King Jr. rehearsed his famous "I Have a Dream" speech with its set of quotational and proverbial statements at the Lincoln Memorial on August 28, 1963, it was billed as the keynote address of the "March on Washington, D.C., for Civil Rights." The press from the United States and abroad was present, a quarter million people had assembled, and Martin Luther King found himself at the largest public event of the civil rights movement. It gave him and his idea of nonviolent struggle for equality, justice, and freedom a national and subsequently an international forum, never to be forgotten by those who were fortunate enough to be present at this momentous occasion, who witnessed the speech on television or listened to it on the radio, read it in the papers the following day or have come across it on film or in print ever since. Not surprisingly, then, much scholarly attention has been directed to this very speech, including two invaluable books, *The Dream: Martin Luther King, Jr., and the Speech That Inspired a Nation*, by Drew D. Hansen, and *King's Dream*, by Eric J. Sundquist. This is not the place to review everything that has been said about this speech, but from the beginning of their various analyses of its content, language, and meaning, scholars have made a point of emphasizing King's use of the intriguing proverbial metaphor "To cash a check" at the beginning of this relatively short address. Even though King did exceed his allotted time by several minutes, there was nobody who took his liberty amiss, judging by the response of the giant crowd. Clearly King's unique check references were a proverbial and rhetorical hit, and it is amazing that he did not use this successful "reaffirmative rhetoric" (Fisher 135-36) based on the check imagery again as he continued to argue for the cause of civil rights in later addresses:

> So we've come here today to dramatize a shameful condition. In a sense we've come to our nation's capital to cash a check. When the architects of our republic wrote the magnificent words of the Constitution and the Declaration of Independence, they were signing a promissory note to which every American was to fall heir. This note was the promise that all men, yes, black men as well as white men, would be guaranteed the unalienable rights of life, liberty, and the pursuit of happiness.
>
> It is obvious today that America has defaulted on this promissory note in so far as her citizens of color are concerned. Instead of honoring this sacred obligation, America has given the Negro people a bad check; a check which has come back marked "insufficient funds." We refuse to believe that there are insufficient funds in the great vaults of opportunity of this nation. And so we've come to cash this check, a check that will give us upon demand the riches of freedom and the security of justice. (Washington 217)

What a stroke of genius to turn to this metaphor of a check after having just described how African Americans have long suffered because of segregation and discrimination! Everybody could relate to this "promissory note" as expressed in the Declaration of Independence that is but one of the "foundational texts" (Rocci 30; see also Burrell and also Aron) of the American history and culture that King repeatedly relied on for his views. The time had surely come that this note would be cashed in, for, as King is quick to cite proverbially, "This note was the promise that all men, yes, black men as well as white men, would be guaranteed the unalienable rights of life, liberty, and the pursuit of happiness." It is, however, somewhat surprising that King at this point of his speech (he will do so later) does not expressly include the proverb "All men are created equal," although he makes up for it by addressing both races, being well aware that many white people were part of the large crowd of civil rights supporters in Washington and elsewhere in the nation. David A. Bobbitt, in his book on *The Rhetoric of Redemption: Kenneth Burke's Redemption Drama and Martin Luther King, Jr.'s "I Have a Dream" Speech* includes three pages on this "check/promissory note cluster" (see also Solomon 72-73), looking at it quite correctly as an "extended metaphor or analogy," but also criticizing King for having oversimplified matters:

> The tenor of this metaphor is the rights owed to African Americans. The vehicle, of course, is the check or promissory note, the later being a financial obligation to pay a certain amount of funds at a specified time. The metaphor predicates social and political rights in financial/economic terms. In other words, King is using a financial vehicle to describe a moral and political obligation. [...] However, [...] there is no simple, routine procedure for "cashing in" upon such fluid concepts as "justice" and "liberty." Thus, King has employed a simplistic, quantifiable economic metaphor to organize the auditors' perspective on a complex, non-quantifiable situation. A complex social/moral obligation involving rights which are as yet unsecured (and for which there is as yet no national consensus as to the specific nature of that obligation) is being predicated in terms of something as quantifiable and routine as cashing a check. When money is owed one can pay the amount owed and the debt is canceled, but how does one pay back a moral or political obligation? The metaphor attempts to predicate a moral claim of social justice in terms of a specific financial obligation. (Bobbitt 75-76)

It would be my conjecture that King would have had no problem with being accused of oversimplifying matters a bit, but his major metaphorical point was, of course, to bring the idea across that African Americans have the right to demand improvements in their socioeconomic lot after decades of injustice and deprivation.

More Proverbial Phrasing

In any case, King is perhaps a bit more direct with his warning in the immediately following cluster of four emotive proverbial phrases, including a variant of Shakespeare's "to be one's winter of discontent," "to blow off steam," "to have a rude awakening," and "to return to business as usual." Relating somewhat to his check metaphor, King certainly chose the perfect proverbial expression to state that the time of returning "to business as usual" has definitely passed:

> We have come to this hallowed spot [the Lincoln Memorial in Washington, D.C.] to remind America of the fierce urgency of now. This is no time to engage in the luxury of cooling off or to take the tranquilizing drug of gradualism. Now is the time to make real the promises of democracy; now is the time to rise from the dark and desolate valley of segregation to the sunlit path of racial justice; now is the time to lift our nation from the quicksands of racial injustice to the solid rock of brotherhood; now is the time to make justice a reality for all God's children. It would be fatal for the nation to overlook the urgency of the moment. This sweltering summer of the Negro's legitimate discontent will not pass until there is an invigorating autumn of freedom and equality.
>
> Nineteen sixty-three is not an end, but a beginning. And those who hope that the Negro needed to blow off steam and will now be content, will have a rude awakening if the nation returns to business as usual.
>
> There will be neither rest nor tranquility in America until the Negro is granted his citizenship rights. The whirlwinds of revolt will continue to shake the foundations of our nation until the bright day of justice emerges. (Washington 217-18)

Mark Vail, in his intriguing study of King's "integrative rhetoric," includes a keen interpretation of this paragraph, stressing the importance of the "economic metaphor" (i.e., the proverbial phrase "to return to business as usual") and also referring to the underlying expressiveness of the other three phrases, albeit without calling attention to their proverbiality:

> In the seventh and eighth paragraphs, King uses language that seems rooted in economic justice, yet its context is that of social justice. King warns that "[t]hose who hope that the Negro needed to blow off steam and will now be content will have a rude awakening if the nation returns to business as usual." This sentence comes in the wake of King's reference to the explosively violent summer of 1963, the "sweltering summer of the Negro's legitimate discontent [that] will not pass until there is an invigorating autumn of freedom and equality." Given King's prior linkage of social and economic justice, "business as usual" acquires a dual meaning with a singular purpose. Black Americans will no longer tolerate the figurative "business"

of social injustice (that is, discrimination), nor will they tolerate the literal "business" of economic injustice. Because of his prior linkage, King can effectively use an economic metaphor in a social context, thereby further galvanizing the integration of social and economic justice. (Vail 69)

While this cluster of proverbial phrases is also new to this address, it is at this point in his speech where King begins to draw on some of the quotations, proverbs, and proverbial phrases that belong to his basic repertoire of fixed rhetorical formulas (Fleer). Referring to the march metaphor of the civil rights movement, he cites the Bible proverb "Let justice roll down like waters and righteousness as a mighty stream" (Amos 5:24) that served him so well during his struggle against segregation and injustice (Sundquist 138), adding much emphasis to his remarks by yet another anaphoric formula:

> And as we walk, we must make the pledge that we shall always march ahead. We cannot turn back. There are those who are asking the devotees of civil rights, "When will you be satisfied?" We can never be satisfied as long as the Negro is the victim of the unspeakable horrors of police brutality.
> We can never be satisfied as long as our bodies, heavy with fatigue of travel, cannot gain lodging in the motels of the highways and the hotels of the cities. We cannot be satisfied as long as the Negro's basic mobility is from a smaller ghetto to a larger one.
> We can never be satisfied as long as our children are stripped of their selfhood and robbed of their dignity by signs stating "for whites only." We cannot be satisfied as long as a Negro in Mississippi cannot vote and a Negro in New York believes he has nothing for which to vote. No, we are not satisfied, and we will not be satisfied until justice rolls down like waters and righteousness like a mighty stream [Amos: 5:24]. (Washington 218-19)

Shortly after this statement, King put his carefully prepared written remarks aside and switched to his "I have a dream" sequence, as Drew D. Hansen has shown in a revealing side-by-side comparison of the written manuscript with the actual oral delivery (271-86). As was his custom, he now relied on his "repertoire of oratorical fragments" or "his own storehouse of oratory" (Hansen 70), knowing intuitively that his "dream" set piece, spoken as an orally performed conclusion (Patton 114-16), would give him the desired conclusion that he had not been able to compose during his work on this all-important address the days and night before its delivery. Here then is the "I have a dream" peroration with but three proverbial statements —"All men are created equal," which he had left out earlier in the speech, and the proverbial phrases "to be judged by the content of one's character and not by the color of one's skin" and "to join hands with someone"—with the latter being cited twice as a verbal sign of true brother- and sisterhood in an America of equality, justice, and freedom:

> So I say to you, my friends, that even though we must face the difficulties of today and tomorrow, I still have a dream. It is a dream deeply rooted in the American dream that one day this nation will rise up and live out the true meaning of its creed—we hold these truths to be self-evident, that all men are created equal.
> I have a dream that one day on the red hills of Georgia, sons of former slaves and sons of former slave-owners will be able to sit down together at the table of brotherhood.
> I have a dream that one day, even the state of Mississippi, a state sweltering with the heat of injustice, sweltering with the heat of oppression, will be transformed into an oasis of freedom and justice.
> I have a dream my four little children will one day live in a nation where they will not be judged by the color of their skin but by content of their character. I have a dream today!
> I have a dream that one day [...] little black boys and black girls will be able to join hands with the little white boys and white girls as sisters and brothers. I have a dream today!
> I have a dream that one day every valley shall be exalted, every hill and mountain shall be made low, the rough places shall be made plain, and the crooked places shall be made straight and the glory of the Lord will be revealed and all flesh shall see it together.
> This is our hope.... With this faith we will be able to hew out of the mountain of despair a stone of hope. With this faith we will be able to transform the jangling discords of our nation into a beautiful symphony of brotherhood.

> With this faith we will be able to work together, to pray together, to struggle together, to go to jail together, to stand up for freedom together, knowing that we will be free one day. . . .
>
> So let freedom ring. . . .
>
> And when we allow freedom to ring, when we let it ring from every village and hamlet, from every state and city, we will be able to speed up that day when all of God's children—black men and white men, Jews and Gentiles, Catholics and Protestants—will be able to join hands and to sing in the words of the old Negro spiritual, "Free at last, free at last; thank God Almighty, we are free at last." (Washington 219-20)

It goes to Eric J. Sundquist's credit that he draws attention to King's formulaic statement "not by the color of their skin" at the beginning of his long chapter with that title in his book *King's Dream* (194-228):

> Even though it does not provide the Dream speech's most famous phrase, one sentence stands alone for the philosophy it appeared to announce and the contentious use to which it has since been put: "I have a dream that my four little children will one day live in a nation where they will not be judged by the color of their skin but by the content of their character." If King's dream began to be realized with passage of the Civil Rights Act of 1964, his apparently clear elevation of character over color proved central to subsequent arguments about the reach and consequences of that landmark legislation. Those thirty-five spontaneous words have done more than any politician's polemic, any sociologist's theory, or any court's ruling to frame public discussion of affirmative action over the past four decades. (194)

Regarding the use of the phrase—Sundquist comes close to calling it a proverbial phrase—he is correct in referring to its "spontaneous" use in the context of this particular speech. It was in fact not included in the original manuscript and King added it during his extemporaneous peroration: "'I started out reading the speech,' recalled Martin Luther King, Jr., then 'all of a sudden this thing came out of me that I have used—I'd used it many times before, that thing about 'I have a dream'—and I just felt that I wanted to use it here. I don't know why, I hadn't thought about it before the speech'" (qtd. in Sundquist 14). King was thus obviously aware of his recycling of the "I have a dream" sequence in a number of variants, and I would assume that he also knew about his previous use of the "character/ skin" phrase in his "dream" peroration of the address in Detroit two months earlier, as I discussed in the preceding essay. If with his reference to "spontaneous words" Sundquist means to imply that the use of the phrase was new in the Washington speech, then he would be mistaken. In fact, as it were, King quite liked its metaphor and meaning, citing it three more times in sermons and speeches during 1967, thereby effectively helping his formulation along the path of becoming a proverbial expression.

But to return to the most famous of King's "I have a dream" speeches, there is no denying the fact that it was this speech delivered at the Lincoln Memorial on August 28, 1963, that will forever be remembered (see Sayenko). Drew D. Hansen has given a summary of why this is so at the beginning of a long chapter entitled the "Sermon" in his book on *The Dream*:

> By the time of the March on Washington, King had been known as a talented preacher for over a decade. When he was in seminary at Crozer, his fellow students would crowd into the chapel to hear him practice his sermons. He had preached at churches around the country by the age of twenty-five, when he took up the pastorate at Dexter. His fame among the black clergy was already so established that his father, the minister of the Ebenezer Baptist Church in Atlanta, received a letter that began: "They told me you have a son that can preach rings around you any day you ascend the pulpit. How about that? If it is so, it is a compliment to you."
>
> But in 1963, King's oratorical ability was, for the most part, unknown outside of the black church and the civil rights movement. Before the March on Washington, most Americans had never heard King preach a complete sermon. King's speech at the march was so powerful in part because it exposed a national audience, for the first time, to his genius as a preacher: his facility with language, his ability to transform material from different sources into set pieces that were uniquely his own, and his mastery of the art of black homiletics.

> The "I Have a Dream" speech was so remarkable not because it was the pinnacle of King's oratorical skill, as if he were merely an average public speaker who happened to be in particularly good form on August 28, 1963. The March on Washington simply provided a national audience with its first opportunity to witness a pulpit performance that those active in the civil rights movement could see many times a year. King transformed a political rally of the nation's citizens at the Lincoln Memorial into a vast congregation. He may have prepared a formal address for the March on Washington, but he ended up preaching a sermon, and his homiletic abilities were responsible for much of the speech's success. (99-100)

From a purely paremiological point of view, I could not agree more with Drew D. Hansen's assessment. This famous speech with its proverbial language is not necessarily his best, and I would argue that the "dream" sequence of his Detroit speech of June 23, 1963, is even more powerful in regard to its reliance on proverbs and proverbial phrases.[1] And, to be sure, yet another version of his "American Dream" speech of July 4, 1965, as well as his Christmas sermon of December 24, 1967, include subsequent variants of his "dream" peroration that come close to, equal, or perhaps also surpass what King spoke proverbially at Washington. All of this should not surprise us if we recall King's rhetorical tendency of recycling and rephrasing his repertoire of set pieces to suit his audience and without doubt also his time constraints.

Later Versions of the "I Have a Dream" Motif

Even though his speech at the end of the March on Washington is the one that rightfully has been canonized as a magisterial rhetorical and emotional accomplishment, it behooves us to take a short glance at what King was able to do with his "dream" imagery linked with proverbial language on the two occasions just mentioned. It was indeed appropriate for Martin Luther King to return to his theme of the "American Dream" with his sermon on the Fourth of July 1965 at Ebenezer Baptist Church in Atlanta. Reminding the congregation that this was Independence Day, he quickly turned to the double proverbial message of the Declaration of Independence that he,

Abraham Lincoln, Frederick Douglass, and now Barack Obama have also used repeatedly (see Mieder 1998, 2000, 2001, 2005, 2009). But there is a difference, of course, in that King links these noble ideas of equality with his uplifting leitmotif of the American dream:

> This morning I would like to use as a subject from which to preach: "The American Dream." [*Yes, sir*]
> It wouldn't take us long to discover the substance of that dream. It is found in those majestic words of the Declaration of Independence, words lifted to cosmic proportions: "We hold these truths to be self-evident, that all men are created equal, that they are endowed by [their] Creator with certain inalienable Rights, that among these are Life, Liberty, and the pursuit of Happiness." This is a dream. It's a great dream. (Carson and Holloran 85-86)

A few paragraphs later he uses his standard proverbial expressions "to pay the price for something" and "the clock is ticking" to stress the challenges that America faces to make the dream of a more perfect union become a reality. His wording is very similar to what he said in his "American Dream" speech of June 6, 1961, showing once again his method of reusing key passages of previous addresses with only minor alterations, usually recalling such set pieces from memory with the possibility of changing things as he saw fit:

> But now more than ever before, America is challenged to realize its dream [of freedom], for the shape of the world today does not permit our nation the luxury of an anemic democracy. And the price that America must pay for the continued oppression of the Negro and other minority groups is the price of its own destruction. [*Yes it is*] For the hour is late. And the clock of destiny is ticking out. We must act now before it is too late.
> And so it is marvelous and great that we do have a dream, that we have a nation with a dream; and to forever challenge us; to forever give us a sense of urgency; to forever stand in the midst of the "isness" of our terrible injustices; to remind us of the "oughtness" of our noble capacity for justice and love and brotherhood. (Carson and Hollaran 187)

Having mentioned the urgency of changing the dream of equality into reality, King literally makes the proverb "All men are created equal" into a leitmotif, citing it a total of nine more times in a number of paragraphs. In the following example, he goes to great rhetorical lengths to explain that this equality means above all that all people are of the same value as human beings, regardless of their intellectual or artistic abilities:

> This morning I would like to deal with some of the challenges that we face today in our nation as a result of the American dream. First, I want to reiterate the fact that we are challenged more than ever before to respect the dignity and the worth of all human personality. We are challenged to really believe that all men are created equal. And don't misunderstand that. It does not mean that all men are created equal in terms of native endowment, in terms of intellectual capacity—it doesn't mean that. There are certain bright stars in the human firmament in every field. [*Yes, sir*] It doesn't mean that every musician is equal to a Beethoven or Handel, a Verdi or a Mozart. It doesn't mean that every physicist is equal to an Einstein. It does not mean that every literary figure in history is equal to Aeschylus and Euripides, Shakespeare and Chaucer. [*Make it plain*] It does not mean that every philosopher is equal to Plato, Aristotle, Immanuel Kant, and Friedrich Hegel. It doesn't mean that. There are individuals who do excel and rise to the heights of genius in their areas and in their fields. What it does mean is that all men are equal in intrinsic worth. [*Yes*] (Carson and Holloran 87-88)

And then he moves on to look at the special role that America plays in giving people of many racial and national backgrounds the same opportunities to succeed in life because they are all equal according to the fundamental creed of this nation:

> And I tell you this morning, my friends, the reason we got to solve this problem here in America: because God somehow called America to do a special job for mankind and the world. [*Yes, sir. Make it plain*] Never before in the history of the world have so many racial groups and so many national backgrounds assembled together in one nation. And somehow, if we can't solve the problem in America the world

can't solve the problem, because America is the world in miniature and the world is America writ large. And God set us out with all of the opportunities. [*Make it plain*] He set us between two great oceans; [*Yes, sir*] made it possible for us to live with some of the great natural resources of the world. And there he gave us through the minds of our forefathers a great creed: "We hold these truths to be self-evident, that all men [*Yes, sir*] are created equal." (Carson and Holloran 92)

There is no need to cite additional paragraphs exemplifying this leitmotif, especially since it appears one final time in the peroration of this particular "American Dream" speech. Even though some dreams have been shattered, including some pressing goals of his own civil rights movement, King is far from throwing in the proverbial towel. Instead, he changes the "I have a dream" anaphora to "I still have a dream" that signifies his unrelenting faith and hope in the progress toward equality and justice. He also adds the biblical proverbial phrase "The lion and the lamb will lie down together" (Isaiah 11:6) to his futuristic vision as a metaphor for all people living in harmony together:

So yes, the dream has [in part] been shattered, [*Amen*] and I have had my nightmarish experiences, but I tell you this morning once more that I haven't lost the faith. [*No, sir*] I still have a dream [*A dream. Yes, sir*] that one day all of God's children will have food and clothing and material well-being for their bodies, culture and education for their minds, and freedom for their spirits. [*Yes*]

I still have a dream this morning: [*Yes*] One day all of God's black children will be respected like his white children.

I still have a dream this morning [*Yes*] that one day the lion and the lamb will lie down together, and every man will sit under his own vine and fig tree and none shall be afraid [Isaiah 11:6].

I still have a dream this morning that one day all men everywhere will recognize that out of one blood God made all men to dwell upon the face of the earth.

I still have a dream this morning [*Yes, sir*] that one day every valley shall be exalted, and every mountain and hill will be made low; the rough places will be made plain, and the crooked places straight; and the glory of the Lord shall be revealed, and all flesh shall see it together.

I still have a dream this morning [*Amen*] that truth will reign supreme and all of God's children will respect the dignity and worth of human personality. And when this day comes the morning stars will sing together [*Yes*] and the sons of God will shout for joy.

"We hold these truths to be self-evident, that all men [*All right*] are created equal, that they are endowed by their Creator with certain inalienable Rights, [*Yes, sir*] that among these are Life, Liberty, and the pursuit of Happiness." (Carson and Holloran 99-100)

His "American Dream" speech of June 6, 1961, did not yet include the "I have a dream" anaphora, but once King created it in November of 1962, he was well aware of its rhetorical effectiveness. In fact, after this speech of August 28, 1963, at the Lincoln Memorial, people were in a way expecting him to employ it. This was definitely the case in the Christmas Eve sermon that he gave on December 24, 1967, at Ebenezer Baptist Church in Atlanta. The sermon contains some of King's quotational and proverbial favorites throughout, to wit "Love your enemies" (Matt. 5:44), "Truth crushed to earth will rise again," and "No lie can live for ever" (Karabegović). The "I have a dream" peroration in and of itself is once again a powerful endorsement for equality, justice, freedom, and peace. While it does not include the proverb "All men are created equal" and the proverbial expression "to join hands with someone" of the Washington speech, it does repeat the important proverbial phrase "to be judged by the content of one's character and not by the color of one's skin." But always finding ways to vary such set pieces of rhetoric, King this time added three of his often-employed Bible proverbs to underscore his message of justice, peace, and harmony:

I have a dream that one day men will rise up and come to see that they are made to live together as brothers. I still have a dream this morning that one day every Negro in this country, every colored person in the world, will be judged on the basis of the content of his character rather than the color of his skin, and every man will respect the dignity and worth of human personality. I still have a dream today that one day the idle industries of Appalachia will be revitalized, and the empty stomachs of Mississippi will be filled, and brotherhood will be more than a few words at the end of a prayer, but rather the first order of business on every legislative agenda. I still have a dream today that one day justice will roll down like water, and righteousness like a mighty stream [Amos 5:24]. I still have a dream today that in all of our state houses and city halls men will be elected to go there who will do justly and love mercy and walk humbly with their God. I still have a dream today that one day war will come to an end, that men will beat their swords into plowshares and their spears into pruning hooks [Isaiah 2:4], that nations will no longer rise up against nations, neither will they study war any more. I still have a dream today that one day the lamb and the lion will lie down together [cf. Isaiah 11:6] and every man will sit under his own vine and fig tree and none shall be afraid. I still have a dream today that one day every valley shall be exalted and every mountain and hill will be made low, the rough places will be made smooth and the crooked places straight, and the glory of the Lord shall be revealed, and all flesh shall see it together. I still have a dream that with this faith we will be able to adjourn the councils of despair and bring new light into the dark chambers of pessimism. With this faith we will be able to speed up the day when there will be peace on earth and goodwill toward men. It will be a glorious day, the morning stars will sing together, and the sons of God will shout for joy. (Washington 257-58; also the last paragraph in King 77-78)

Conclusion

By the end of 1967, the "I have a dream" anaphora, modified to "I still have a dream" after its (inter)national exposure at the Lincoln Memorial on August 28, 1963, at Washington, D.C., had doubtlessly become King's rhetorical signature phrase. Of course, it represents but one of his quotational and proverbial leitmotifs that made his sermons, speeches, letters, essays, and books such effective and memorable statements in the cause of civil and human rights. Quotations turned proverbs, as well as Bible proverbs, folk proverbs, and a plethora of proverbial expressions, are an intrinsic part of King's rhetorical prowess, providing his messages with colorful metaphors and authoritative strength. His noble dream of an America and a world interconnected by equality, justice, freedom, love, and hope had to be expressed through language so that the nonviolent movement for civil and human rights could march forward (Miller). Individual words and sentences were needed to bring these dignified ideals across, and there can be no doubt that proverbs and proverbial phrases as ready-made expressions served King extremely well in adding imagery and expressiveness to his numerous oral and written communications (Mieder, *Making*). His dream needed words and deeds, and being a master of both, Martin Luther King was and remains the visionary champion of making a way out of no way for all of humanity that thanks to him has come a long way but still has a long way to go. Moving on with an adherence to the biblical triad of "faith, hope, and love" and the acceptance of the African American proverb "Making a way out of no way" (Mieder, *American Proverbs* 111-28; see also Prahlad) will keep Martin Luther King's proverbial dream alive for future generations as they confront their fate in the world house of brotherly and sisterly mutuality.

Note
1. For some relevant examples of my own work on proverbs, see the pieces cited below.

Works Cited

Aron, Paul. *We Hold These Truths ... And Other Words That Made America.* Rowman & Littlefield, 2008.

Bobbitt, David A. *The Rhetoric of Redemption: Kenneth Burke's Redemption Drama and Martin Luther King, Jr.'s "I Have a Dream" Speech.* Rowman & Littlefield, 2004.

Burrell, Brian. *The Words We Live By: The Creeds, Mottoes, and Pledges That Have Shaped America.* Free, 1997.

Calloway-Thomas, Carolyn, and John Louis Lucaites, editors. *Martin Luther King, Jr., and the Sermonic Power of Public Discourse.* U of Alabama P, 1993.

Carson, Clayborne, and Peter Holloran. *A Knock at Midnight. Inspiration from the Great Sermons of Reverend Martin Luther King, Jr.* Warner, 1998.

Fisher, Walter R. "A Motive View of Communication." *The Quarterly Journal of Speech*, vol. 56, 1970, pp. 131-39.

Fleer, David, *Martin Luther King, Jr.'s Reformation of Sources: A Close Rhetorical Reading of His Compositional Strategies and Arrangement*. Dissertation. U of Washington, 1995.

Garrow, David J., editor. *Martin Luther King, Jr.: Civil Rights Leader, Theologian, Orator*. 3 vols. Carlson, 1989.

Hansen, Drew D. *The Dream. Martin Luther King, Jr., and the Speech that Inspired a Nation*. HarperCollins, 2003.

Karabegović, Dženeta, "'No Lie Can Live Forever': Zur sprichwörtlichen Rhetorik von Martin Luther King." *Sprichwörter sind Goldes wert: Parömiologische Studien zu Kultur, Literatur und Medien*. Edited byWolfgang Mieder, U of Vermont, 2007, pp. 223-40.

King, Martin Luther, Jr. *The Trumpet of Conscience*. Harper & Row, 1967.

Mieder, Wolfgang. *American Proverbs: A Study of Texts and Contexts*. Peter Lang, 1989.

_____. *Not by Bread Alone: Proverbs of the Bible*. New England P, 1990.

_____. *"A House Divided": From Biblical Proverb to Lincoln and Beyond*. Uof Vermont, 1998.

_____. *The Proverbial Abraham Lincoln: An Index to Proverbs in the Works of Abraham Lincoln*. Peter Lang, 2000.

_____. *"No Struggle, No Progress": Frederick Douglass and His Proverbial Rhetoric for Civil Rights*. Peter Lang, 2001.

_____. *Proverbs Are the Best Policy: Folk Wisdom and American Politics*. Utah State UP, 2005.

_____. *Sprichwörter sind Goldes wert: Parömiologische Studien zu Kultur, Literatur und Medien*. U of Vermont, 2007.

_____. *Yes We Can": Barack Obama's Proverbial Rhetoric*. Peter Lang, 2009.

_____. *"Making a Way Out of No Way": Martin Luther King's Sermonic Proverbial Rhetoric*. Peter Lang, 2010.

_____, et al., editors. *A Dictionary of American Proverbs*. Ohio UP, 1992.

Miller, Keith D. *Voice of Deliverance: The Language of Martin Luther King, Jr. and Its Sources*. Free, 1992.

Patton, John H. "'I Have a Dream': The Performance of Theology Fused with the Power of Orality." In Calloway-Thomas and Lucaites, 1993, pp. 104-26.

Prahlad, Sw. Anand. *African-American Proverbs in Context*. UP of Mississippi, 1996.

Rocci, Andrea. "Doing Discourse Analysis with Possible Worlds [Applied to a Fragment of Martin Luther King's 'I Have a Dream' Speech]." *Discourse, of Course: An Overview of Research in Discourse Studies*. Edited by Jan Renkema, Benjamins, 2009, pp. 15-35.

Sayenko, Tetyana. "On the Pragmatic and Prosodic Structure of an Inspirational Political Address [i.e., Martin Luther King's 'I Have a Dream']." *Rhetorical Aspects of Discourses in Present-Day Society*. Edited by Lotte Dam et al., Cambridge Scholars, 2008, pp. 129-53.

Solomon, Martha. "Covenanted Rights: The Metaphoric Matrix of 'I Have a Dream.'" *Martin Luther King, Jr., and the Sermonic Power of Public Discourse*. In Calloway-Thomas and Lucaites, 1993, pp. 68-84.

Sundquist, Eric J. *King's Dream*. Yale UP, 2009.

Vail, Mark, "The 'Integrative' Rhetoric of Martin Luther King Jr.'s 'I Have a Dream' Speech." *Rhetoric & Public Affairs*, vol. 9, 2006, pp. 51-78.

Washington, James M., editor. *A Testament of Hope: The Essential Writings of Martin Luther King, Jr*. Harper & Row, 1986.

"The Samaritan Way" in Martin Luther King's Final Public Address

Raymond Blanton

In an earlier essay in this volume, I stressed the importance of Martin Luther King's reliance on key metaphors in his sermons and speeches. In particular, I emphasized the ways he employed archetypal images of roads—images related not only to literal and figurative movement but also to the larger progress of the civil rights movement in general. In the present essay I wish to focus on a related metaphor, one especially pertinent to King's final public speech. This metaphor involves the so-called Samaritan Way and appears in the speech King delivered to striking sanitation workers in Memphis, Tennessee, on the evening of April 3, 1968. The next evening, at 6:01 P.M., King was struck down by an assassin's bullet. His own life had ended, but the movement he had led continued without him. Often that movement proceeded in accordance with "The Samaritan Way," an ethic of crucial importance to King himself.

"Something Is Happening"

It had been more than two months since the sanitation workers strike in Memphis had begun, involving more than thirteen hundred people. It was a dire moment for an already poor people, now two months without salaries and no preexisting strike fund to assist them in their cause. Moreover, the Memphis strike had been plagued by poor organization from the beginning. Its disastrous first march had ended with the demonstrators fleeing police. But this was also a difficult time both for King and for the movement he was leading. Nonviolence as a method had begun to wane as insistence on Black Power grew, and in the months before coming to Memphis, King and his followers had gained little ground in Chicago, where they had hoped to successfully challenge slum conditions and overcome economic exploitation.

Nevertheless, against the advice of his inner circle, King announced in late March that he would be traveling to Memphis to support the sanitation workers' strike. On the morning of his famous speech, King's Eastern Airlines flight in Atlanta had been delayed because of a bomb threat. That afternoon, after checking in at the Lorraine Motel, he and his aides attended a meeting with black ministers, where they received news that a local federal judge had blocked their march and issued an injunction. As Osborn notes, "All these furies were swarming about King's head as he stepped onto the stage at Mason Temple" (150). In fact, King had been considering not speaking that night and sending his most trusted friend, Ralph Abernathy, in his place. But after Abernathy phoned King at the motel to urge him to reconsider, King obliged, giving us not only his last public address but also one of the most memorable speeches he ever delivered.

"I'm delighted," he told his audience, "to see each of you here tonight in spite of a storm warning. You reveal that you are determined to go on anyhow. Something is happening in Memphis, something is happening in our world" ("I See" 279). These opening lines introduce us to a peculiar but important insight into the address, especially given the troubling circumstances for all involved. Plainly, and paradoxically, King's tone throughout the speech is one of delight: he uses the term *happy* on nine different occasions to describe being in his hearers' midst as part of what God was doing. To help situate the "happening," King guided his listeners on a journey, a "mental flight," through eight different periods of human history, using the refrain, "I wouldn't stop there. I would go on..." (279) as he added each new "period" (that is, a well-balanced, lengthy, and rhetorically impressive sentence).

King establishes the scene by describing a series of encounters with the Almighty, who, King proposes, asks him what age he would like to live in among all the eras of human history. Consistent with his frequent use of archetypal road imagery, King begins with the most prevalent mythic theme of the civil rights movement, the Exodus. Alongside the Hebrews, King imaginatively traverses the paths out of Egypt and across the Red Sea into the wilderness toward the Promised Land. Next King moves us through the ancient origins of rhetoric in Greece to Mount Olympus, where Plato, Aristotle, and Socrates are assembled in the Parthenon, discussing eternal issues of reality. From there, King moves us swiftly through the Roman Empire, the Renaissance, and on into the Reformation, where his namesake, Martin Luther, nails the ninety-five theses to the doors of All Saints' Church in Wittenberg, Germany. On King's sixth stop, he guides us through the time of Abraham Lincoln's Emancipation Proclamation, and on the seventh he moves us into the twentieth century with the First Inaugural Speech of President Franklin Roosevelt, who on March 4, 1933, delivered the line "The only thing we have to fear, is fear itself." From there, King proceeds through the Great Depression and brings us to his present moment, where he accounts for the conditions and circumstances of his own day.

"Strangely enough," King finally replies to the Almighty, "if you allow me to live in the second half of the twentieth century, I'll be happy: Now that's a strange statement to make, because the world is all messed up. The nation is sick. Trouble is in the land. Confusion all around. That's a strange statement. But I know, somehow, that only when it is dark enough, can you see the stars. And I see God working in this period of the twentieth century in a way that men, in some strange way, are responding—something is happening in our world" ("I See" 280). By providing a panoramic perspective, King indicates the significance of the "happening" by noting that both on an international and on a domestic scale, people from all walks of life are standing up for the cause in South Africa, Kenya, Ghana, New York City, Atlanta, Jackson, and Memphis. Then, King transitions from recent "happenings" to what *has* to happen to actualize the movement's goals—to attain the ultimate order that transcends the dialectical tensions of race in American culture and human history.

Coming Together/Antagonistic Cooperation

In the middle section of the speech, King emphasizes two important themes. The first is the need to come together through marches and songs. Second, in promoting this effort to come together, King urges his listeners to follow through to the end of the line. I will now focus on an essential benefit and one dilemma associated with these two themes. First, just as King concludes his "mental fight," he outlines an additional reason for his strange happiness. "I'm happy," he indicates, "because we are being put into a place where we are going to have to grapple with the problems that men have been trying to grapple with through history, but the demands didn't force them to do it. Survival demands that we grapple with them" ("I See" 280). King says, "It is no longer a choice between violence and nonviolence in this world; it's nonviolence or nonexistence. That is where we are today" ("I See" 280). Two aspects of this statement are especially notable. First, just three days before making these remarks, King had delivered his "Remaining Awake Through a Great Revolution" sermon, which was given on Passion Sunday at the National Cathedral (Episcopal) in Washington, D.C. King there had uttered these exact words about nonviolence and nonexistence and called for a "world perspective" that would involve developing an ethical commitment to make the neighborhood of the world into a brotherhood:

> But somehow, and in some way, we have got to do this. We must all learn to live together as brothers. Or we will perish together as fools. We are tied together in the single garment of destiny, caught in an inescapable network of mutuality. And whatever affects one directly affects all indirectly. For some strange reason I can never be what I ought to be until you are what you ought to be. And you can never be what you ought to be until I am what I ought to be. This is the way God's universe is made; this is the way it is structured. (268)

But in the Memphis address King also answers one of the questions he had raised in 1967 in his presidential address to the Southern Christian Leadership Council: "Where Do We Go from Here?" In this speech, King had indicated that we must "first honestly recognize where we are now" to consider where we go from here (245). But where is "here"? Notice the connection—in theme, tone, and language—between this phrasing and the introduction of King's "I See the Promised Land" address. In that address, after he indicates the dialectical tension between nonviolence and nonexistence, he emphasizes, "[This] is where we are today." In both addresses, we find an urgency and determination in his language that we have "got to do this," for the destiny of the United States is tied up with the destiny of every other nation ("Remaining" 272-73).

At this crossroad in the Memphis address, King turns his attention to what has to happen for the "happening" to continue on toward its local and ultimate aims. "Now, what does all of this mean in this great period of history? It means that we've got to stay together. We've got to stay together and maintain unity" ("I See" 280). At this point, King shifts his focus to the march and the power of song in the movement, with an emphasis on action verbs such as *went, go, move,* and *march*: "Now we're going to march again, and we've got to march again in order to put the issue where it is supposed to be. And force everybody to see that there are thirteen hundred of God's children here suffering" ("I See" 281). More specifically, King emphasizes that he intends to "make the invisible visible," which can only be done by putting the strikers' bodies and souls in *motion* ("Remaining" 274-75). Of particular note, King recalls the Birmingham march and how the marchers there would move out of the 16th Street Baptist Church every day by the hundreds, marching as Bull Connor sent dogs forth. And they went before the dogs, singing, "Ain't gonna let nobody turn me round" ("I See" 281). When Bull Connor turned the water hoses on them, they went on singing, "Over my head I see freedom in the air" ("I See" 281). When Bull Connor stacked them into the paddy wagons, they went on singing, "We Shall Overcome." And even when they were in jail, they went on singing, the jailers being moved by their prayers and songs (for parallel phrasing, see Acts 16:25). It is at this point, having stressed the need for unity and reminding the people about the importance of marching and song, that King notes,"Now we've got to go on to Memphis just like that" ("I See" 282).

The Relevance of Kenneth Burke
But how do people come together in the midst of intense conflict caused by America's racial tensions? For an answer, I look to a

short essay written in response to the turmoil of this same period—Kenneth Burke's "Responsibilities of National Greatness." As Gregory Clark asserts:

> In a nation of displaced people where roots are often not deep, culture and identity are both in perpetual process. That gives Americans trouble. Haunted as we are with calls to collective mission, we share an insistent need to identify ourselves around a stable set of "national values, ideals, and expectancies." But that is difficult to do for people who are always in the process of inventing themselves. . . . The American identity crisis intensifies in contentious times. (43)

These were the conditions that animated the times in which both Burke and King were living. For Clark, Burke's essay presented a strategy offering antagonistic people the chance to cooperate just long enough to see oneself in the other's actions and the other's actions in oneself. According to Burke, as well as to King, Americans needed an attitude that would help them come together. For Burke, this alternative American identity is directed toward "consummation," that is, a move from self-expression toward a focus on others that would, ideally, lead to an understanding shared by both self and others together. Though Burke believed that we can never fully achieve this goal in its fullness, he felt that we may encounter one another in ways that motivate our pursuit of the ideal. In looking beyond ourselves to this function of sociality, we encounter one another by acting together, becoming consubstantial, with each identity merging one into the other. Put differently, and using Ralph Ellison's language, the civic projects of both Burke and King seek to guide people into productive rather than destructive encounters, toward "antagonistic cooperation" (see Chapter 2 of Crable). By stressing our need to come together, Clark further underscores the importance of archetypal language in our sequential move toward the ultimate order:

> If aesthetic form is a kind of journey that takes someone through a sequence of questions and answers that must be accommodated by new understanding along the way, then consummation is the

culmination of that journey, arrival at a destination where in our interactions no adjustment is needed for us to understand each other. Burke's metaphor for that journey is an "Upward Way" that leads from alienation, separation and conflict to, ultimately, "unification, promise, and freedom" [where] minds and bodies are bound together as one by their very differences, in an experience so fully shared that it seems as if there were no separation of people at all. (46)

In "Responsibilities of National Greatness," Burke pointed to the "notable risks and dangers which must be recognized if democracy is to function at its best" (47). Clark, elaborating on Burke's views, remarks that it "requires considerable effort for us to assess in every experience we encounter, however innocuous it might seem, which values, ideals, and expectancies it brings to life, and who they bind together as well as who they push away" (70).

The particular dilemma of coming together is that we do not always do so successfully. Burke therefore urges each of us to subject both our corporate and our unconscious identifications to careful scrutiny and to reflect on these puzzling identifications in relation to our sense of citizenship. Though we recognize the unlikelihood that we will always come together meaningfully, we still want things to be better. Clark explains that "Burke readily acknowledged the practical constraints that contain such aspirations, but he still claimed them. While he didn't expect them to be realized, he still urged us on in the effort of trying" (133). This "abiding sense of search" as Edward Strickland called it (see Clark 133), moves, in Burke's language, toward the "end of the line"—phrasing that aligns seamlessly with King's own exhortation:

> I ask you to follow through here. . . . As I move to my conclusion . . . to give ourselves to this struggle until the end. Nothing would be more tragic than to stop at this point in Memphis. We've got to see it through. And when we have our march, you need to be there. Be concerned about your brother. ("I See" 284)

In this "abiding sense of search" there will be uncertainty and conflict. Though we cannot come together with all, we may become consubstantial with a select few, in a "mythic" experience that takes us beyond our expectations. Despite the fact that we can only make connections with one another from "unreliable concepts and terms," life goes on. And so must we, toward a better life, whatever the cost (Clark 137).

The Samaritan Way

> 25 And, behold, a certain lawyer stood up, and tempted him, saying, Master, what shall I do to inherit eternal life? 26 He said unto him, What is written in the law? how readest thou? 27 And he answering said, Thou shalt love the Lord thy God with all thy heart, and with all thy soul, and with all thy strength, and with all thy mind; and thy neighbour as thyself. 28 And he said unto him, Thou hast answered right: this do, and thou shalt live. 29 But he, willing to justify himself, said unto Jesus, And who is my neighbour? 30 And Jesus answering said, A certain man went down from Jerusalem to Jericho, and fell among thieves, which stripped him of his raiment, and wounded him, and departed, leaving him half dead. 31 And by chance there came down a certain priest that way: and when he saw him, he passed by on the other side. 32 And likewise a Levite, when he was at the place, came and looked on him, and passed by on the other side. 33 But a certain Samaritan, as he journeyed, came where he was: and when he saw him, he had compassion on him, 34 And went to him, and bound up his wounds, pouring in oil and wine, and set him on his own beast, and brought him to an inn, and took care of him. 35 And on the morrow when he departed, he took out two pence, and gave them to the host, and said unto him, Take care of him; and whatsoever thou spendest more, when I come again, I will repay thee. 36 Which now of these three, thinkest thou, was neighbour unto him that fell among the thieves? 37 And he said, He that shewed mercy on him. Then said Jesus unto him, Go, and do thou likewise. (Luke 10, King James Version)

In the body of his Memphis speech, King, the rhetor leading souls, instructs his listeners in exactly what they must do and how they must do it. First, they should go out in unity, respectfully but with determination. Then, they must anchor their direct action in economic withdrawal while also building economic strength in the black community. And finally, they need to invest personally in the desperate plight of the sanitation workers by marching on a "dangerous road" (Osborn 153). After King calls the people to see these aspects of the movement through to the end of the line, he gives them a perspective by incongruity and then introduces a mythic ideal that embodies that perspective. The incongruity, "dangerous unselfishness," refers back to a theme in King's "On Being a Good Neighbor" speech. Here, I argue, King is not simply using the parable of the Good Samaritan as a conclusion or as some circumstantial theme for his address. Rather, more importantly and substantively, King is again directing the people's attention, and ours, to the perfection of this mythic ideal of the Upward and Downward Way.

Specifically, King introduces two new questions to those discussed, in the parable, by Jesus and the lawyer. King's audience had to answer these questions, and so do we. The first question asks, "If I stop to help this man, what will happen to me?" This question is concerned mostly with the self. It recalls the priest and the Levite from the parable and presupposes a cost the individual is unwilling to bear. The second question asks, "If I do not stop to help this man, what will happen to him?" This question places the emphasis upon the other rather than the self, on need over nationality. It implies the practical questions some of us must face as we attempt to enact the Samaritan ethic, questions King outlined in "On Being A Good Neighbor": "We so often ask,'What will happen to my job, my prestige, or my status if I take a stand on this issue? Will my home be bombed, will my life be threatened, or will I be jailed?' The good man always reverses the question" ("On Being" 26). In his final speech, King emphasizes which question is most important:

> That's the question before you tonight. Not, "If I stop to help the sanitation workers, what will happen to all of the hours that I usually spend in my office every day and every week as a pastor?" The question is not, "If I stop to help this man in need, what will happen to me?" "If I do not stop to help the sanitation workers, what will happen to them?" That's the question. ("I See" 285)

As King approached his final words, he returned to his "mental flight" from the opening of the speech. This time, though, King focused on important moments and marches of the movement. Once again emphasizing his happiness at being a witness to the movement's progress, he remembers the Greensboro sit-ins of 1960, the events of Albany, Georgia in 1962, the marches in Birmingham, Washington, and Selma, and finally, Memphis. In King's ascent to the "mountaintop," his climb toward freedom was about more than civil rights, it was also a battle for his and the nation's soul (Burns x).

I contend that the Samaritan parable is an important counterpart to the Exodus myth that played such a significant role in the civil rights movement. The Exodus myth and the Samaritan parable work together through the entirety of King's civic and sermonic discourse as moral compasses, guiding his listeners toward their future aims by emphasizing both memory and aspiration. Osborn argues that the Good Samaritan is a kind of balance to the Exodus narrative. Where the Exodus narrative supplies King's listeners with a collective identity, the Good Samaritan provides a model of action to emulate. And, more importantly, given the Samaritan's social status as a racial other, the parable reminds the audience of their *own* need to embody the Samaritan ethic. On one hand, given the discriminatory treatment of African Americans, the parable seems most obviously intended for a white audience. This is not inaccurate. But it is also not the primary objective of King the *psychagogic* rhetor. That is, the parable is directed at his primary audience—*all* Americans. King focuses on need over nationality at all times.

After King raises these two new questions by evoking the parable of the Good Samaritan, he turns, as Osborn notes, to a "vertical metaphor": "Let us rise up tonight with a greater readiness. Let us stand with a greater determination. And let us move on, in these powerful days, these days of challenge, to make America what it ought to be. We have an opportunity to make America a better nation" ("I See" 285). This vertical orientation implies the Upward Way, guiding us toward the ultimate order. It also, however, suggests the Downward Way, where the vision of the mythic image acquired can be enacted ethically. Osborn argues, for instance, that while the Exodus narrative offered the hope of America as the Promised Land, actualization of that hope could only be had by the kind of action best exemplified in the parable of the Good Samaritan. Osborn notes:

> [The Exodus narrative] offers cultural, collective identity for black people, while the [GoodSamaritan parable] deals with personal moral obligation. But more than just the counterpart of the Exodus narrative, the Good Samaritan story functions as its enabling condition. The Exodus myth will become reality; will carry listeners to the Promised Land, *if* they are willing to follow with full-hearted commitment the moral example of the Good Samaritan. (158)

In essence, all of King's civic and sermonic discourse, not merely this speech, is based on the collective identity of the Exodus myth and progresses developmentally, just as Osborn argued, on the Upward Way. In turn, the Samaritan ethic becomes a mythic image of the ultimate order. Most importantly, note that in the parable the directional focus is *down,* from Jerusalem. When en route to Jerusalem, on the Upward Way, one encounters the divine other and acquires the mythic image beyond the ideas the Law embodies—an image the Samaritan enacts paradigmatically. In other words, King's use of the Samaritan ethic is the grand concluding image of his public life. Having been to the "mountaintop" and seen the Promised Land, King acquired a vision along the Upward Way. In turn, on the Downward Way, King enacts that vision with a new language of the ultimate order in the Samaritan ethic.

Final Thoughts on the Memphis Address

In concluding my focus on the Samaritan in King's discourse, I return to the most renowned words of the Memphis address:

> Well, I don't know what will happen now. We've got some difficult days ahead. But it doesn't matter with me now. Because I've been to the mountaintop. And I don't mind. Like anybody, I would like to live a long life. Longevity has its place. But I'm not concerned about that now. I just want to do God's will. And He's allowed me to go

up to the mountain. And I've looked over. But I want you to know tonight, that we, as a people will get to the Promised Land. And I'm happy, tonight. I'm not worried about anything. I'm not fearing any man. Mine eyes have seen the glory of the coming of the Lord. ("I See" 286)

As prophetic or even eerie as these words may seem, they actually reach back to the origins of the movement: on Sunday, January 27, 1957, a bundle of twelve sticks of dynamite was found on the porch of King's home. Because of an apparently defective fuse, the bomb did not explode, though it was still smoldering when it was found. During his Sunday sermon that same morning, more than ten years prior to the final moments of "I See the Promised Land," King used his near-death experience to recall an even earlier moment, crucial to the movement's development. In an article titled "King Says Vision Told Him to Lead Integration Forces," our only record of the sermon, King recalled a sleepless night in January 1956 when, just as rationality had almost left him, "Almost out of nowhere ... I heard a voice that morning saying to me: 'Preach the Gospel, stand up for the truth, stand up for righteousness" (qtd. in Selby 124).

Almost a year after that experience, King used that memory and his recent near-death experience to give a vision for the movement:

> Since that morning I can stand up without fear. So I'm not afraid of anybody this morning. . . .Tell Montgomery they can keep shooting and I'm going to stand up to them; tell Montgomery they can keep bombing and I'm going to stand up to them. . . . If I had to die tomorrow morning I would die happy, because I've been to the mountain top and I've seen the promised land and it's going to be here in Montgomery. (qtd. in Selby 125)

For Selby, this sermon is the "defining moment" of King's public role as civil rights leader, framing the movement in the language of the Exodus with King as the Moses figure. This example shows that in giving attention to isolated speeches or marches we can miss the underlying connective threads that hold the movement together and propel its rhetorical meaning and significance. In the same manner that Selby has argued for the significance of the Exodus narrative in King's sermons and speeches, I have argued for the importance of the Good Samaritan parable. In fact, I contend, alongside Osborn, that without the Samaritan ethic, the entire movement, to use Burke's sentiment, becomes a "damned lie" (qtd. in Clark 45). However, beyond offering a mere application point or some mere delightfully momentary epiphany, my aim has been to help us acquire a glimpse of King's larger design—a design that would lead his listeners toward a mythic image along the Upward Way. Having acquired this vision, we ourselves must now take the Downward Way, where we will most assuredly encounter others on life's roadside. Perhaps we will all someday share in the same delight King felt at the "mountaintop," before he descended into the arms of his dear friend Ralph Abernathy: "Mine eyes have seen the glory of the coming of the Lord" ("I See" 286).

The Samaritan Ethic

Throughout my recent work, I have argued that the ethos of the road as a rhetorical encounter with the other produces a particular ethic. That is, in progressing developmentally along the Upward Way, we glimpse an ultimate order—an archetypal image or vision. Then, along the Downward Way, we enact the ethic resulting from the ethos of the road. King uses road imagery to promote a rhetorical encounter with the other—an encounter he hoped would be rooted in the Samaritan ethic. Collectively, these two ethics recall the archetype of the road depicted in Plato's *Phaedrus*, where Socrates and Phaedrus go for a walk on the roads outside Athens and contemplate the nature of the soul. Using Plato's notion of *psychagogia*, I have argued that the road archetype helps overcome our trained inability to perceive the significance of road imagery in American culture. I have sought to shift our attention away from the cultural myths of the nineteenth and twentieth centuries and toward the road as a rhetorical encounter with the other. When listening, watching, or reading the sermonic discourse of King, we are encountering more than individual texts of historical eloquence. Rather, we are encountering the Samaritan ethic, an ethic that can help us transcend the dialectical jangle of white and black and focus on our common humanity.

Works Cited

Blanton, Raymond J. "Marching, Singing, and Road Imagery in Martin Luther King's Involvement in the Civil Rights Movement." In *Martin Luther King, Jr.* Edited by Robert C. Evans, Salem, 2018, pp. tk.

Burke, Kenneth. "The Responsibilities of National Greatness."*The Nation*, vol. 225, July 17, 1967, pp. 46-50.

Burns, Stewart. *To the Mountaintop: Martin Luther King's Mission to Save America, 1955-1968*. HarperSanFrancisco, 2004.

Clark, Gregory. *Civic Jazz: American Music and Kenneth Burke on the Art of Getting Along*. U of Chicago P, 2015.

Crable, Bryan. *Ralph Ellison and Kenneth Burke at the Roots of the Racial Divide*. U of Virginia P, 2012.

King, Martin Luther, Jr. "I See the Promised Land." In Washington, pp. 279-86.

_____. "On Being a Good Neighbor." *A Gift of Love: Sermons from Strength to Love and Other Preachings*. Beacon, 2012, pp. 21-32.

_____. "RemainingAwake Through A Great Revolution." In Washington, pp. 268-78.

_____. *The Strength to Love*. In Washington, pp. 491-517.

_____. "Where Do We Go from Here?" In Washington, pp. 245-52.

Osborn, Michael. "The Last Mountaintop of Martin Luther King, Jr." In *Sermonic Power of Public Discourse*. Edited by Carolyn Calloway-Thomas and John Lucaites. U of Alabama P, 1993, pp. 147-61.

Plato. *Phaedrus*. classics.mit.edu/Plato/phaedrus.html.

Selby, Gary S. *Martin Luther King and the Rhetoric of Freedom: The Exodus Narrative in America's Struggle for Civil Rights*. Baylor UP, 2008.

Washington, James M. *A Testament of Hope: The Essential Writings and Speeches of Martin Luther King, Jr.* HarperOne, 1986.

Martin Luther King and Whiteness: Reconsidering "Care for the Other" Rhetoric

Kristine Warrenburg Rome

Martin Luther King Jr.'s life and leadership have been critiqued, analyzed, and interpreted by numerous academics across various disciplines. However, only relatively recently has much major work been done on King's rhetoric. Little of that work has focused on communication ethics from a critical cultural perspective. My own project began by considering the ethic of "care for the other," a term associated with the French philosopher Emmanuel Levinas. In particular, I have tried to locate this ethic in the rhetoric of King's very last address, "I See the Promised Land," which was delivered in Memphis, Tennessee, on April 3, 1968, not long before King's assassination (Washington 279-86). As my project developed, however, it became evident that ignoring the "situational context" of King's striking last words would limit full understanding of his speech. I needed to draw not only on Levinas's thinking but also on other ways of explaining the significance of King's words.

The situational context of the "I See the Promised Land" speech foregrounds, most prominently, issues of race. King's final address occurred during the rise of the black power movement, and King was speaking mainly to an African American audience. Furthermore, King was in Memphis on April 3, 1968, to support the Poor Peoples Campaign, so issues of materiality, class, and economics complicate the already complex racial context. "Care for the Other," therefore, involves, in this case, caring about the race and class of the people King was addressing. This concern is especially evident when King links the present 1968 situation of the striking sanitation workers in Memphis with the larger destiny of the civil rights movement. King knew that this fateful fight might proceed even if he were no longer alive to lead the struggle. At the time of the Memphis speech, King faced numerous threats of murder. However, he was less concerned with his own life than with establishing a path that people could follow toward their own promised lands.

The Radical King

King demonstrated care through his criticism. As Michael Eric Dyson has put it,

> We have surrendered to romantic images of King at the Lincoln Memorial inspiring America to reach, as he reached with outstretched arms, for a better future. All the while we forget his poignant warning against gradual racial progress and his remarkable threat of revolution should our nation fail to keep its promises. (15)

The iconic King, the "I Have a Dream" King, the "I See the Promised Land" King, are only fragments of King's story. Dyson suggests that perpetuating an incomplete legacy feeds a "national amnesia" that benefits whites. Therefore, rather than reemphasize King simply as the great seeker of equality, I hope to explore King's realization that racial power structures are reinforced by the idea that whiteness is the key criterion of what is considered "normal." By investigating how King rejected whiteness in his "I See the Promised Land" address, I hope to illustrate how crucial race is not only to his thinking in this particular speech but also how society was (and is) structured. King's move to embrace black solidarity was relevant to the rise of the black power movement in 1968 and is also relevant to current identity constructions and expressions of power. Recognizing this other side of King—as one who spoke out against white power structures, white privilege, and America's racist sentiments—means considering what has been silenced or left out of most academic discussions. King rejected whiteness while also forging a true, memorable, timeless ethical message. To dismiss either of these efforts would be to deny his true dream. His rhetoric on April 3, 1968, not only showed traces of Levinasian ethics but also illustrated his mistrust of white America and his move toward black solidarity. To dismiss either element would be to disregard the situational context that contributed to King's overall message.

King and *The Racial Contract*

Examining King in this way presents opportunities to expand the philosophical insight of a Levinasian ethic to consider its potential racial implications. Future research would benefit by considering what Levinas's "care for the other" would look like if viewed through a racial lens. In other words, what happens to Levinas's theory when the face of "the other" is black? I hope to demonstrate, here, how race is a key undercurrent in all aspects of social being—politically, morally, epistemologically, and rhetorically.

According to Charles W. Mills in *The Racial Contract*, race is (or should be) foundational in most considerations of American society. If, as Mills suggests, "racism is *itself* a political system, a particular power structure of formal or informal rule, socioeconomic privilege, and norms for the differential distribution of material wealth and opportunities, benefits and burdens, rights and duties," then a broad theoretical framework is needed to situate discussions of race and white racism. Mills's book offers such a framework. He argues, in contrast to traditional conceptions of the "social contract," that the "racial contract" is one way to begin overcoming the traditional lack of discussion about racial justice. He explores race as a stand-alone category involving its own logic. Mills argues that the traditional idea of a social contract (a contract between "equals") was unstable from the start because it treated nonwhites as inferiors (3). Scholars in many fields, especially those interested in critical white studies, have approached many themes inherent in Mills' work, including ideas of invisibility/normativity,[1] material wealth,[2] interconnectedness of race/class/gender,[3] identity construction,[4] and power/expressions of power.[5] However, surprisingly few scholars in communication studies have turned to Mills's ideas. One notable exception, however, is Mark McPhail in a valuable essay titled "A Question of Character: Re(-)signing the Racial Contract." Drawing on McPhail's ideas, I will here consider how Martin Luther King Jr. dramatized the racial contract in his "I See the Promised Land" address.

Analysis: April 3, 1968

King memorably told his audience of nearly 3,000 at the Masonic Temple in Memphis that

> [l]ongevity has its place. But I'm not concerned about that now. I just want to do God's will. And He's allowed me to go up to the mountain. And I've looked over. And I've seen the Promised Land. I may not get there with you. But I want you to know tonight, that we, as a people, will get to the promised land! (Washington 286)

The next day, he was assassinated. In fact, it has often been said that King seemingly delivered his own eulogy the night before he died.

Typical discussion of King's final speech is concerned with honoring his legacy—a legacy of nonviolence rooted in "dreams" of equality among all humans. However, King's last speech also offered direct calls to action and challenges to whiteness. He dramatized the racial contract rhetorically before Mills had even coined that term, reclaiming the moral status of black personhood by rejecting subhuman stereotypes projected onto African Americans. King strengthened this reclaiming of individual black humanity by connecting it to the overall group identity of blackness.

The Racial Contract: Moral Dimensions

As a moral system that dictates social behavior, the traditional social contract exists prior to any political systems. It establishes codes that citizens are supposed to use to regulate their behavior. These codes are founded on ideals of *"freedom and equality of all men in the state of nature"* and thus exist prior to political codes (Mills 14; italics in original). King used white people's beliefs in traditional social contract theory to highlight and challenge their racism. He did so, in Dyson's words, "by suggesting that the moral values of American culture lie beyond race" (35). In the Memphis speech, for instance, he contrasted biblical ideals with American social reality. He asserted that because black people are

> God's children, we don't have to live like we are forced to live. It's all right to talk about the "streets flowing with milk and honey," but God

has commanded us here to be concerned about the slums down here, and his children who can't eat three square meals a day. It's all right to talk about the new Jerusalem, but one day, God's preacher must talk about the new New York, the new Atlanta, the new Philadelphia, the new Los Angeles, the new Memphis, Tennessee. This is what we have to do. (Washington 282)

Although King often extolled the ideal absence of any kind of racial prejudice, he also insisted in this speech on the need for black solidarity. He rejected the kind of imperceptive "color blindness" that involved ignoring the realities of racial hatred and racial discrimination. As Dyson writes:"King preached to blacks that their struggle was not between white and black but between right and wrong. By pegging black struggle to a universal moral foundation, King strongly affirmed black humanity, a fact that is today ignored by ahistorical advocates of [imperceptive] color-blindness" (35).

King was able to evoke moral codes that relieved whites of the crimes and/or guilt associated with racist ideology while at the same time he reaffirmed the personhood of blacks by making their struggle a universal cause. He hoped to teach people to think of themselves first and foremost as individual persons rather than primarily as members of particular races. But race, for him, was never unimportant or something to be ignored.

Mills emphasizes the necessity, especially for African Americans, of claiming the moral status of personhood. Blacks can do so by "challenging the white-constructed ontology that has deemed one a 'body impolitic,' an entity not entitled to assert personhood in the first place" (118). This emphasis on personhood is even implied by the way King juxtaposes references to humanity and inhumanity. Describing the challenges he and other marchers faced in Birmingham, he says,

> we just went on before the *dogs* and *we would look* at them; and we'd go on before the *water hoses* and *we would look* at it, and we'd just *go on singing* "Over my head I see freedom in the air." And then we would *be thrown* in the paddy wagons, and sometimes we were *stacked in there like sardines in a can*. And they would *throw*

> *us in,* and old Bull would say, "Take 'em off," and they did; and we would just go in the paddy wagon *singing,* "We Shall Overcome." (Washington 281-82; emphasis added)

By highlighting the way King juxtaposes humane conduct (such as looking and especially singing) within humane abuse (as in the references to dogs, water hoses, being thrown, and being stacked), we can see how he works rhetorically to reconstitute black individuals as persons rather than as subpersons. Similarly, King said that "whenever men and women straighten their backs up, they are going somewhere, because a man can't ride your back unless it is bent" (Washington 286). African Americans, in other words, should not allow themselves to be treated like animals but should claim their status as persons. To do so, according to Mills, they would need to engage in self-reflection. They would need to move beyond "the internalization of subpersonhood prescribed by the Racial Contract and recognize [their] own humanity, resisting the official category of despised aboriginal, natural slave, colonial ward" (118). According to Mills, persons seeking personhood have to learn "basic self-respect" (118). King works to reclaim such self-respect, for himself and others, when he says:

> We aren't engaged in any negative protest and in any negative arguments with anybody. We are saying that we are determined to be men. We are determined to be people. We are saying—We are saying that we are God's children. And that we are God's children, we don't have to live like we are forced to live. (Washington 280)

One way King hoped blacks would gain self-respect was through solidarity: "we've got to stay together. We've got to stay together and maintain unity" (Washington 280). King would have agreed with Mills's statement that "[p]articularly for blacks, ex-slaves, the importance of developing self-respect and demanding respect from whites is crucial" (119).

A final way for a nonwhite person to assert herself or himself is by emphasizing what Mills calls "the *somatic* aspect of the Racial Contract—the necessary reference it makes to the body." Mills refers to "the *body politics* that nonwhites have often incorporated into their struggles" (120). King would have agreed with this attention to the body, as when he stressed the need for the *right kind* of physical behavior:

> The issue is injustice.... Now, we've got to keep attention on that. That's always the problem with a little violence. You know what happened the other day, and the press dealt only with the window-breaking. I read the articles.... Now we're going to march again, and we've got to march again, in order to put the issue where it is supposed to be—and force everybody to see that there are thirteen hundred of God's children here suffering, sometimes going hungry, going through dark and dreary nights wondering how this thing is going to come out. (Washington 281)

Violence, he implies, actually works *against* real progress. It only invites a violent response. In contrast, peacefully marching bodies disrupt normal civil society and force attention to the need for justice. King resisted the stereotype of blacks as violent and wanted them to present themselves instead as morally astute and courageous. Marching, he thought, was one of the best ways African Americans could assert their dignity, their power, their status as persons, and their power as collective, raced bodies.

King would also have agreed with Mills's emphasis on the *moral* component of the racial contact. According to Mills, moral codes exist prior to politics. King sought to remind whites of their commitment to a Christian moral code by frequently invoking the Bible and employing biblical imagery. This strategy, of course, also helped enhance the humanity of black individuals, and it was designed to persuade whites, too, to see African Americans as children of God—as fellow human beings. By using biblical language and other methods to reconstitute blacks as persons (in the minds of themselves and others) rather than as subpersons, King set the stage for moving from the moral component of the racial contract to the political. As Mills suggests, and as King believed, if people are to participate in the political they must first establish themselves as equal to others in personhood.

The Racial Contract: The Political

Mills argues that the racial contract operates politically through systems of classification by which people are categorized, judged, and controlled. King, working through the civil rights movement, sought to make blacks equal citizens partly by both challenging laws and changing them. King would have agreed with Mills that the "terms of the Racial Contract" treat nonwhite persons as "morally, epistemically, and aesthetically" inferior to whites, even though nonwhites were, at least in a figurative sense, "signatories to the Contract" (118) and were forced to abide by it. King often asserted that America had failed to meet the agreements laid out, for instance, in the Constitution, the Declaration of Independence, and the Emancipation Proclamation. Thus, after mentioning a scheduled court date on which he would fight an oppressive injunction, King proclaimed, "All we say to America is, 'Be true to what you said on paper'" (Washington 282). He continued,

> If I lived in China or even Russia, or any totalitarian country, maybe I could understand some of these illegal injunctions. Maybe I could understand the denial of certain basic First Amendment privileges, because they hadn't committed themselves to that over there. But somewhere I read of the freedom of assembly. Somewhere I read of the freedom of speech. Somewhere I read of the freedom of press. Somewhere I read that the greatness of America is the right to protest for right. And so just as I say, we aren't going to let dogs or water hoses turn us around, we aren't going to let any injunction turn us around. We are going on. (Washington 282)

Aptly summarizing how the civil rights movement acted in and through components of the racial contract (morally and politically), Houston Baker Jr. writes, "In the South, the scene had altered from medieval morality to legally civil, twentieth-century premodernity" (31). But even after the passage of the landmark Civil Rights Act of 1965, normative, hegemonic power structures permeated and regulated U.S. society. As Baker notes, the "real stakes of modernism were in the ethnically divided cities of the north and west, where there were jobs, economic security, gleaming cars, and sturdy homes: symbols of a fulfilled American dream" (31). Blacks supposedly enjoyed full and equal legal rights in such places, but in reality they did not.

King, of course, had come to realize this by 1968. That was one reason he had recently been fighting in Chicago against segregated housing and other forms of economic injustice (see Grossman). Whites, he understood, enjoyed certain social, cultural, and material privileges simply because they were white. King knew all about "white privilege" long before that particular phrase was circulating academically (see Crenshaw 255). King's emphasis on the material and monetary realities of race can be seen in his final speech, especially when he relates racial equality to economic advancement. In fact, Dyson has claimed that "[o]ne of the greatest pitfalls of idolizing the 'I Have a Dream' speech" of five years earlier is that doing so means "failing to grapple with King's views on compensation to blacks" by obscuring King's "dramatic change of heart and mind about the roots of white racism" (29). By 1968, King had come to realize, more than ever, the connections between racial and economic injustices. Such connections lie at the heart of the racial contract. According to Baker, by 1968 King was emphasizing "the immediate necessity to achieve full citizenship rights *now*, in *this* world. Economic impoverishment and social segregation," he believed, "had to be eliminated" as soon as possible (29).

This economic emphasis would not have surprised Mills, who writes that "the economic dimension of the Racial Contract is the *most* salient, foreground rather than background, since the Racial Contract is calculatedly aimed at economic exploitation" (32). Thus, it is not surprising that for King (in Dyson's words) "compensatory measures that were truly just—that is, [that] took race into account while also considering class—had the best chance of bringing healing to our nation's minorities and to the white poor" (29). According to Dyson, however, "King's Poor People's Campaign was a hard sell, perhaps because it forced those who were used to thinking about race to think also about class, while forcing those who puzzle over economic inequality to think about race" (79). At the intersection of race and class is King's call to action, a place to climb toward or turn away from the mountaintop.

The interconnectedness of race and class in King's April 3, 1968, address is relevant when considering how King, through his construction of black identity, conflates these elements into one identity for the striking sanitation workers (black = poor; poor = black). He says that "if something isn't done, and done in a hurry, to bring the colored peoples of the world out of their long years of poverty, their long years of hurt and neglect, the whole world is doomed" (Washington 280). Later he notes, "Now, we are poor people. Individually, we are poor when you compare us with white society in America. We are poor" (282-83). In fact, King might have agreed with Mills that *"Whiteness is not really a color at all, but a set of power relations"* (127; italics in original). As King suggests ways his audience could challenge whiteness through the direct action of economic withdrawal (such as boycotts), he challenges the power structures rooted in the assumption that whiteness is normal. For example, consider King's calls to action to challenge power when he says,

> Now the other thing we'll have to do is this: Always anchor our external direct action with the power of economic withdrawal.
> And so, as a result of this, we are asking you tonight, to go out and tell your neighbors not to buy Coca-Cola in Memphis. Go by and tell them not to buy Sealtest milk. Tell them not to buy—what is the other bread? —Wonder Bread. And what is the other bread company, Jesse? Tell them not to buy Hart's bread…. We are choosing these companies because they haven't been fair in their hiring policies; and we are choosing them because they can begin the process of saying they are going to support the needs and rights of these men who are on strike (Washington 283)

Beyond stressing the need for economic withdrawal of the black public from dominant white organizations, King acknowledges the power of the black economic pool: "We have an annual income of more than thirty billion dollars a year, which is more than all of the exports of the United States, and more than the national budget of

Canada. Did you know that? That's power right there, if we know how to pool it" (Washington 283). Furthermore, King stresses that African Americans don't need to rely on violence to gain power; instead, they need money:

> We don't have to argue with anybody. We don't have to curse and go around acting bad with our words. We don't need any bricks and bottles. We don't need any Molotov cocktails. We just need to go around to these stores, and to these massive industries in our country, and say, "God sent us by here, to say to you that you're not treating his children right. . . . And our agenda calls for withdrawing economic support from you. (Washington 283)

King, still working within the white capitalist structure, calls for direct action from the black public to pool their economic power and redistribute it to build up black businesses:

> But not only that, we've got to strengthen black institutions. I call upon you to take your money out of the banks downtown and deposit your money in Tri-State Bank. We want a "bank-in" movement in Memphis. Go by the savings and loan association. . . . Put your money there. You have six or seven black insurance companies here in the city of Memphis. Take out your insurance there. We want to have an "insurance-in." (Washington 283)

Analysis of King's April 3, 1968, speech illustrates how American society remained racially and economically unequal even after such legislation as the Civil Rights Act of 1965. King called for boycotts and other kinds of economic withdrawal. He sought to highlight the invisibility of white capitalist structures that control power via institutions. No matter what the color of the people running them, these institutions had the power to prevent economic and racial justice.

The Racial Contract: Epistemological Aspects
If we acknowledge that whiteness is socially constructed in the very heart of democracy, we must also reflect upon what it means to be

white, who creates the terms of whiteness, and what privileges come with membership in the dominant race. According to Dyson, King himself "viewed the tension between America the Emancipator and America the Enslaver as the fundamental issue of [the nation's] self-identification that must be resolved" (40). According to Mills, because white is dominant and normalized as natural, anything other than white is invisible and, thus, structured around (or "other than") whiteness. Furthermore, white people, by "unquestioningly 'going along with things,' by accepting all the privileges of whiteness with concomitant complicity in the system of white supremacy, . . . can be said to have consented to Whiteness" (107). King's last message reflected concern for the perpetuation of hegemonic power found in systemic politics, morality, and epistemological rhetoric.

The universality of whiteness is highlighted when we consider that its defined position is everything (Nakiyama and Krizek 631). In the words of James W. Perkinson, "If 'being made black' is an experience of a kind of 'hyper-consciousness'—a doubling of awareness that distends and dilates...," then being white could be considered as a "double-*un*consciousness." This is because white "identity is generally lived, that is to say, as a kind of 'artless ignorance,' an almost incorrigible lack of awareness of either one's racial position or of the actual cost to others of one's prosperity" (89). Similarly, Thomas K. Nakayama and Robert L. Krizek argue that in

> the realm of categories, black is always marked as a colour (as the term "coloured" egregiously acknowledges), and is always particularizing; whereas white is not anything really, not an identity, not a particularizing quality, because it is everything—white is no colour because it is all colours." (631)

For all these reasons, the way King constructed black identity is essential in understanding his move to undermine whiteness. How King constructed black identity in relation to class as well as how he challenged the norm of "black as other" through his rhetoric illustrates how he dramatized the racial contract. King's speech on April 3, 1968, highlighted some of the ways nonwhites could work together to gain power. Two of those ways involved reconstructing their identity as persons (not as subpersons) and by seeing themselves as part of a larger group of economically disadvantaged people (and regain some of that power with collective economic boycotts). Dyson, referring to King's efforts beyond Memphis, notes that King

> criss-crossed the nation in one campaign after another, urging blacks not to hate whites even as he helped to unravel the tightly woven fabric of Southern apartheid. King viewed nonviolence as both a way of life and a way of undoing unjust laws. It was also an effective means to challenge immoral social codes that made blacks second-class citizens. (33)

King dramatized the racial contract in his final address on April 3, 1968. He did not *only* promote a legacy of justice or solely present a Levinasian turn toward/or for the Other. He rejected the kind of naïve, imperceptive color blindness that involved an inability to even *see* black persons as persons, and he understood that racial healing would not happen in the United States until our society, as a whole, recognized its deeply rooted racist ideologies. King understood the black struggle in terms of universal moral codes (such as right versus wrong) but at the same time he used rhetoric to challenge the normativity of whiteness and injustice of economic oppression. If we remember only the idealized King and never question the dominant legacy of a color-blind King, we understand only a fragment of his message concerning race relations. As Dyson says, we must not forget that "two weeks before his death, he announced that '*yes it is true... America is a racist country.*' This," Dyson continues, "is a far cry from the King who assured whites of their basic humanity, who was convinced that we must separate white sinners from the sin of white supremacy" (39).

The racial contract is real. It is historically situated in a series of events essential to the making of the modern world. Colonialism, slavery, genocide, segregation, and so forth are real lived events that contributed—and continue to contribute—to the way we live. Thus, how we remember particular historical moments, like King's last public address, and what elements of those moments are included in or left out of academic and public discussion are essential concerns for rhetorical studies. "Let us develop a kind of dangerous unselfishness," King claims in his final criticism of hegemonic power found in a U.S. intersection of race and class (Washington 284). Such a lingering last call reminds us of the heightened risk and responsibility embedded in care for the other.

Notes

1. See, for instance, Crenshaw; Goodman; Lewis; Martin et al.; Perkinson; and Shome.
2. See Delgado and Stefancic; Flores and Moon; Lewis; and Lipari.
3. See Avant-Mier and Hasian and also Crenshaw.
4. See Avant-Mier and Hasian; Houston; and Jackson.
5. See Martin et al.

Works Cited

Avant-Mier, Robert, and Marouf Hasian Jr. "In Search of the Power of Whiteness: A Genealogical Exploration of Negotiated Racial Identities in America's Ethnic Past." *Communication Quarterly*, vol. 50, 2002, pp. 391-409.

Baker Jr., Houston A. "Critical Memory and the Black Public Sphere." *Public Culture*, vol. 7, 1994, pp. 3-33.

Bates, Beth T. "The Upheaval of Jim Crow: African Americans and the Struggle for Civil Rights in the 1960s." In *The Columbia Guide to America in the 1960s*. Edited by D. Farber and B. Bailer, Columbia UP, 2001, pp. 79-90.

Crenshaw, Carrie. "Resisting Whiteness' Rhetorical Silence." *Western Journal of Communication*, vol. 61, 1997, pp. 253-78.

Delgado, Richard, and Jean Stefancic. *Critical Race Theory: An Introduction*. New York UP, 2001.

Dyson, Michael E. *I May Not Get There With You: The True Martin Luther King, Jr*. Simon & Schuster, 2000.

Farber, David, and Beth Bailey. *The Columbia Guide to America in the 1960s*. Columbia UP, 2001.

Flores, Lisa A., and Dreama G. Moon. "Rethinking Race, Revealing Dilemmas: Imagining a New Racial Subject in Race Traitor." *Western Journal of Communication*, vol. 66, 2002, pp. 181-207.

Goodman, Diane J. *Promoting Diversity and Social Justice: Educating People from Privileged Groups*. Sage, 2002.

Grossman, Ron. "Commentary: The Tense Months Before Martin Luther King, Jr.'s Assassination." *The Chicago Tribune*, 1 Apr. 2018. www.chicagotribune.com/news/opinion/commentary/ct-perspec-flash-mlk-king-assassination-0401-20180327-story.html. Accessed 12 Oct. 2018.

Houston, Marsha. "When Black Women Talk with White Women: Why Dialogues Are Difficult." In *Our Voices: Essays in Culture, Ethnicity, and Communication*. Edited by Alberto Gonzalez et al., Roxbury, 1997, pp. 187-95.

Jackson II, Ronald L. "White Space, White Privilege: Mapping Discursive Inquiry into the Self." *Quarterly Journal of Speech*, vol. 85, 1999, pp. 38-54.

King, Martin Luther, Jr. "I See the Promised Land (3 April 1968)." In *A Testament of Hope: The Essential Writings and Speeches of Martin Luther King, Jr.* Edited by James Melvin Washington. Harper, 1986, pp. 279-86.

Levinas, Emmanuel. *Ethics and Infinity: Conversations with Philippe Nemo*. Duquesne UP, 1985.

Lewis, Amanda E. "What Group?" Studying Whites and Whiteness in the Era of "Color Blindness." *Sociological Theory*, vol. 22, 2004, pp. 623-46.

Lipari, Lisbeth. "Fearful of the Written Word:" White Fear, Black Writing, and Lorraine Hansberry's *A Raisin in the Sun* Screenplay." *Quarterly Journal of Speech*, vol. 90, pp. 81-102.

Martin, Judith N., et al. "Exploring Whiteness: A Study of Self Labels for White Americans." *Communication Quarterly*, vol. 44, 1996, pp. 125-44.

McPhail, Mark L. "A Question of Character: Re(-)signing the Racial Contract," *Rhetoric & Public Affairs*, vol. 7, no. 3, 2004, pp. 391-405.

Mills, Charles W. *The Racial Contract*. Cornell UP, 1997.

Nakayama, Thomas K., and Robert L. Krizek. "Whiteness: A Strategic Rhetoric." *Readings in Rhetorical Criticism*. Edited by Carl R. Burgchardt. Strata, 2005, pp. 628-47.

Nemo, P. (Interviewer). *Ethics and Infinity: Conversations with Philippe Nemo*. Duquesne UP, 1982.

Perkinson, James W. *White Theology: Outing Supremacy in Modernity*. Palgrave Macmillan, 2004.

Shome, Raka. "Outing Whiteness." *Critical Studies in Media Communication*, vol. 17, no. 3, 2000, pp. 366-70.

Poems Inspired by Martin Luther King Jr.: A Series of Close Readings

Robert C. Evans

Since his tragic death from an assassin's bullet in 1968, Martin Luther King Jr. has increasingly become not only an iconic figure in American culture but also a significant figure to many creative writers. This has been true not only in the United States but throughout the world. Trudier Harris explored many aspects of King's literary impact in a 2014 book entitled *Martin Luther King, Jr., Heroism, and African American Literature.* In that volume, Harris surveyed King's many appearances in poems, essays, and novels written by black writers. Not long after Harris's book appeared, however, a whole new collection of poems featuring King, or meant to pay tribute to him, was published in England. Edited by Carolyn Forché and Jackie Kay, this new text was entitled *The Mighty Stream: Poems in Celebration of Martin Luther King.* Containing the work of eighty-eight distinct authors (many of them very well-known writers) and running to 224 pages, this anthology is one of the most substantive literary tributes to King ever published, particularly since many of the contributors are not even Americans, and some of them are not even black. Martin Luther King, in the years since his death, is fast becoming what Abraham Lincoln has been since his own assassination: a symbol of freedom not only in popular culture but in the works of important creative writers.

My purpose in this essay is to offer close readings of several poems published in *The Mighty Stream*, especially poems that explicitly mention King or allude to him in less obvious ways. I will be paying particular attention to works that seem successful not simply as tributes to a great man but as worthy works of art. If literature can be defined as "writing that is interesting *as* writing," then many of the works printed in *The Mighty Stream* qualify as literature, not simply as historical, sociological, or cultural commentary. We remember Walt Whitman's great poem about Lincoln—"When Lilacs Last in the Dooryard Bloom'd"—less because it was a poem about Lincoln (there were and are thousands of those) than because it is a powerful piece of *writing* crafted by an exceptionally talented *writer*. Thus my focus here is literary, not contextual. Operating more or less as a formalist (the kind of critic interested more in art than in messages), I hope to explore the craftsmanship of these poems *as poems*.

Nikky Finney's "Red Velvet"

The brief biographical note about Nikky Finney published at the end of *The Mighty Stream* (hereafter *TMS*) mentions her various publications and reports that one of them "won the National Book Award for Poetry in 2011" (218). This is not surprising, for although Finney's poem "Red Velvet" is one of the longest works in *The Mighty Stream*, it is also one of the most impressive. Its main focus is not Martin Luther King but rather Rosa Parks, the middle-aged woman whose unplanned but open defiance of segregation led, in 1955, to the famous Montgomery Bus Boycott—a protest that propelled both her and King to national attention. King was quickly selected to lead the boycott after Parks was arrested for politely but firmly refusing to give up her seat in the "colored" section of a public bus so that the seat could be taken by a waiting white. When Parks stayed put, the bus driver had her arrested—a decision that led the black community to boycott the public transportation system. This boycott was the opening salvo in the increasingly powerful civil rights movement that helped topple the whole system of legal segregation in the South.

"Red Velvet," as its title suggests, emphasizes that Parks was a talented seamstress who had spent most of her adult life making and repairing clothes, especially for white customers. The poem opens with a memorable metaphor, calling the bus a "rolling box with wheels" (*TMS* 61) —phrasing far more vivid than the simple word "bus" would have been, and phrasing that also, perhaps, will make some readers think of the boxcars notoriously used to transport victims of the Holocaust during World War II. In any case, the phrase already makes the bus seem somehow inhuman and inhumane.

Another effective metaphor appears a few lines later, when Finney mentions that passengers were expected to pay an "Indian Head" (not the more common term, a five-cent "nickel,") while boarding the bus (*TMS* 61). This phrase is not only precise and vivid but may also, perhaps, make some readers recall the miserable plight of Native Americans. They, like African Americans, were long the subjects of official discrimination and violence. Ironically, an "Indian head" was used on the five-cent piece during the first half of the twentieth century to make U.S. coinage seem distinctively "American." Even more ironically, the same rationale was also used to justify putting images of bison on other five-cent coins. It seems odd, in retrospect, that the two images chosen to commemorate and celebrate America were images of humans and animals nearly driven extinct during the course of the nation's early history.

Finney next describes what happened after African Americans paid their nickels:

Then, walk to the door at the end of the bus.
Then, reboard the bus through the Black back door.
(Then, push *repeat* for fifty years.) (*TMS* 61)

Here the use of "Then" repeated at the beginning of each line (a device known as *anaphora*) effectively emphasizes the sense of a longstanding, monotonous, dehumanizing routine—a routine that had existed during the whole time (before the Parks-inspired boycott) that Montgomery had had a public transportation system. Finney subtly emphasizes verbs, the strongest parts of speech, and she also, in the second quoted line, skillfully combines alliteration, assonance, and internal rhyme to add extra music to her phrasing: "*Th*en, re**boar**d *th*e **b**us *th*rough *th*e **B**lack **b**ack d**oor**" (my emphases). A line like this shows a poet's skill, not simply the desire to make some political or social point. Paradoxically, however, any point made using poetic skill is likely to be all the more effective as a piece of political propaganda.

Sometimes, Finney correctly notes, white drivers would pull away before black passengers could reach the rear doors, even though the passengers had paid their nickels. The poem thus reminds us that individual maliciousness often intensified an already malignant system of social discrimination. The poem's speaker, using a verb whose subject(s) is/are left unspecified, notes that Parks (and/or others) was/were "Fed up with buses driving off— without *them*— / just as *her* foot lifted up, grazing, the steel step" (TMS 61; my italics). The imprecision of the grammar here clearly seems deliberate: Finney wants readers to realize that the injuries (to dignity and potentially to the body) suffered by Parks were suffered by many others. The reference to a "steel step" vividly reinforces the dangers blacks faced when dealing with vicious white drivers.

Throughout the poem, Finney consistently uses effective language. Her phrasing is usually simple, clear, and direct; she often employs balanced phrases to emphasize key points. She alternates sentence lengths and often uses fragments to put maximum emphasis on verbs. The poem is long but never seems lethargic, and it provides a remarkably full overview of the personalities and events associated with the bus boycott. In one passage, Finney creates a strong sense of social and racial claustrophobia by continually repeating a key phrase. Speaking of Parks, Finney writes,

> She had grown up in a place:
>   where only white people had power,
>   where only white people passed good jobs on
>   to other white people,
>   where only white people loaned money
>   to other white people,
>   where only white people were considered human
>   by other white people (*TMS* 61-62)

Here the anaphora (the repeated "where only") and the continual references to "white people" help reinforce the reader's strong sense of enclosed, confining, systematic racial oppression. Finney could easily have made the same points without using so much repetition, but the repeated phrasing makes readers *feel*, not simply understand, what it was like to be literally surrounded and constricted by white power.

Finney presents Rosa Parks as a very talented seamstress, someone capable of working carefully with fabrics to create and repair clothes. Eventually it seems clear that Finney is using these talents as an extended metaphor for different aspects of Parks' personality: her ability to bring things together, to unite different colors and kinds of fabric, and to work with various kinds of "bias" (a word that refers to "an oblique diagonal line, especially across a woven fabric" [dictionary.com] but which also seems clearly a pun on *racial* bias). Parks, Finney makes clear, was a mature, intelligent woman at the time she was arrested; she might not have been so defiant during her younger years.

So many examples of effective phrasing appear in Finney's poem that it would be difficult to list them all. At one point, for instance, she skillfully uses repetition to emphasize how long Parks "waits and waits" for the bus to arrive. Later, she imaginatively addresses Parks, saying Parks "heard / 'Nigger Gal' more times than you can stitch your / manners down." In a striking simile that also exhibits Finney's talent for balanced phrasing, the speaker says to Parks, "You have smelled fear cut through / the air like *sulfur iron* from the *paper mills* (my italics, to emphasize the balance in syntax, rhythm, and meter [*TMS* 62]). Finney, again addressing Parks, says that "By forty-two, your biases are flat, your seams are inter- / locked, your patience with fools, razor thin" (*TMS* 63)—phrasing that memorably uses balanced syntax, emphatic adjectives, and especially clever enjambment, with the linking hyphen appearing at the very end of a line, as if sewing the lines together.

For the first time, a hint of Parks's capacity for personal anger enters the poem in the reference to "fools"—that is, *white* fools. The most obvious fool in the poem is clearly the driver of the bus who (admittedly on the orders of his superiors) had Parks arrested. In "real life" the driver was James F. Blake, but Finney, perhaps as a gesture of historical mercy, never uses his name. Apparently in later decades he eventually changed his views and conduct (as so many white Southerners did), and so it is perhaps as an act of kindness that Finney leaves him unidentified. But apparently Blake had had an encounter with Parks years before the incident that led to the boycott. He, it seems, was the driver who actually once drove off after she had paid her fare and was about to enter the back door. Finney alludes to this fact but, again, spares Blake the everlasting shame of recording his name in her poem.

In fact, Finney's treatment of whites in general is fairly balanced. She does, to be sure, indict the system of white power and prejudice (in lines already cited), but she also mentions that Park worked, in part, for "nice, well-meaning white women" (*TMS* 63)—women who were probably not vicious racists but who had simply grown up taking the whole system of racial segregation for granted, without giving it much conscious thought. Similarly, when Finney mentions white males spitting near Parks and "narrowly missing" her clothing (*TMS* 62), it is possible to conclude that if they had actually *intended* to soil her clothes, they could have done so. Instead, their behavior seems to have been either stupidly ignorant or deliberately disrespectful but not an outright, obvious attack. It is the white bus driver who comes off especially badly in this poem, although even *he* can seem polite when he threatens Parks with removal: "*Well—I'm going to have you arrested*"—to which *she* responds, in another example of Finney's penchant for balance: "*Well—you may go on and do so*" (*TMS* 63). Is Parks being sarcastic here? Or is she being dignified and polite? Readers are left to decide for themselves, and it is this kind of ambiguity that often makes Finney's poem so rich and suggestive.

Martin Luther King enters the poem explicitly only in one passage—a passage that, for once, is not especially clear:

> You are arrested on a Thursday. That night in
> Montgomery, Dr King led the chant, "There
> comes a time when people just get tired." (He
> wasn't quite right, but he was King.) He asked
> you to stand so your people can see you. You
> stand. *Veritas!* You do not speak. . . . (*TMS* 63)

In what senses was King not "quite right"? His word "tired," after all, could be taken both literally and figuratively. Also, why the use of an italicized Latin word to proclaim the simple idea of *truth*?

Searches of *veritas* in various biographies of Parks have turned up no leads. In any case, the rest of the poem is as lucid as can be, and it seems interesting that the one open reference to King is made merely in passing, so that the emphasis stays on the unassuming heroine of an event that was, in many ways, the most important event of her life—and, for that matter, of his.

Throughout the poem, Finney vividly creates "you are there" effects. She doesn't simply tell us about Parks and the famous incidents but helps us *see* them. Consider, for example, this passage, describing Parks's approach to the court house—a passage that also contains an attractive touch of humor:

> A trim black velvet
> hat, a gray coat, white gloves. You hold your
> purse close: everything valuable is kept near
> the belly, just like you had seen your own mother
> do. You are pristine. Persnickety. Particular. (*TMS* 64)

Persnickety—what a splendid word! It would have seemed amusing simply by itself but is all the more comic by being part of an alliterative series. We are reminded that Parks was not a well-known rebel or rabble-rouser but a self-respecting woman who had simply had enough. More humor quickly ensues:

> A girl in the crowd, taught not to
> shout, shouts, "Oh! She's so sweet looking! Oh!
> They done messed with the wrong one now." (*TMS* 64)

The abrupt juxtaposition of that last line with the one that precedes it creates a funny, ironic shock: Parks will be all the more threatening to the power structure precisely *because* she seems so prim and proper. By adding humor, Finney displays her tonal range and helps emphasize how the whole incident was both tragic *and* ridiculous, how the authorities were both overbearing *and* absurd.

In another effective passage in a generally effective poem, Finney warns not only the Montgomery authorities but also (white) readers in general that

> You cannot keep messing with a sweet-looking
> Black woman who knows her way around velvet.
> A woman who can take cotton and gabardine,
> seersucker and silk, swirl tapestry, and hang
> boiled wool for the house curtains, to the very
> millimeter. A woman made of all this is never to
> be taken for granted, never to be asked to move
> to the back of anything, never ever to be arrested.
>
> A woman who believes she is worthy of every
> thing possible. Godly. Grace. Good. (*TMS* 64)

Here, as throughout the text, Finny uses anaphora, colloquial diction (as in "messing with"), precise and vivid details, and a powerful sense of rhythm to great effect. And she also cleverly reminds us, in the final three words, of her earlier list of comic alliterative adjectives ("pristine. Persnickety. Particular"). In this line, however, the alliterated words have an entirely different and more serious tone. Finney, who praises Parks for her ability to stitch different parts together into striking designs, demonstrates the same talent herself. This skill is especially evident in the poem's final lines, where Finney complexly depicts the seamstress speaking with pins in the corners of her mouth and "through her softly clenched teeth / . . . *You do what you need to do & / So will I*" (*TMS* 65).

Benjamin Zephaniah's "I Have a Scheme"
Finney's poem could hardly differ more, in substance, attitude and tone, from Benjamin Zephaniah's deliberately comic "I Have a Scheme." Zephaniah is described, at the end of *The Mighty Stream*, as "an oral poet, novelist, children's writer, and reggae artist" who is the author of several books and who holds a "chair in Creative Writing at Brunel University in West London." That last fact is important, since many aspects of Zephaniah's poem allude to British culture. Indeed, even the word "scheme" tends to mean not a devious plot (as Americans usually understand that term) but rather "a plan, design, or program of action" or even "a visionary or impractical project" (dictionary.com). The second quoted meaning complicates

and ironizes the first. Readers will have to decide for themselves, by the end of the poem, whether the "scheme" mentioned here is a practical plan or an impractical project.

In either case, the poem is funny. Zephaniah, refreshingly, alludes to King's famous "I Have a Dream" speech not in hushed or respectful tones but with a big and winning smile on his face. In a sense, the very fact that a poem as irreverent as this could even be written may suggest how much progress has been made in race relations since King's assassination. Zephaniah feels no need to advocate for multiculturalism or argue about it; instead he can *joke* about it, as if most of his readers will not feel threatened or offended by his humor.

The poem begins by riffing on the "I Have a Dream" speech in numerous ways. It frequently employs the standard comic technique of unexpected reversals to provoke smiles and even laughter, as when the speaker says "There is a tunnel at the end of the light" (*TMS* 73). This sentence might seem to set an ominous tone, but in fact all the rest of the poem is laughingly lighthearted. The speaker says, for instance,

> I see a time
> When angry white men
> Will sit down with angry black women
> And talk about the weather . . .
> I see a time
> When words like affirmative action
> Will have sexual connotations (*TMS* 73)

Zephaniah's main method, perhaps, is to challenge stereotypes and reverse expectations, as when the speaker foresees a time when "black people all over this blessed country of ours / Will play golf"—a time when "Afro-Caribbean and Asian youth / Will spend big money on English takeaways" (*TMS* 73). Occasionally the poem alludes to serious issues, as when the speaker imagines police officers armed with dumplings or when he foresees an era when "Immigration officers will just check that you are all right" (*TMS* 73). The poem thus reminds us of issues of police brutality and ethnic discrimination, but then the very next line foresees a time when "all black people will speak Welsh" (*TMS* 73).

One especially evident trait of Zephaniah's poem is his sheer inventiveness, particularly his ability to undercut stereotypes, as when the speaker says, "I see thousands of muscular black men on Hampstead Heath / walking their poodles / And hundreds of black female Formula 1 drivers / Racing around Birmingham in pursuit of a truly British way of life" (*TMS* 74). The poem goes on like this, but one measure of its success is that it is never predictable or tedious. Zephaniah invents one striking phrase after another, and by the time the poem concludes, most readers will have laughed out loud or at least broken into broad smiles. No other poem in *The Mighty Stream* has this kind of comic impact, and "I Have a Scheme" is all the more memorable for being so humorous. One comes away from it realizing just how much, and in how many ways, life *has* improved for people of all races, ethnicities, genders, and classes in the time since King's death. And one also comes away feeling that even more progress might be possible if people would simply relax, laugh, and try to treat one another as friends.

"Ghost," by Tim Seibles

At the opposite end of the spectrum from Zephaniah's "I Have a Scheme" is a poem titled "Ghost," by Tim Seibles, a well-known poet whose work has been nominated for the National Book Award. In Seibles's poem, Martin Luther King himself is the speaker. His language is clear, simple, and direct, as in the poem's opening words:

> Do you remember
> that unchecked faith?—
> the world itself, a promise:
> a child, you dream something
> and it glistens. You wake up
> and can't believe it
> isn't there. (*TMS* 90)

However, the clarity and simplicity of this poem are arguably flaws, at least if one compares Seibles's poem with the kind of poem one *could* imagine King speaking in his own voice. King, after all, was one of the great orators (and, in a sense, poets) of his time or any other era. Surely a poem in which King is the imagined speaker could be more eloquent and overpowering than the poem Seibles has produced. Perhaps, in fact, Seibles *intended* to present a different kind of King than the one most readers and listeners are used to. Perhaps he meant to take us inside King's own head, to give us the man's private thoughts and ways of thinking rather than a polished public performance. It is difficult, for instance, to imagine the public King saying anything like this, at least when delivering a speech:

> Even heading to Selma,
> seeing those troopers
> across the bridge, it took
> all I had not to holler
>
> *Who are we kidding? These fools*
> *will never change.* (*TMS* 91)

Ultimately, of course, readers will have to decide for themselves the effectiveness of Seibles's poem, especially when it is read alongside others in *The Mighty Stream*. Finney and Zephaniah will seem, to many readers, tough acts to follow.

"Sleeping on the Bus," by Martín Espada

Martín Espada's poem "Sleeping on the Bus," like many of the other most effective works in *The Mighty Stream*, relies heavily on anaphora ("How we drift . . . how we shrink . . . how we wait . . ." [*TMS* 81]) to impart a strong sense of rhythm and skillfully create an almost chanting effect. Espada's opening stanza emphasizes the dreary, mundane experiences common in most bus stations today but then forcefully shifts to the experiences of the famous freedom riders of the 1960s who risked—and actually suffered—beatings and arrests when they tried to integrate buses and bus terminals in the Deep South:

> How we forget the bus stations of Alabama,
> Birmingham to Montgomery,
> how the Freedom Riders were abandoned
> to the beckoning mob, how afterwards
> their faces were tender and lopsided as spoiled fruit,
> fingers searching the mouth for lost teeth,
> and how the riders, descendants
> of Africa and Europe both, kept riding
> even as the mob with pleading hands wept fiercely
> for the ancient laws of segregation. (*TMS* 81)

The speaker's use of "we" implicates both himself and his readers in this collective forgetfulness, but this stanza is especially effective because of its vivid imagery (particularly the image of "faces . . . tender and lopsided as spoiled fruit") and its surprising phrasing, notably regarding "the mob with pleading hands [who] wept fiercely." Espada makes the mob sound almost intensely religious in their passionate devotion to "the ancient laws of segregation," thereby offering an unexpected "take" on people who are usually depicted simply as crude, unfeeling villains. Espada's words manage to convey how deeply these people were committed to their own entrenched, traditional beliefs and how paradoxically threatened they felt at the mere thought of blacks and whites riding buses together. Espada's poem then memorably shifts back to the bus riders of today, who don't recall the risks once involved in merely traveling by bus. For them (for *us*),

> . . . the singing and clapping
> of another generation
> fade like distant radio
> as we ride, forehead
> heavy on the window,
> how we sleep, how we sleep. (*TMS* 82)

Like many of the other most effective poems in *The Mighty Stream*, Espada's lyric doesn't simply preach (if it preaches at all, as Seibles's poem perhaps does). Instead, it uses a specific situation, haunting rhythms, and vivid imagery to force readers to relive the past rather than simply and openly condemning it.

"Call and Response," by Fred D'Aguiar

Certainly one of the most memorable and sophisticated poems of all the lyrics included in *The Mighty Stream* is Fred D'Aguiar's lengthy but carefully structured work, "Call and Response" (*TMS* 94-96). Looking for all the world like a sonnet sequence and featuring challenging rhyme schemes, this text is divided into two parts, each consisting of four stanzas. But whereas the first four stanzas are comprised of twelve lines each, the final four consist of fourteen lines apiece. Fourteen-line stanzas, of course, are associated with standard sonnets, and standard sonnets are often associated with the theme of love. D'Aguiar seems to be playing a subtle structural game, especially when one realizes that the first four stanzas are spoken (stunningly) by the bullet racing toward King's body while the final four are spoken by King himself. This is an astonishing and unforgettable conceit, and the poem's phrasing is often just as memorable as its overall design. Consider, for example, the opening stanza's opening lines:

> Dear Martin, I wish you had never been found.
> Telescope and direction, aim, hammer, grudge,
> Velocity and malice sent me, your bloodhound. (*TMS* 94)

Here and throughout the poem, D'Aguiar wastes few words and manages to create complex tones, beginning with the paradoxical opening words ("Dear Martin"). The rest of line 1 makes the bullet sound almost regretful (not, as would be thoroughly predictable and stereotypical, *merely* malicious). D'Aguiar packs these lines with vivid, concrete nouns, some referring to material things, others to human emotions. He violates normal syntax, as if the bullet literally and figuratively has no time to waste. The ensuing lines forcefully stress vivid verbs as the bullet heads toward its target:

> As I **burned** through space, **left** my own sound
> In my wake, **parted** strands from my site, **dodged**

> Time, **split** particles, my Hummingbird instant
> For your slow, finger wet in mouth test of falling,
> **Swept** aside by my speed inside your constant,
> I knew where I would end up, what my blunt
> Instrument must do to your routine, more calling
> Than career, to that bigger dream you coined,
> **Robbed** of you, **grabbed** by me, us **joined**.
>
> (*TMS* 94; my bold-faced emphasis)

There is so much to admire here that it is hard to list all the carefully crafted details. One notices, for instance, the skillful alliteration ("calling . . . career . . . coined"); the subtle play on the cliché "blunt / Instrument," which is here given brand new, sickening life; the balanced wordplay and soundplay of "Robbed of you, grabbed by me"; and especially the devastating abruptness and simplicity that ironically describe the moment of murderous impact: "us joined." These lines show a real poet at work—someone interested more in art than in argument because he knows that it is art that makes any argument stick in the mind. An entire essay could easily be devoted to the whole of "Call and Response," but such an essay will, for the time being, have to be postponed.

As in all the other details of this work, D'Aguiar has shown real thoughtfulness in selecting his title. The words *call and response*, of course, refer to a typical method of preaching in African American churches. In this method, the preacher makes a statement to which members of the congregation spontaneously and openly respond. As with so much else in this poem, D'Aguiar's title achieves real irony. Here it is the bullet that symbolizes a kind of call, to which King issues a kind of response. The first stanza of the work's second section, spoken by King, opens as follows:

> **Rest** in *me*. **End** your journ*ey*. **Let** my <u>flesh</u> *be* your <u>bed</u>
> If you promise to **sleep**, never **rise** to **erase** another day.
> Much like the one where you searched out my voice
> On your <u>blind drive</u> to a different place, person, <u>time</u>.
>
> (*TMS* 95; my diverse emphases)

Here again D'Aguiar employs an impressive range of poetic techniques. Once more he stresses key verbs (which I have placed in bold). The opening line, in particular, shows how skillfully he employs assonance (echoed vowel sounds, which I have underlined), and internal rhyme (which I have highlighted by italicizing); in line 2 he cleverly alliterates *r* and *s* sounds in "rise" and "erase"; in that same line he uses the startling metaphor of "eras[ing]" an entire "day"; and then, in the final quoted line, he ends with an emphatic trio of heavily stressed nouns. If one had to choose a single poem from *The Mighty Stream* that is not only about King but also a piece of artfully written poetry, surely D'Aguiar's "Call and Response" would be that poem. It is a text that deserves much more extended attention than I can pay it here.

"American Sonnet for My Past and Future Assassin," by Terrance Hayes

Terrance Hayes's "American Sonnet" resembles D'Aguiar's poem in some ways but not in others. The title suggests at least two similarities, and the opening sentence consists of the sort of striking language D'Aguiar might use: "When MLK was shot, his blood changed to change / Wherever it hit the floor" (*TMS* 140). Hayes suggests that some of King's closest associates (he specifically mentions Jesse Jackson and Ralph Abernathy) profited financially from having witnessed King's death. But he also notes that even "A maid sold the penny she found for a pretty penny on / The black market" (*TMS* 140). This sentence seems less skillful than the one quoted above, not only because the cliché "a pretty penny" remains a cliché but also because of the (intended? unintended?) reference to the "black market." All in all, Hayes's writing, here at least, seems less impressive than D'Aguiar's and also less technically remarkable and tightly coherent. The final line, however, is nicely balanced: "This country is mine as much as an orphan's house is his" (*TMS* 140).

"The Preachers Eat Out" and "Brevity," by Camille T. Dungy

Camille T. Dungy is represented by four poems in *The Mighty Stream*, and all four are superbly written and therefore memorable. One, "The Preachers Eat Out," is accompanied by an italicized reference to *"Vernon Johns,"* a famously defiant African American preacher of the civil rights era and the man who preceded Martin Luther King as the minister at Montgomery's Dexter Avenue Baptist Church before being dismissed by the staid middle-class congregation. One wonders what might have happened if Johns, rather than King, had still been prominent in Montgomery when Rosa Parks was arrested for defying segregation. As Dungy's poem suggests, Johns did not easily suffer fools.

The poem is fourteen lines long and will therefore, ironically, remind many readers of the sonnet form, a form often associated with love. This poem, however, deals with quite different emotions:

> There were maybe four of them, perhaps five.
> They were headed, where? It does not matter,
> only, they were not home yet, were not near
> anyone who could have cared. So hungry,
> they stopped there anyway. And when they heard,
> *We don't serve your kind,* one among them laughed,
> *That's okay. We're not hungry for our kind.*
> *We've come for food.* And when the one waitress
> who would serve them—she had children at home
> and these were tips—finished breaking their plates
> behind the building, he called her over
> to the table. *Lady, my one regret*
> *is that we don't have appetite enough*
> *to make you break every damned plate inside this room.* (*TMS* 144)

Like many poems in *The Mighty Stream*, this one benefits from clear, straightforward diction, but one also notices various subtleties of phrasing, as in the sound-similarities of *where, were, near, cared, there,* and *heard* in the first four lines. Also impressive are the opening line's studied indifference to details; the sudden shift of syntax in the first sentence of line 2; the return to the earlier indifference in the rest of that line; the lapse into a hurried fragment in lines 4 and 5; and the clever, defiant humor of lines 7 and 8. Perhaps the most interesting passage, however—at least in terms of psychological complexity—involves the waitress's behavior. At first she seems a sympathetic figure in several senses of that adjective: she appears, initially, to sympathize with the black ministers, and then she also herself seems worthy of sympathy since she has "children at home." But then, in Dungy's brilliant use of enjambment in the shift from line 9 to line 10, we learn that far from genuinely caring about the ministers, the waitress sees them quite simply as sources of income—as "tips." And then, in a detail that will shock many present-day readers, we learn that the restaurant's policy is to break the plates used by any black people it is forced to serve. The waitress, who had initially appeared as perhaps somewhat noble, now seems extraordinarily petty. But then, giving the screw just one more turn, we realize that she is probably simply doing what her bosses expect her to do. The italicized response, by one of the ministers (Vernon Johns?) that closes the poem is funny in its own justifiably bitter way, so that the poem ends with one more complicated, complicating emotion. This complexity is *especially* complex because the same man who seems bitter in the concluding lines was the one who had earlier joked. Dungy's work (at least the texts printed in *The Mighty Stream*) consistently implies shrewd perceptions expressed in richly memorable language.

Certainly one of the most memorable of all the poems published in *The Mighty Stream* is another one by Dungy. This work, appropriately titled "Brevity," reads as follows:

As in four girls; Sunday
dresses: bone, ash, bone, ash, bone, ash, bone. (*TMS* 145)

The "four girls," of course, are the four young black girls who were killed in the infamous 1963 bombing of a church in Birmingham, Alabama. This incident, which shocked the nation, ironically helped promote (rather than retard, as the bombers hoped) the cause of civil rights. Dungy's poem is itself shocking. A longer work might not have worked as effectively as this one does. The very brevity of "Brevity" stunningly mimics the quickness of the blast itself. In an instant, the bomb destroyed the young girls' lives. When reading this poem, one thinks of Ezra Pound's famous two-line lyric "In a Station of the Metro." But whereas that legendary poem emphasizes a sudden, overwhelming perception of beauty, Dungy's poem deliberately creates the opposite effect. The poem's final words—"bone, ash, bone, ash, bone, ash, bone"—are breathtakingly effective, partly because of the contrast between hard and soft sounds and partly because the very last word is hard rather than soft. Of all the poems in *The Mighty Stream*, this one is perhaps the easiest to remember and the hardest to forget.

Conclusion

The Mighty Stream is certainly one of the most interesting of all the literary responses so far generated by the legacy of Martin Luther King. This book, however, is probably not the last that will feature King as a character, historical figure, or source of inspiration. King has now entered the pantheon of agreed-upon American heroes in a way that few other figures, especially in the twentieth century, seem to have done. Among American heroes in general, perhaps only Abraham Lincoln rivals him in broad cultural acceptance and prestige. The reputations of Washington and Jefferson are no longer sacrosanct, and it is interesting that it is King, not Washington, Jefferson, or Lincoln, who now has a federal holiday dedicated solely to his memory. He is, therefore, likely to be increasingly both a literary and a historical figure, and *The Mighty Stream* may itself one day be seen as simply one item in an even mightier stream of future books.

Works Cited

Forché, Carolyn, and Jackie Kay, editors. *The Mighty Stream: Poems in Celebration of Martin Luther King*. Bloodaxe, 2017.

Harris, Trudier. *Martin Luther King, Jr., Heroism, and African American Literature*. U of Alabama P, 2014.

Critical Reactions to Abby Mann's Televised Miniseries on Martin Luther King Jr.

Sam Dunton

Until the 2014 release of the well-received film *Selma*, directed by Ava DuVernay, the film about Martin Luther King Jr. that had probably received the widest public notice was an NBC television miniseries written and directed by Abby Mann. This miniseries, titled simply *King*, was three times as long as DuVernay's film and was broadcast on three separate nights in February 1978. Coming not long after the immensely successful telecast of *Roots*, an ABC miniseries dealing with African American slavery, *King* seemed sure to attract a similarly large audience. In fact, however, the ratings for the first night's broadcast, on February 12, were abysmally low. The show ranked sixty-fourth out of sixty-four programs in the ratings that week. Although this fact nonetheless meant that the series was seen by roughly twenty-five million people, *King*'s relative failure shocked many television critics and television executives, especially the executives at NBC.

Even before the miniseries was broadcast, it had aroused enormous controversy. Many close associates of Martin Luther King believed that the production had unjustly omitted or deemphasized their own contributions to the civil rights movement. They also felt that the contributions of other persons—especially those of a white lawyer named Stanley Levison—had been grossly exaggerated. Most important, however, were the beliefs of many of King's associates that the script and the program presented King himself as weak and confused and as dominated by whites like Levison. Many black leaders, even before the series was broadcast, alleged that it would present King as a latter-day Uncle Tom. When the series was finally broadcast, many felt that the finished product did in fact present King in this demeaning way.

In contrast, numerous other viewers—especially many professional television critics and newspaper columnists—came to exactly the opposite conclusion. They felt that Mann's film had managed to capture and convey the essence of King's courage and greatness, both as an individual and as a public figure. They noted that King's widow, Coretta Scott King, had strongly endorsed the film, that other associates of King were extremely pleased with it, and that two of King's own children had roles as actors in the series. None of this praise, however, helped the film win the kind of mass audience that Abby Mann and NBC had hoped and expected it would achieve. The controversy about the series may even have discouraged many viewers—especially black viewers—from tuning in. Various other explanations for the failure of the series have been offered, including white racism, a reluctance to watch a program with an obviously depressing ending, and a reluctance to relive the pain of one of the most controversial eras in American history.

Why, however, should any of this matter except to historians? The answers are simple: *King* is widely available on an inexpensive DVD and is, therefore, still likely to be viewed by anyone looking for a well-produced film about King and the civil rights movement. In addition, the film is also easily accessible on the internet and can thus be viewed for free or at a very minimal cost. Finally, for all the reasons just mentioned, the film is still likely to be used by teachers and students in classroom discussions concerning Martin Luther King Jr., and his legacy.

My purpose in this essay, then, is to survey some typical reviews of *King*—beginning with negative assessments, then moving to mixed reactions, and finally ending with positive responses to Mann's film. By doing so, I hope to provide students, teachers, and other viewers of the film with some sense of the kinds of reception the series first aroused and the kinds of responses it can still arouse today.[1]

Negative Reactions

Many of the most forceful negative reactions to the film were offered months before it was even broadcast. Numerous leaders of the African American community condemned the series on the basis of what they had heard about it or simply after having read the script.

Defenses of the project by Mann, by King's widow, by his children, and by other civil rights leaders did little if anything to discourage attacks. My main focus here, however, is on negative reactions to the actual broadcast itself.

One of the earliest negative reviews was published in the *Baltimore Sun* on February 10, 1978. The author of this review, Bill Carter, had obviously seen the film before its nationwide broadcast two nights later. The headline given to Carter's assessment—"'King'—Such Wasted Potential"—aptly summarizes Carter's opinions. Carter called the film "an underwhelming movie" and condemned it for being "sloppy, choppy and disjointed" (21). This series, according to Carter, "takes a story of power and high emotion and defuses it with scenes of dramatic flabbiness" and thus wasted a rare opportunity to deal effectively with an important topic. King's personality and the events in which he participated did give the film, in Carter's view, some genuine "power," but he called *King* "an ultimate disappointment, not because it is bad television, but because it is a hollow echo of the grandeur of the man it is attempting to portray." Carter argued that the "fault rests squarely on the shoulders of Abby Mann, a screenwriter of impeccable credentials, who became so consumed with his personal commitment to the 'King' project that he made his film a victim of his own self-indulgence." Especially unfortunate, in Carter's view, was the fact that

> Mann was so overcome with his role in the "King" legacy that he decided to direct this film himself. And that's where he committed artistic suicide at the expense of what could have been an extraordinary TV event. "King" is one of the few movies that even an average viewer should be able to tell is poorly directed. It is afflicted with a chronic disease: Nonsensical transitions. The scenes are put together like a finger painting. A piece here, a piece there. Some of it fits, some it doesn't, but that doesn't seem to bother Mann in the least. Scenes are narrated by off-camera voices that are never identified. Some you can figure out, some you can't. Scenes take place in offices and rooms that are never identified. The whole first episode is stuffed with characters who are never named. (21)

Like practically everyone else who reviewed the film, Carter strongly praised the "towering presence of Paul Winfield" in the title role. "Winfield's work," Carter continued,

> is even more admirable when compared to the vapid performances of many of the other characters—most notably Cicely Tyson, who brings no life whatever to the flatly written part of Coretta King. Ossie Davis isn't bad as Martin, Sr. But many of the other black leaders are depicted as just so many mannequins moving through the scenes as though attached to strings. (21)

In the final analysis, according to Carter, "the film leans more toward cant than characterization. There is so much in the story of 'King' that is moving and inspiring that the film is worth watching for all its flaws. But it is impossible not to be disappointed. The film has too much Abby Mann and not enough Martin Luther King."

A slightly less harsh review of the series was offered by Tom Shales in *The Washington Post*. Shales, one of the country's best-known television critics, asserted that Mann's film "starts out as a cumbersome and heavy-handed situation tragedy, but eventually evolves, in about its fifth hour . . . into a stirring and absorbing portrait of a man and a mission perfectly matched" (n.p.). But even the film's conclusion, Shales said, "doesn't inspire the tremendous emotional release one hopes for and expects. This is probably because writer Abby Mann mounts a high horse of sanctimonious preciousness at the start and insists on parading his own credentials as a proudly guilty liberal." Mann, according to Shales, "is a slickly skillful dramatist," and Shales even confesses that the miniseries might possibly have been comparable to *Roots* "if only the script had been shaped by a competent director," to which Shales adds, "It wasn't." Despite the film's focus on Dr. King, Shales turns his own focus to the supporting characters, such as the Kennedy brothers, noting that it "doesn't make King any more heroic a figure to portray John and Robert as spineless vacillators on the civil rights issue. . . ." Later he claims that in Mann's series the "role of Coretta Scott King in the movement and in shaping King's role may have been overstressed." Still, Shales did find satisfaction in

Winfield's performance. Shales conceded, "To the credit, perhaps the salvation, of 'King,' the title role is played with striking empathy and consistent conviction by Paul Winfield." However, despite the fact that he considered Winfield "outstanding," Shales continued to question Mann's motives and the film's effectiveness.

Shales denounced Mann for his "half-whispered way" of insinuating that the FBI participated in a conspiracy to assassinate Dr. King. "A documentary-style drama on prime-time network television," Shales explained, "does not seem just the forum for raising such speculation." Shales saw *King* as a personal platform for Mann rather than as an educational and moving piece on a legendary historical figure. In fact, Shales said that Mann "seems more concerned with advertising his own concern, and his own real or imagined credibility, than in telling King's story faithfully and movingly." Mann's alleged shortcomings as a historian were driving points for Shales, who ripped into the director for misrepresenting and distorting reality. Shales explained that often "the conflict between good storytelling and accurate history arises," and he also explained that the realities behind the miniseries "are strong enough and certainly important enough to have been presented in less gimmicky and obfuscating ways." For Shales, *King* fell far short of its potential.

Even shorter reviews, such as one by the *Baltimore Afro American*'s Ida Peters, packed a real punch. Peters echoed Shales by questioning the authenticity of the film, saying, "I think as a news person during the King years, the TV failure [of Mann's film] came about because it told the story from a white viewpoint and not like it 'really was'" (16). Peters focused on an issue not widely discussed in many negative reviews of the film: the misgivings some African Americans felt about the Caucasian writer and director. Peters and others felt that Mann was unable to connect and relate fully to the sufferings of black Americans. Peters expressed her disdain for the film by saying that the "white press service says it was beautifully acted. It wasn't. It was a mess. It made me so mad I turned the set off." Clearly, for some audiences, the film's alleged failure to fully encompass the history and life of Dr. King was too much to bear.

Strong negative positions were also expressed by Marion Lepkin of the *Winnipeg Free Press*, who concisely called *King* an "obscenity. And the obscenity went on during two whole hours for three whole nights" (26). But Lepkin was bothered less by the film itself than by the frequent and tawdry commercials: "It was as if the Pope's Christmas sermon had been interrupted to advertise Andy Gumps Prophylactic and Pessary Shop." Other reviewers, such as Reese Cleghorn in the *Detroit Free Press*, also criticized *King*. Cleghorn asserted that "despite some real strengths," this miniseries "again showed the shortcomings of the TV medium," although "Mann seemed blissfully unaware of that" (8). Cleghorn also condemned the series for storytelling that "wrenched at the truth . . . just as the TV reporting of the time did." He condemned "Mann's unwillingness to let the most extraordinary ebb and flow of those events speak for themselves" and also said that "Mann stripped out the subtleties and sometimes the bone and marrow of the [civil rights] movement." He claimed that "the drama hardly touched upon the great saga of human emergence all across the South," asking, "What about the little people who, once they began to shake off old shackles of the mind and spirit, found extraordinary courage to go out without a visit from Dr. King and change their own worlds?"

Although David Foil of *A-8 Town Talk* first described "King" as "an inspiring and humbling experience," he also claimed that the film "did not amplify history, merely verify it" (8). He thought it "failed to dig into the story of Dr. King's life and times with much passion or sensitivity" and faulted its "saintly soap opera style," its "obvious dialogue," and its "simple, cut-and-dried approach." Still, Foil did applaud the acting of Winfield and Tyson as Dr. King and Coretta King, praising Winfield in particular for "an amazingly recessive performance" in which "the character was warm, paternal, troubled," which Foil considered "the best choice" for anyone trying to act the role of King. Foil also called Tyson "warm and supportive throughout as Coretta King." Thus, despite criticizing Mann's writing, Foil ended on a positive note: "'King' may be just what audiences needed to see now. It spoke for something good and noble, largely through King's words and Winfield's heroic performance. That alone made it rare good viewing on network TV." Chris Stoehr, however, in the *Detroit Free Press*, condemned the film's allegedly "rambling, often confusing story line" and suggested that the film's flaws may have been partly responsible for its massive failure in the ratings.

By far the most interesting negative reactions to the film, however, were offered by a series of prominent black civil rights leaders interviewed by *Jet*, a magazine aimed at African Americans. These figures included many intimate associates of King. Almost without exception they condemned Mann's film in the strongest possible terms. For example, King's close comrade Ralph David Abernathy called the film "nothing more than a distortion of history" (qtd. in Smallwood and Perry 12). Of the movie's influence on younger audiences, Abernathy said: "It is most unfortunate that young people who did not know Dr. King and even unborn generations may get a totally distorted image of this great man from this movie" (qtd. inSmallwood and Perry 12).

Also in *Jet*, E. D. Nixon, who was portrayed in the film and who was at one time the president of the NAACP, explained that "parts of it were wrong" and continued, "If you're going to make the movie, then deal with truth" (qtd. inSmallwood and Perry12). The Reverend Wyatt Walker said, "My omission [from the film] is minor compared to the great damage that has been done to Martin's personality. After seeing three hours of it, I wanted to scream" (qtd. in Smallwood and Perry 13). Rosa Parks commented that the film "overemphasized ... violent scenes" and mentioned that "it wasn't a happy thing to look at" (qtd. in Smallwood and Perry13). The Reverend Joseph Lowery, a friend of King, claimed "The film was historically inaccurate to the point of cruelty." Lowery thought the movie showed King as "weak, uneasy and constantly depressed and depending on others for strength" (qtd. in Smallwood and Perry 14). King's secretary, Dora McDonald, said Mann's work "did not show the greatness of the man" (qtd. in Smallwood and Perry15), and Dr. Kelly Smith of the SCLC and Vanderbilt's Divinity School said the film "fell far short of the Martin Luther King whom I knew."

Smith continued, "Some essential things were left out, such as the truly deep involvement that Dr. King had with the SCLC" (qtd. in Smallwood and Perry 16).

John Lewis, who was beaten in the Selma march and was chairman of the Student Nonviolent Coordinating Committee, stated the film was "a great distortion of history. . . . It tarnished the man and the movement" (qtd. in Smallwood and Perry 13). More positively, Marian Edelman, a former lawyer for the Mississippi NAACP, said "It reminded me of how horrible the fear was in those Mississippi days. I had forgotten that I was scared all the time" (qtd. in Smallwood and Perry 13). Reverend Fred Shuttlesworth also weighed in with another positive reaction: "The film was an effort to bring forth to the consciousness of the country what King really meant. . . . Maybe it'll mean something to us now" (qtd. in Smallwood and Perry 14). Still, he added, "it left something to be desired from the Dr. King I really knew. King was an intellectual. . . . They showed him agonizing to the point where you'd have thought he was a person given to ravages of depression" (qtd. in Smallwood and Perry 14). The Reverend C. T. Vivian stated that the film "will divide the strongest tie that Black America has with Africa—Martin Luther King. That's what makes them respect us and Abby Mann will destroy that link with his film" (qtd. in Smallwood and Perry 15). Hosea Williams, director of the SCLC, asserted, "I regret that the youth of today saw Dr. King portrayed as he was in the film. The producers, directors and writers gave King a scary, Uncle Tom image whites want him to have" (qtd. in Smallwood and Perry 15).

Jet also interviewed the student who had been responsible for desegregating the University of Mississippi, James Meredith, who asserted that "Somebody was trying to control the images and impressions of history and you don't control history if you're going to deal with it at all" (qtd. in Smallwood and Perry 16). Ralph Abernathy's wife, Juanita, claimed "The film was a conglomeration of lies and a distortion of history. It was awful" (qtd. in Smallwood and Perry 16-17). Finally, *Jet* quoted Dr. L. D. Reddick, author of the King biography *Crusader Without Violence,* as alleging that Mann's work was "a crude caricature of the man and should be withdrawn from public showing" (qtd. in Smallwood and Perry 17). All in all, the reactions quoted by Smallwood and Perry were the harshest collection of responses the film ever received. They were almost uniformly negative.

Mixed Reactions

Not all reviews of the film, however, condemned it. Various reviewers, such as Diane Mermigas in the *Arlington Heights Daily Herald*, perceived both faults and strong points of *King*. Mermigas called *King* "a just and proper monument to the man and his times," largely due to "Winfield's spellbinding performance" (5). She thought Winfield succeeded by "portraying [King] not as a demigod but as a man of frailties and weaknesses whose astonishing inner strength leads him to great accomplishments." Mermigas felt that the film's major flaw "is that it is so exclusively Mann's," observing that "the viewer is restricted to Mann's account of King's rise to power." She also found various supporting roles problematic: "The characterizations of the Kennedy brothers are unjustifiably weak and two-faced," but she concluded that the film's faults could not detract from its "starkly honest profile of King's silent uncertainty" (5). High praises were also offered by Lisa Tuttle, who asserted, in the *Akron Beacon Journal*, that the "combination of Abby Mann's script and Paul Winfield's inspired performance nearly bring Martin Luther King to life again" (64). Tuttle felt, however, that a key failure of the film was Mann's decision to "direct it himself." She thought another person "could have brought a much-needed second point of view." Nonetheless, she boldly predicted *King* would be "one of the most memorable television programs of 1978" (64).

An article simply titled "'King' Reaction Mixed Among Viewers in Cenla [i.e., Central Louisiana]" from *The Town Talk* of Alexandria, Louisiana, interviewed one man who "expressed fear the film would stir up old memories among members of both black and white communities" (A8). Another interviewee considered the film "well-handled" but asserted that "the program was definitely slanted in favor of King. It was designed to make him the hero." In the same article, others disagreed and claimed that "it took a lot of courage" for Mann to present the film. On the same page of *The Town Talk*, an article by David Foil ("'King' Rated Last in Nielsen Survey") nevertheless called the film a "beautifully acted biography" (A8). A reviewer for the Winchester *Evening Star*, who focused mostly on the character roles and the actors who played them, exclaimed: "Okay, give Paul Winfield his Emmy award now." However, the critic also asserted that "The Kennedys, President John F. (William Jordan) and his Attorney General brother, Robert (wildly overacted by Cliff DeYoung), don't come off too well . . . ." (14).

A series of letters to the editor published in the *Los Angeles Times* ("More Words about King") also offered varied views. One reader (Trish Van Devere) was so surprised by the program's poor ratings that she claimed to be "shocked to the point of questioning the entire validity of the 'rating system'" (52). She lamented the ratings' disregard for the "talents of Abby Mann or the exquisitely performed, inspiring story of a courageous human being." Another viewer (Norm Pliscou) called the film a "beautifully done television presentation," while Jay Berinstein applauded *King* as "one of the most significant movies of our time." However, another viewer who submitted a letter to the *Times*—Don Cornelius, the popular African American television host—condemned the film for a "ridiculously misleading, and at times downright insulting, so-called story of King's life." Cornelius claimed that the miniseries lacked "even a hint of [the] real essence" of King's life. But a different viewer (Gloria Garner) had the final word: "Please tell Abby Mann that maybe the ratings were poor, but I'm sure the ones who watched learned so much" (52).

Positive Reactions

Despite some harshly critical reactions and disappointing ratings, Mann's series was also flooded with positive reviews. Gary Deeb, for instance, in the *Colorado Springs Gazette Telegraph*, proclaimed, "A superb six-hour biography of Martin Luther King will explode on your television screen." Deeb felt confident that "complaints by [Ralph] Abernathy and others that the movie depicts Dr. King as 'cowardly,' 'docile,' and 'weak' won't stand up to public scrutiny...."

[In this film,] Dr. King is a majestic leader who nevertheless possesses human frailties and occasionally agonizes over major decisions." Deeb summed up his view by saying, "In other words he's no plaster saint" (34D).

In another review, Diane Mermigas, who had already offered some mixed opinions, now maintained in the *Arlington HeightsDaily Herald* that "Mann successfully has kept typical Hollywood sensationalism and sentimentality out of his 'King'...." Mermigas also observed that "Mrs. King and United Nations Ambassador Andrew Young are just two of the persons who confided with Mann on the project, [and] who have seen the film and have supported it wholeheartedly," according to Mann ("'King producer'" 5). Similarly positive about the film (but not about the commercial interruptions) was Marion Lepkin in the *Winnipeg Free Press*, who wrote, "The King biography is powerful stuff. Writer-director Abby Mann orchestrated the production, his directional baton firmly controlling the pace of the drama, the rise and fall of dramatic tensions matching the rhythms of King's oratory" (26). Like some other critics, Lepkin complained about the number and nature of commercials, but she greatly admired the film itself.

An anonymous reviewer in Ohio's *Lima News* described the final hours of the series as a "monumental, illuminating saga of America, north and south, during the 1950s and 1960s" ("'King,' Part 3", 17). The critic suggested that "[o]ne of the most devastating scenes shows the gruesome death of two Memphis garbage workers, but this bit of TV violence, unlike violence on most other shows, is dramatically valid" because it "reminded viewers that the tragic deaths were clearly the result of the prevailing racist attitudes of the period." The critic even argued that "Mann deserves to win the Emmy and virtually every other TV award in sight" (17). Another review, in the *Alton* [Illinois] *Telegraph*, praised the film as "a stunning, illuminating and deeply moving modern morality play, superbly acted by the entire cast" ("'King.' Part I.," 32). The author claimed that "one of the many strengths of Mann's screenplay is that the protagonists are not the usual TV cardboard cutouts" and called this program "one of

American television's most distinguished productions of the past decade." Similarly, David Piety, a reviewer for the Ohio *Journal Herald*, called the series "more documentary than drama" but said that he "sensed no shortcoming on these grounds" (10). The author also observed: "The three-part show ... recreated in vivid fashion an ugly and turbulent and intensely exhilarating chapter in America's social history" and lamented, "It is unfortunate that the King show did not enjoy a wider audience" (10). Kay Gardella, in the New York *Daily News*, similarly said that "Americans who did not watch this six-hour film missed a compassionate biography ... and one of the single finest performances by an actor you will see all year" (69). Bill Frank, of the Wilmington, Delaware, *Morning News*, explained that he was "terrifically impressed with the film" and said that he "failed to see any indication or hint that Dr. King was being portrayed . . . as a coward," as some of the film's critics had claimed. Frank stated: "Since most of the film was written, directed and produced with what I thought was loving care, reverence and respect for Dr. King, I for one fail to see any intentional slur upon the character of Dr. King." In fact, Frank concluded that King "emerged from the six-hour film as one of the most notable Americans in our 200-year history" (12).

In a similarly positive review in the *Minneapolis Star*, Don Morrison claimed that the film "unquestionably broke new ground for television" because it "was considerably different from any prior television effort to re-create or seriously explore recent history" (47). This series, in Morrison's opinion, "did not offer the usual cautious apologetics or qualifications, nor try to document every statement that could be challenged, nor utter those nervous 'on the other hands' that suggest the real truth is always up for grabs." Although Morrison commented on some "gaps of needful data" left by Mann and considered the film spotty in showing the logic of characters," he also clarified that "NONE of those important deficiencies really affected the force of what I had to believe and accept as essential truth." He went on to add, "The tactics of the show were worthy of the man it celebrated," partly because King himself had used television so effectively during the struggle for civil rights. Disagreeing with critics of the film, Morrison said that the series "exhibited the same type of unassailable conviction" as King himself had shown "and acted on it in a remarkably unflinching manner for a popular mass medium mostly bent on pleasing everyone." Further, the author remarked: "It invoked a tough, intractable position and didn't back down from it or waste time trying to justify the self-evident moralities involved." Morrison persisted, saying that the film "tried to avoid sentimental hero worship that lets us escape into the lazy fantasy that the good guys always can prevail over the bad guys and don't need our help" (47).

Dick Shippy, in a widely published syndicated article that appeared, for instance, in the *Akron Beacon Journal* proclaimed about *King* that "America was favorably impressed…. Or should have been," but he regretted that this "celebration of decency and courage of the outstanding American of the [past] quarter-century was completely done in by a western and a Burt Reynolds movie" (64). Like many others, Shippy applauded Winfield, saying his casting "was a master stroke in the delineation of this portrait." Shippy also claimed that "any defects and-or defections could not mar 'King' as a stirring tribute to greatness" (64). A review in the *Pittsburgh Post-Gazette* ("Winfield's Emmy") also delighted in Winfield's performance, saying, "It is impossible to imagine his portrayal … can be matched much less topped by any other actor in any TV drama this season." The unnamed author also argued that "[Mann's] literate script and painstaking recreation of history was matched by the incisiveness of his direction." The review likewise praised Tyson and Ossie Davis, who played King's wife and his father, respectively, for their "outstanding performances" and additionally commended, in general, the "able support by members of the large supporting cast" (41).

Brian O'Meara, in the *Ottawa Journal*, called Mann's film "the most moving television experience I've had in a long while" (67). O'Meara admitted that "Men like Martin Luther King are complex and elusive," but he added that although "Mann doesn't ignore personal faults . . . he does accentuate the traits that made King a great man. That's fair" (67). In the *Detroit Free Press*, Joe Urschel, sounding a similarly positive note, described *King* as "a truly epic depiction of the King story. And like King himself, the show is controversial and unsettling. But above all, it is inspiring" (34). Urschel argued that "'King' takes very little license with the facts, and thus retains a high degree of believability," but he also mentioned "some obvious distortions." Still, Urschel not only relished Winfield, saying that he "completely assumes the buoyant spirit and power of Martin Luther King," but also called most of the supporting cast "strong." Urschel believed that perhaps "the most important quality" of *King* was that it allowed people in the seventies to "view the King story from a point nearly 10 years after his assassination and more than 29 years since the start of his crusade" (34).

Cecil Smith in the *Los Angeles Times* also praised the miniseries, arguing that although "Mann's film…has been attacked by various leaders of the black movement … as diminishing" King's stature, "[t]his is blatant nonsense" (12). Smith also credited Winfield, praising his "towering performance" and claiming that "to say that this film lessens the importance of Martin Luther King Jr. is preposterous." Smith also commended Mann's positive impact on the cast, saying that "his directorial effort seems to draw from them their full effect" (12). In the Louisville *Courier Journal*, Tom Dorsey described the film as "documentary-style" and "highly emotional," arguing that it "does away with the plaster-saint image and shows us a man full of hopes, fears and human frailties" (C1). Dorsey said the film "moves relentlessly through dozens of fascinating political sidelights," referring to how "Lyndon Johnson befriends, then turns on, King" and also mentioning an incident when "King's phones are tapped to blackmail him" (C2). Dorsey concluded by saying that the film's "final moments are not pretty, but they are honest and powerful like the rest of the six hours" (C2).

Barbara Holsopple, in *The Pittsburgh Press*, praised Winfield's and Tyson's "excellent performances," and specifically admired Winfield for the way he "skillfully balances the public fire and private agony of Dr. King" ("'King' Powerful" 4). Holsopple also suggested that the film was "heightened by the use of voice-overs by real persons" and by the "use of black-and-white newsfilm" (5). Meanwhile, Tim Weller, a reporter for the Michigan *Times Herald*, called the film "the best ever of its genre," specifically because "Mann refused to portray the civil rights leader as a pious, one-dimensional man" (3). This opinion, of course, could not differ more from the opinions of the negative critics who panned the docudrama as an embarrassing travesty.

Conclusion

If nothing else, this survey of responses to Abby Mann's *King* shows that people can look at the same thing and perceive it in entirely different ways. Some critics loved *King*; some hated it; others had ambivalent reactions. Students, teachers, and general viewers who watch the miniseries can benefit from being familiar with this entire range of viewpoints. The evidence the different reviewers presented to support their claims often differs significantly, but sometimes the very same evidence is used to make strikingly different arguments. This, of course, is true of many debates, and so the arguments about *King* can provide insights into the larger ways in which people think, decide, and debate.

Note

1. My work supplements and extends some of the work done by Jennifer Fuller, partly by providing much more additional evidence than she could include.

Works Cited and Consulted

Carter, Bill. "'King': Such Wasted Potential." *The Baltimore Sun*, 10 Feb. 1978, p. 21.

Cleghorn, Reese. "Civil Rights Movement Yet to Be Done Justice; TV's 'King' Flattened Out an Era." *Detroit Free Press*, 17 Feb. 1978, p. 8.

Deeb, Gary. [Untitled column.] *Colorado Springs Gazette Telegraph*, 4 Feb. 1978, p. 34D.

Dorsey, Tom. "'King': An Honest Look at the Man." *The Courier-Journal* [Louisville, KY], 10 Feb. 1978, pp. C1-C2.

Foil, David. "'King' Lacked Passion, Sensitivity." *The Town Talk* [Alexandria, LA], 15 Feb. 1978, p. A8.

Frank, Bill. "'King': An Evaluation." *The Morning News* [Wilmington, DE], 17 Feb. 1978, p. 12.

Fuller, Jennifer. "Dangerous Fictions: Race, History, and 'King.'" *Cinema Journal*, vol. 49, no. 2, 2010, pp. 40-62.

Gardella, Kay. "Television." *Daily News* [New York, NY], 17 Feb 1978, p. 69.

Holsopple, Barbara. "Industry 'Shocked' 'King' Dead Last in National Nielsen Ratings." *The Pittsburgh Press*, 15 Feb. 1978, p. c22.

_____. "'King' Powerful Drama of a Man and His Work." *The Pittsburgh Press*, 12 Feb. 1978, pp. 4-5, TV section.

"'King.' Part I." *Alton Telegraph* [Alton, IL], 11 Feb. 1978, p. 32.

"'King.' Part 3." *Lima News* [Lima, OH], 14 Feb. 1978, p. 17.

"'King' Rated Last in Nielsen Survey." *The Town Talk* [Alexandria, LA], 15 Feb. 1978, p. 8.

"'King' Reaction Mixed Among Viewers in Cenla [i.e., Central Louisiana]." *The Town Talk* [Alexandria, LA], 15 Feb. 1978, p. A8.

Lepkin, Marion. "TV's 'King' a Noble Victim of Sadly Badly Placed Ads." *Winnipeg Free Press* [Winnipeg, MB, CAN], 17 Feb. 1978, p.26.

Mermigas, Diane. "Even with All Its Flaws, 'King' Packs a Wallop." *Arlington Heights Daily Herald* [Arlington Heights, IL], 11 Feb. 1978, Sec 3, p. 5.

_____. "'King' Producer and Actor Hope Their Film Encourages Nonviolence." *Arlington Heights Daily Herald* [Arlington Heights, IL], 11 Feb. 1978, Sec 3, p. 5.

"More Words About 'King.'" *The Los Angeles Times*, 6 Mar. 1978, p. 52.

Morrison, Don. "TV Shows Courage in 'King' Portrait." *The Minneapolis Star*, 16 Feb. 1978, p. 47.

"NBC's 'King' Starting Three-Night Run." *Winchester Evening Star* [Winchester, VA], 11 Feb. 1978, p. 14.

O'Meara, Brian. "King Program Sovereign Fare." *Ottawa Journal* 67 [Ottawa, ON, CAN], 15 Feb. 1978, p. 67.

Peters, Ida. "I'm Not Crying over 'King.'" *Baltimore Afro American*, 18 Feb. 1978, p. 16.

Piety, Harold. "King Show Recalled an Ugly, Turbulent Era." *The Journal Herald* [Dayton, OH], 17 Feb. 1978, p. 10.

Shales, Tom. "'King,' a Controversial Portrait." *Washington Post*, 11 Feb. 1978. www.washingtonpost.com/archive/lifestyle/1978/02/11/king-a-controversial-portrait/b9b5ce65-b3bd-42a6-b21d-8ab9c4095868/?utm_term=.d042b911ac62.

Shippy, Dick. "Stirring TV Drama 'King' a Fine Tribute to Greatness." *The Akron Beacon Journal* [Akron, OH], 16 Feb. 1978, p. 64.

Smallwood, David, and Harmon Perry. "TV Film of King Provokes Anger of His Top Associates." *Jet*, 9 Mar. 1978, pp. 12-17.

Smith, Cecil. "'King'—A Salute with Honor and Love." *The Los Angeles Times*, 13 Feb. 1978, Part IV, p. 12.

Stoehr, Chris. "'King': Still Too Close for Prime-Time Comfort." *Detroit Free Press*, 16 Feb. 1978, p. 2.

Tuttle, Lisa. "Last Two Parts of 'King' a Must-See." *The Akron Beacon Journal* [Akron, OH], 16 Feb. 1978, p. 64.

Urschel, Joe. "'King' Triumph—If Not Quite Truth." *Detroit Free Press*, 12 Feb. 1978, p. 34.

Weller, Tim. "TV Special 'King' Called Best Program Since 'Roots.'" *The Times Herald* [Port Huron, MI], 15 Feb. 1978, p. 3.

Wilson, John M. "The Anguish of Reliving the Martin Luther King Drama." *The New York Times Archives*, 12 Feb. 1978, p. 31.

"Winfield's Emmy Seems Assured." *Pittsburgh Post-Gazette*, 15 Feb. 1978, p. 41.

Martin Luther King's *A Testament of Hope*: A Survey of Critical Reactions

Bryan Warren

One of the most impressive—and certainly one of the longest—contributions to scholarship on Martin Luther King Jr. was made by James M. Washington. In 1986, Washington edited a massive collection of King's speeches, sermons, interviews, essays, and even selections from books. *A Testament of Hope: The Essential Writings and Speeches of Martin Luther King, Jr.* clocked in at more than 700 pages. It has never gone out of print and is now available in an inexpensive paperback edition. For most people interested in King, Washington's anthology provides by far the best value for the money. And, since it puts at readers' fingertips a huge proportion of King's work, reviewers responding to Washington's efforts inevitably commented not only on the book itself but also, often, on King's ideas and career as a whole. My purpose in this essay, therefore, is to survey some of the ways people reacted to *A Testament of Hope* when it first appeared and then again, years later, when it was reprinted. Particularly noteworthy are the cautionary reviews the book received. These deserve to be better known by teachers and students, especially. Surveying reviews of this book is, therefore, worthwhile for that reason alone.

Early Reviews: Roger Wilkins

A particularly important early review of Washington's book was written by Roger Wilkins, a leading advocate for civil rights for African Americans. Wilkins's review was published in the *Washington Post*, one of the nation's major newspapers. (It was also printed in Britain's *Guardian*.) According to Wilkins, *A Testament of Hope* demonstrated "powerfully that in his lifetime and in most memories, King was underrated" (n.p.). King was remembered, Wilkins thought, mainly as a speaker and a leader, but Washington's collection helped reveal that "King had a piercing intellect which he employed relentlessly in examining, analyzing and criticizing a nation that had wronged him and his people, but which he loved with a Christian passion" (n.p.). In Wilkins's opinion, it was not

> surprising that King's intellect is largely unremarked since our pictures of him are mainly filtered through white lenses. Whites have a hard time ascribing intellectual gifts to blacks, who are often described as eloquent, passionate and articulate, but rarely as acute, reflective, analytical or brilliant. King was brilliant. (n.p.)

Wilkins expressed wonder at the sheer "mass of the written legacy of King's brief public career, which began in December 1955 and ended in April 1968" (n.p.). Especially when considering all the other demands on King's time, Wilkins said that "the volume and quality of this intellectual work is breathtaking" (n.p.). He thought that King's

> earliest writings—his narrowest—can be characterized not just as descriptions of the Montgomery bus boycott and elucidations of his nonviolent philosophy, but also as an urgent search for intellectual tools to break out of the fences that surrounded him. He laid hands on the philosophy of nonviolence and the ideas of Tillich, Gandhi and Niebuhr, among others, as crowbars to break out of fundamentalism, segregation and oppression. (n.p.)

But these early writings, in Wilkins' opinion, "have nothing of the power and the sweep of his later vision" (n.p.). Instead, Wilkins argued that as King aged and became more experienced, "he began to include the social impotence of the white church in his list of concerns. Then, with his thought under siege from segregationists, other black leaders, the concept of black power, racism in the North and the poison of the Vietnam War, King's vision flowered and grew—always from the twin seeds of Christianity and nonviolence" (n.p.). Wilkins considered many of King's ideas "still fresh today" and said that they even "contain lessons that could instruct contemporary black conservatives who seem to believe that they have invented the idea of black self-help" (n.p.). Wilkins contended that King's mind, although starting "from the narrow structures of Baptist fundamentalism and southern segregation," had "battled through wave after wave of orthodoxy and opposition to cut past the two prevailing ideologies of his time to a deeper and richer vision of his beloved America" (n.p.). He had become not just "a champion of southern blacks" but also an advocate for all of America's poor and a "force for peace and American decency" in the world as well (n.p.).

Early Reviews: Edmonds, McKibben, Fishman, Gilkes, Gottshall, Franklin, Garrow, and Tierce

Less completely positive than the Wilkins review was a brief notice published in *Library Journal*, in which Anthony O. Edmonds called the book's structure "confusing" (146). He claimed that its organization—"by literary genre"—was unfortunate, and he also suggested that it contained too much "repetitious material." He nevertheless called it "the best one-volume compendium of King's written legacy" (146). Bill McKibben, in a review for the *New Yorker*, also noted that what made it "startling" was to see how often King repeated quotations and passages, "especially for his thundering perorations" (108). McKibben claimed, however, that King used these tested passages to keep his speeches "ringing in the ears of his readers." He noted, in particular, that King often quoted William Cullen Bryant and frequently echoed the concluding lines from James Russell Lowell's "powerful" hymn "Once to Every Man and Nation," which was a "product of the abolition era" (108). But rather than faulting King for repeating himself, McKibben seemed to admire his instincts to rely on material he knew had been effective in previous speeches.

In a more substantial review, T. A. Fishman offered some background information about the anthology. He observed, for example, that it was compiled at the request of King's widow, Coretta Scott King. He also noted various topics stressed in the collection, such as the "necessity of passive resistance, the need for eloquent speakers, and the difficulties caused by internal conflicts within the movement" (n.p.). Fishman reported that, according to

Washington, King "as a public figure" sometimes received help when inventing and composing his works," but he argued that the volume should nonetheless be celebrated as a record of "the principles [King] espoused and the ideals for which he stood" (n.p.). Fishman relayed Washington's view that the volume's chronological structure allowed readers to "chart aspects of King's philosophical development," showing how his thoughts and expression changed in response to "the changing political and social climate of America" (n.p.;).[1] Despite these changes, however, Fishman thought that King's focus—"the necessity of nonviolent civil disobedience in order to accomplish the greater good of racial equality"—remained strong and evident throughout *A Testament of Hope*.

While agreeing with some other critics that the book's organization is flawed, Cheryl Townsend Gilkes argued that this shortcoming merely "reflects the difficulty with which King's thought is placed into discrete editorial categories" (274). She asserted that the anthology would be useful for students, writing that it could "provide an opportunity, especially in seminars, to reflect upon thinking that evolved over time, wrestled with complex issues, and never settled comfortably with simple answers to difficult and still-perplexing" problems (275). She also claimed that the book would help readers "gain an appreciation" for King's diverse, widespread audience (275). Perhaps most important, she pointed out the value of King's scholarship and praised his "clear, highly communicable, consistent, but complex responses to his critics and his circumstances" (275).

Rich Gottshall, in a review for the *Indianapolis Star*, also commended Washington's anthology. He argued that unlike some other recent work on King, this book allowed readers to "draw their own conclusions" about him through samplings of his writings (102). By reading *A Testament of Hope*, Gottshall asserted, readers would be able independently "to see his logic, to feel his passions, to understand his brilliance" (102). He thought the book's "strongest" portions consisted of King's sermons and suggested that readers take the sermons slowly, "reading each word at a time, and imagining them spoken with the power of one of America's greatest orators"

(102). Gottshall argued that even if a reader had never heard Dr. King speak, the "power of his oratory is unmistakable" and would be evident simply from reading *A Testament of Hope* (102). Robert Franklin, in a review for the *Journal of Religion*, claimed that the volume "delivers precisely what its title promises" (430). He said that Washington applied his "deft editorial skills" to King's "vast literary corpus" (430). Although he lamented that Washington's introductory essay was "too brief," he claimed that Washington did effectively place King in "historical and cultural context" (431).

David J. Garrow, a major King scholar, reviewed the book for the *Journal of Church and State*. Garrow credited Washington with performing a "valuable service" by bringing together a "sizeable number" of "oftentimes obscure and hard to obtain" magazine articles and public speeches (537). He called King's sermons "far and away the most valuable sources for appreciating and understanding" central elements of King's story (537). However, he lamented that only a small number of the sermons, some of which existed in rare texts or on audiotapes, had been published. Garrow regretted that Washington's collection lacked many "immensely valuable unpublished" sermons, which he claimed were "numerous" and especially "helpful" for understanding "the last three years of King's life" (537). Garrow suggested that this circumstance could have arisen from literary property concerns of King's widow, Coretta, and of the King estate. He asserted that the sermons' absence was "most unfortunate" and said that, while the reprinted pieces from the 1950s and early 1960s gave an "excellent picture" of King's thinking, the post-1965 pieces failed "to convey . . . the emotional richness or growing political radicalism that are evident in the unpublished King sermons from those later years" (537). Garrow closed his review by stating that Washington's "useful" annotations made clear that King's major books and magazine articles were often drafted with assistance, but he observed that this kind of assistance was common in the writings of almost all major public figures of the last half-century. He argued that because the sermons were largely written by King himself, they carried "yet further special value." In Garrow's view, the sermons represent "a far purer trove" than the works written with others' assistance since the sermons were delivered "both extemporaneously and from a superb memory" (538).

In an assessment published in the *South Atlantic Review*, Mike Tierce gave an often mixed judgment of Washington's book. He claimed that Washington was correct to assert that "the general public and students in various colleges, universities, and seminaries need a handy set of the published writings of King" (167-68). He credited the volume with helping to "establish King as one of the most significant American writers of the past twenty-five years" (168). Tierce went on to call the anthology "ideal" for any reader "engaged in serious study of King's writings" (168). He praised the "excellent" bibliography and claimed that it would facilitate "scholarly research" (168). But he also called the anthology "mammoth" and asserted that, for the general public and for students, it would be "simply too long" (168). Tierce claimed that the selections of King's philosophical arguments had a "repetitious nature" that would frustrate most readers by forcing them to rehash material that was sometimes even repeated "word-for-word" (168).

Tierce's objections to *A Testament of Hope* did not concern simply its size. He argued that, while Washington included King's "essential writings," the volume contained "one significant omission": it lacked King's inaugural address to the Montgomery Improvement Association, a speech that occurred three days after Rosa Parks's arrest in December 1955. Tierce asserted that this speech "christened the Civil Rights Movement" and demonstrated that King had the rhetorical skills to "be its most effective spokesman" (169). He did concede that parts of the speech are included in King's book *Stride Toward Freedom* (excerpted in *A Testament of Hope*) but called Washington's "failure to reprint the entire text" a "glaring oversight" (169).

However, Tierce did commend Washington for putting together a volume that, despite its "weaknesses," left "little doubt" that King deserved literary attention, especially in college classrooms (169). He regretted that student exposure to King is typically limited to brief notices in history and sociology textbooks that "supply two or three photographs of King, . . . reprint a few notable excerpts from his writings, and offer biographical blurbs about his role in Montgomery, Birmingham, and other civil rights confrontations" (169). Tierce went on to say that students "should be surprised" to find King's writings absent from "customary anthologies" used in American literature courses (169). He called this absence a "terrible oversight" and objected to arguments that King's writings are of only "historical and political importance" and are not significant as literature. He mentioned Bradford, Winthrop, and Lincoln as writers typically read in American literature courses and whose importance was also "chiefly historical and political." Tierce asserted that King was "very likely the most historically and politically influential American writer of the last twenty-five years" (169). He declared that "any figure who [could] use his writing skills to hold a nation's attention as King did" deserves literary recognition (169). Tierce ended by calling King's inclusion in American literature anthologies "essential" and claimed that there "simply is no defensible reason for continuing to ignore the literary value of King's writings" (170).

Later Reviews: Ralph Luker

The reviews already cited appeared in either 1986 or 1987, shortly after the original publication of Washington's anthology. But Ralph Luker, in an important 1993 review for *Church History*, provided perhaps the most substantive and searching response to *A Testament of Hope*. He called the collection "an important anthology of Martin Luther King's published work" and praised Washington for compiling "the most important King texts . . . into a single handy and hefty volume" (303-04). He noted that Washington had divided the book partially thematically and partially by genre in order to help readers "grapple with the sheer bulk and disparate character of the material" (304). Luker also reported that Washington had organized the documents "chronologically" and that he had "added an introductory essay, a bibliography of primary sources by and secondary sources on King, and editorial notes placing each document in historical context" (304). Luker argued that the volume's size was both a strength and a weakness. He suggested that a reader could be almost certain to find any key text associated with King in the book, but he argued that only a "splendid cross-indexing of biblical references, names, quotations, places, subjects, and themes" could help solve the problem of the volume's sheer bulk (304). Luker worried that King's major passages on "religious, social, and political thought" could be lost among the extensive selections of his sermons, speeches, essays, interviews, and books (304).

Perhaps most important, Luker pointed out errors in the book's introductory essay, notes, and index. He noted, for instance, how "almost randomly" the index either "correctly located, ignored, [or] found references to names and places in King's texts where they did not exist" (304). King often referred to people simply by using their last names, but the index (according to Luker) frequently misidentified those persons. Luker noted that Washington, unfortunately, had failed to make any of the needed corrections in the updated paperback edition although he *had* made changes to the introductory essay. In fact, Luker claimed that the revised edition added even more flaws, and he called the bibliography "frozen in time" (305).

However, Luker's commentary on the flaws of the book did not stop there. He claimed that the volume's largest shortcoming was that it "makes little contribution to King scholarship" (305). In particular, he mentioned that the book briefly refers to "sealed FBI tapes and Ralph Abernathy's controversial autobiographical revelations," calling these references "gratuitous without being illuminating" (305). Luker detailed how Washington acknowledged the "interrelated problems of ghost writing and . . . repetition and unacknowledged borrowing in King's texts" but regretted that Washington never discussed King's "method of composition" (305).

Luker concluded his reservations about the book by wondering what should be made of King's repeated "invocation of memorable lines from William Cullen Bryant, Thomas Carlyle, Victor Hugo, James Weldon Johnson, and James Russell Lowell" (305). He questioned whether such repetitions should be seen as "poetic expressions" of his beliefs or "misleading signs" of King's real thoughts (305). Finally, Luker argued that while Washington's book "will continue to make important King texts accessible to the public," scholars would find more value in Clayborne Carson's ongoing series for the University of California Press, *The Papers of Martin Luther King, Jr.*

Final Thoughts

A Testament of Hope still has enormous value, especially as an inexpensive text for classroom use and for general readers. It is remarkably comprehensive, putting at one's fingertips an enormous selection of King's writings. For most purposes, it is still a text very much worth owning. One hopes, however, that when it is next reprinted, the errors cited by Luker will be addressed. Doing this will help make *A Testament of Hope* even more worth purchasing than it already is.

Note

1. For another comment on the chronological organization, see Claude Sitton: "King's persuasiveness comes through again and again in this 676-page collection . . . . [Instead of the thematic structure of the book, a] simple chronological format would have enabled the reader to follow more easily the progression of King's thoughts . . . . However, each item in the table of contents is dated by year, enabling the diligent to trace that path" (17).

Works Cited or Consulted

"Books." Review of *A Testament of Hope: The Essential Writings and Speeches of Martin Luther King, Jr.*, edited by James M. Washington. *Antioch Review*, vol. 49, no. 3, Summer 1991, p. 470. *EBSCOhost*, search.ebscohost.com/login.aspx?direct=true&db=lfh&AN=9604022509&site=ehost-live. Accessed 23 Oct. 2018.

Edmonds, Anthony O. Review of *A Testament of Hope: The Essential Writings and Speeches of Martin Luther King, Jr.*, edited by James M. Washington. *Library Journal*, 1 Apr. 1986, p. 146.

Fishman, T. A. "Testament of Hope." Review of *A Testament of Hope: The Essential Writings and Speeches of Martin Luther King, Jr.*, edited by James M. Washington. *Identities & Issues in Literature*,

Sept. 1997, p. 1. *EBSCOhost,* search.ebscohost.com/login.aspx?direct=true&db=lfh&AN=103331INI16280209303362&site=ehost-live. Accessed 23 Oct. 2018.

Garrow, David J. Review of *A Testament of Hope: The Essential Writings and Speeches of Martin Luther King, Jr.,* edited by James M. Washington. *Journal of Church and State,* vol. 29, no. 3, 1987, pp. 537-38.

Gilkes, Cheryl Townsend. "A Testament of Hope. The Essential Writings of Martin Luther King, Jr. (Book)." Review of *A Testament of Hope: The Essential Writings and Speeches of Martin Luther King, Jr.,* edited by James M. Washington. *Journal for the Scientific Study of Religion,* vol. 26, no. 2, June 1987, pp. 274–275. *EBSCOhost,* search.ebscohost.com/login.aspx?direct=true&db=aph&AN=4897451&site=ehost-live. Accessed 23 Oct. 2018.

Gottshall, Rich. "Civil Rights Leader Portrayed in New Volumes." Review of *A Testament of Hope: The Essential Writings and Speeches of Martin Luther King, Jr.,* edited by James M. Washington. *The Indianapolis Star,* 9 Feb. 1986, p. 102. www.newspapers.com/image/106183438. Accessed 23 Oct. 2018.

Hornbaker, Alice. "King's Writings Illuminate Mission." Review of *A Testament of Hope: The Essential Writings and Speeches of Martin Luther King, Jr.,* edited by James M. Washington. *Cincinnati Enquirer,* 12 Jan. 1986, F-4 *Tempo,* p. 2. www.newspapers.com/image/101761797. Accessed 18 Oct. 2018.

Luker, Ralph. Review of *A Testament of Hope: The Essential Writings and Speeches of Martin Luther King, Jr.,* edited by James M. Washington. *Church History,* vol. 62, no. 2, 1993, pp. 303-05.

McKibben, Bill. "God Within the Shadow." Review of *A Testament of Hope: The Essential Writings and Speeches of Martin Luther King, Jr.,* edited by James M. Washington. *New Yorker,* vol. 63, no. 7, Apr. 1987, pp. 102–12. *EBSCOhost,* search.ebscohost.com/login.aspx?direct=true&db=aph&AN=12691669&site=ehost-live. Accessed 23 Oct. 2018.

Sitton, Claude. Review of *A Testament of Hope: The Essential Writings and Speeches of Martin Luther King, Jr.,* edited by James M. Washington. *The New York Times Book Review,* 16 Feb. 1986, pp. 16-17.

Tate, Eleanora E. "A Life of Courage and Compassion Chronicled in New Books." Review of *A Testament of Hope: The Essential Writings and*

Speeches of Martin Luther King, Jr., edited by James M. Washington. *The Des Moines Register*, 19 Jan. 1986, p. 21. www.newspapers.com/image/132053512. Accessed 23 Oct. 2018.

Tierce, Mike. Review of *A Testament of Hope: The Essential Writings and Speeches of Martin Luther King, Jr.*, edited by James M. Washington. *South Atlantic Review*, vol. 51, no. 4, 1986, pp. 167-70.

Washington, James M., editor. *A Testament of Hope: The Essential Writings and Speeches of Martin Luther King, Jr.* Harper, 1986.

Wilkins, Roger. "The Mind of Martin Luther King, Jr." Review of *A Testament of Hope: The Essential Writings and Speeches of Martin Luther King, Jr.*, edited by James M. Washington. *The Washington Post*, 19 Jan. 1986, www.washingtonpost.com/archive/entertainment/books/1986/01/19/the-mind-of-martin-luther-king/5c8fd225-2b87-40a7-8ba8-2fc30315464b/?utm_term=.7316c4b63c94. Accessed 23 Oct. 2018. [Also published, with the same title, in *The Guardian* [England], 23 Feb. 1986, p. 18.

Williams, Rev. Cecil. "The Dream Lives On." Review of *A Testament of Hope: The Essential Writings and Speeches of Martin Luther King, Jr.*, edited by James M. Washington. *The San Francisco Examiner*, 19 Jan. 1986, pp. 1, 4.

Martin Luther King: An Interview with Charles Johnson

Marshall D. Buford

MDB: I wondered if you have any initial thoughts about Martin Luther King as an orator.

CJ: Well, in the nineteenth century, if I'm not mistaken, oratory was very important. It was a skill; it was something that one worked at. You see it beautifully in Frederick Douglass, for example, even in Booker T. Washington and the speeches and talks he gave. They didn't have the advantage of microphones for big crowds; they had to project just using their voices. In my mind we don't have anybody right now that's standing at the microphone and giving speeches who can equal those nineteenth-century oratorical skills. I think we could probably say it's a lost art. It probably became a lost art when television began to dominate. . . . Great speeches are rare these days but King's speeches, some of them, are very beautiful. They are clear; they lift the spirit; they give us a vision of what America could possibly be if it had lived up to its ideals as expressed in our secular sacred documents, such as the Declaration of Independence and the Constitution. King was a powerful speaker, and during the march on Washington his "I Have a Dream" speech was televised and President Kennedy was watching it and he was just impressed by how powerful this man was as an orator. That speech, like all the speeches and sermons King delivered, begins with a quiet, almost academic statement of his thesis. Then it builds, often using key-word repetition—"I have a dream"—to drive home his point repeatedly, and the speeches finally end in a crescendo of emotion fused with intellectual acuity.

MDB: Are there any speeches besides the "I Have a Dream" speech which you think equal that one?

CJ: Oh, absolutely. I mean the "I Have a Dream" speech is always quoted, and you know that's not the speech he prepared the night before. He abandoned the speech he stayed up working on and just went with a theme or a refrain he had been using in other speeches—you know, about America issuing a bad check to black people. One of the speeches I do refer to a lot (I believe he gave it during his interview as a minister; it got him the job in Montgomery) was one he also delivered at St. Paul's Cathedral when he was on his way to receive the Nobel Peace Prize. This speech is about "the three dimensions of a complete life." Here—I'll read it; I actually wrote something about it quite recently. . . . In this speech he reminded his audience that the first dimension of a complete life involved self-acceptance and the development of one's personal resources and doing a life's work "so well that the living, the dead, or the unborn couldn't do it any better." The second dimension was learning that "there is nothing greater than to do something for others." And the third dimension for King, as a theologian and the nation's most prominent preacher and moral voice in the 1960s, was a quest for the divine because "we were made for God and we will be restless until we find rest in him." My wife recently pointed out to me that that line—"we will be restless until we rest in God"—that's actually from St. Augustine. So King is actually paraphrasing. That's very impressive also.

I studied a lot, before I wrote my novel *Dreamer*, in the three volumes of the papers of King. They were coming out as I worked on that novel. I prepared for writing that book for seven years, all total, but especially for two years before I wrote a single word. So I looked at all that material, including his letters home when he was a high school student. You've got everything about King in there, even his height and weight. I've read the speeches and the sermons; I did scansion on the sermons to see the rhythm of King's voice, how he actually pronounced things. I went to the Lorraine Motel, where he was killed, as I worked on *Dreamer*.

That novel is about the Chicago campaign and the last two years of his life. I remember that campaign because I was a senior in high school in a suburb of Chicago called Evanston. I remember King coming. It was his first and only Northern campaign, and I chose to portray it because most people don't talk about that campaign. King and his followers really weren't successful and electrifying in Chicago as they had been in Birmingham and Montgomery. During this entire campaign he was kind of outmaneuvered there, in Chicago, by Mayor Richard Daley. I know that area; I know that world; I grew up in that world and worked as a reporter for the *Chicago Tribune* during my undergraduate days. . . . I was a high school senior when he came, and to be perfectly honest, as a young black male in Chicago I felt attracted more to Malcolm X than I did to Martin Luther King Jr. because I didn't believe in turning the other cheek if somebody attacked me or somebody that I loved. King's nonviolent approach didn't sit well with many younger black people in the sixties. . . .

You know, King is very often portrayed in a one-dimensional way as just a civil rights leader for black Americans. But wasn't there more to this man? Did he say other things about how we should live?. . . Didn't he say things that would be useful to my son in the eighties, when he was growing up? Of course he did. This very speech that I was just reading to you from—"The Three Dimensions of a Complete Life"—that speech is applicable to everybody, to any human being. So in *Dreamer* I said "Let me just see if I can give a portrait of King that is different than the one that's airbrushed— you know, where all his scars and sweat and spiritual struggles have been erased from his face. . . . He was thirty-nine, I believe, when he was assassinated. So what motivated me was my deep desire to understand King better and to present a portrait of King that shows the profiles that we normally don't see. *Dreamer* is the only novel I can think of or that I know about that actually portrays King as a theologian and philosopher, in his fullness, as well as a civil rights activist and leader.

I examine three stages in King's life—first when he shows up in Montgomery. He's the new minister in town. There are older ministers who could have led the Montgomery Improvement Association or the bus boycott but one wasn't in town or others were unavailable. so King got this leadership role. . . . Next, . . .there's another King that emerges by the time he gets the Nobel Peace Prize, . . . and he suddenly sees himself as an international advocate for peace. That's the second King that I see. And then, toward the end, which is the period my book covers—the last few years of his life—he becomes even larger than that. He becomes the one man who could combine the civil rights movement with the antiwar movement and the labor movement. He goes to Memphis to help the black garbagemen, who are not in a labor union. So he could have become this powerful figure, really, by combining those three threads (labor, civil rights, and antiwar) in the late sixties.

MDB: What sort of secondary sources did you use? How did you find out the nitty-gritty details of his life?

CJ: Well, I literally read everything that I could get my hands on regarding King, including all his papers. . . . I read biographies of King and studies of King as a theologian; I listened to his speeches and sermons. I went to the places where he was born and died. One very good book is *Let the Trumpet Sound* by Stephen Oates. . . . I love *Let the Trumpet Sound* because it's a very powerful history book written as a suspenseful story. . . .

MDB: During the years that you spent doing research, did you find that there were any other civil rights leaders who were on a par with King who were maybe overshadowed by his fame and time on TV?

CJ: Well, I think Adam Clayton Powell felt a certain competition with King. King himself would look at the newspapers and when there was a poll taken about who is the greatest civil rights leader and it would be him he would say to himself "Well, I shouldn't be like this; I shouldn't be so vain and competitive with others," but he felt pleased that he always came out on the top of those polls. He was a young guy. Think about it for a minute: in the 1950s, following World War II, we were looking for youth, we were looking for young people, like a young president (JFK), right? We were looking for new people, and then in the sixties you get the Beatles. We were looking for youth and vitality, and that's King. Now there had been other civil rights leaders around for a while, for decades, such as the guy [A. Philip Randolph] who organized the Pullman porters. It goes all the way back to early in the century with those really heroic black men and women who prepared for King during the era of segregation. His father—"Daddy King"— was certainly in that group; so was, definitely, W. E. B. Du Bois and the founders of the NAACP. The NAACP would get a test case that you could bring into the courts, that showed the egregious nature of discrimination and segregation. And that approach—that legal approach—was very effective and it was what really brought to an end the Montgomery bus boycott, because that case dragged on for a year until the Supreme Court, I believe, made a decision. That was the NAACP approach.

Well, the approach of King and the Southern Christian Leadership Conference was to go into a community and dramatically demonstrate the discrimination. For example, they would break a law by going into a place to get a meal or something. If you were black, you weren't supposed to eat with whites. Restaurants were segregated. King and the SCLC dramatized the problem. It was the age of television, so to see violence used against them, particularly in Birmingham, was electrifying. Those two approaches were supposed to work together—the active approach of the SCLC and King and the legal approach of the NAACP. . . . And there's one more layer that's on top of all of this: it was televised for the world and therefore seen by the Russians, by the Soviets, so they could point their finger at America during the Cold War and say "Well, you talk about freedom, about what you stand for, America, but look at how you treat your blacks." So that was another element in the mix during that period of time.

MDB: Are there films that you would recommend that people watch if they want to get a better idea of the period?

CJ: Yes, there's a lot of them out there but I guess the series *Eyes onthe Prize* would give a pretty good overview.

MDB: Are there any other fictional books, like *Dreamer*, that you would recommend?

CJ: There's another novel that has a disguised version of King, by Julius Lester, titled *All Our Sins Forgiven*, but that's not really the same kind of book as *Dreamer*, and there's a play by Katori Hall entitled *The Mountaintop*. Actually, people in the civil rights movement didn't want her to do that play because of the way she portrays King. I have thought about this and I think one of the reasons people of my generation—black writers in my generation, the baby boomer generation—didn't really pick up on King as a subject for dramatization was because a lot of us tilted toward Malcolm X. We didn't really embrace King's idea of integration. One thing I point out in *Dreamer* as essential for King was nonviolence. Nonviolence is a way of life, which is something that Congressman John Lewis talks about. Nonviolence wasn't just a civil rights tactic; it was supposed to be a way of life. Another idea important to King was *agape*, the love that is an unselfish love, like that of a mother for her child. *Agape* is the kind of love that King talked about. But most writers of my time were more interested in Malcolm X. Malcolm X was not a nonviolent kind of guy when it came to protecting your own. But King's vision is greater; it's deeper; it's learned. Take a look at "Letter from Birmingham Jail," which he wrote without research material. He wrote it on scraps of paper and toilet paper. That is a learned man: his knowledge was at his fingertips for him to do that and under such duress, in such a pressured situation. But it became one of the most important documents in American history.

MDB: Concerning *Dreamer*: **we were talking about King and his charismatic speeches. That's what drew me to him the most, and in your book you say his sermons were "a shimmering creation" that were "so beautiful that they could convert the wolf of Gubbio." So I read that and I'm like "yes, exactly right—except that it didn't." Racist white people were the people who needed to be converted, and he didn't do it; he didn't get them to change.**

CJ: Well, yes and no, in my opinion. The example I used for agape is this: how do you love somebody like George Wallace in the fifties? He's an unlovable man standing in the door to prevent integration in the schools. But you see a change in Wallace by the seventies. You see a change in laws. . . . There were people whose lives were changed completely by King, transformed by him. I know such a person, a photographer who knew King. But there certainly existed a group of people who were not changed. In King's time there were Southern Democrats and they fled the Democratic Party after the Civil Rights Act and the Voting Rights Act, and Nixon brought them into the Republican party with his "Southern Strategy." So they moved over to the Republican Party's far right wing. The civil rights movement transformed those two parties in the sixties and they wouldn't exist as they do today if that hadn't happened.

MDB: In *Dreamer*, **you mentioned that the average Negro was making forty-seven hundred dollars per year and the cheapest apartments in the slums cost about ninety dollars a month. But the Chicago operations were costing ten thousand dollars per month. Where was the money coming from?**

CJ: They raised money in churches. Harry Belafonte out in Hollywood was getting other actors that he knew to support the movement. King donated the $54,000 prize money he received for the Nobel Peace Prize to SCLC, CORE, SNCC, the NAACP, and the National Council of Negro Women for Nonviolence.

MDB: You mention that King lived in one place—you sort of call it a urinal—where people were just peeing in the doorway and it was just a total firetrap. Were you saying that he lived there to try to keep himself as sort of a "man of the people" and not staying in the hotels?

CJ: Yes, that's absolutely right. He would move his family into a place like that, and the effect on his children and Coretta was grim. I mean, it was depressing, but at the same time he moved in there to make a point.

MDB: My final question is this: do you believe that he knew he was going to be killed and that his death would advance the cause?

CJ: Immediately after his death, areas in cities all over America erupted with violence. The black militants who had been opposed to King—the black power people like Stokely Carmichael—said that here was the apostle of nonviolence killed violently, so nonviolence doesn't work. That's when the shift happened, in sixty-eight. The idea of nonviolent resistance was dismissed and you had all these guerilla warfare groups, such as the Black Liberation Army and the Symbionese Liberation Army, pursuing their violent approaches. I think that's wrong, sure, but Gandhi was also killed and so was Jesus. History points to the fact that some of the advocates for nonviolence met violent ends. But it's important to realize, I believe, that no one could kill their ideals and the transformative impact that Gandhi had on India and that King had on America and the entire world.

Martin Luther King: Interviews with People Who Personally Heard Him Speak

Donna Yvette Smith

Editor's note. In the following interviews, Donna Yvette Smith, a longtime resident of the Tuskegee and Montgomery, Alabama, areas, speaks with some even longer-time residents—people who often personally heard Martin Luther King speak and whose lives were directly affected by his efforts to promote civil rights. The interviewees include the following: (1) Janice Dickson, a member of the Golden Life Center at Greater St. Mark Missionary Baptist Church in Tuskegee, Alabama; (2) Annabelle Freeman, also a member of Golden Life; (3) Joyce German, born 1949, a retired medical laboratory technician; (4) Lollie Henderson, another member of the Golden Life Center; (5) Gwen Johnson, also a member of the Golden Life Center; (6) Shirley Mills, one more member of the Golden Life Center; (7) Pastor C. P. Noble, born 1944, a retired educator who has been the pastor of Greater St. Mark Missionary Baptist Church in Tuskegee, Alabama, for forty-one years; (8) Vera Smith, born 1946, a retired nurse who spent her career working for the V.A. Hospital, now known as CAVHCS (Central Alabama Veterans' Health Care System) in Tuskegee, Alabama; (9) Ethel Williams, born 1922, a retired seamstress, mother of six, grandmother of 22, great-grandmother of 27, and great-great grandmother of 5. Most members of the Golden Life Center are now in their eighties.

DYS: When did you see Dr. King speak?

Gwen Johnson: I don't know what day of the week it was but it was the [televised] March on Washington.

Lollie Henderson: When he made the speech, uh, I think it was the "Mountaintop." I was in high school.

Ethel Williams: I never got a chance to see him, but I did attend a mass meeting. Some years ago they were held here in different churches in Tuskegee. We couldn't get in because of the crowd, but I could hear him speak [while I stood] on the outside. People were sitting on cars and whatever . . . it was exciting.

Annabelle Freeman: I was young—I don't remember the age, but I remember that the campus had their Homecoming, or either graduation, one of the two, and he was there, but it was so crowded that my mom had kids and we all didn't go down to really see him, but we could see him from afar off.

Shirley Mills: I saw Dr. King during the bus boycott. Here in Macon County he would come up to Greenwood and I think Mt. Olive [church], and the youth choirs would sing at these gatherings, and we were members of Solomon Chapel at that time. Mr. Phillips would take us, and that's how I got to see him.

DYS: For those of you who got to see or hear him, what was the situation around his speech or sermon?

Ethel Williams: It concerned civil rights. They were having the mass meetings.

Janice Dickson: I can remember when blacks didn't have laws, and Martin Luther King spoke on behalf of blacks, saying "Why? They have a conscience. They can think, they can feel—why shouldn't they have laws?"

DYS: Do you remember what it felt like to hear him speak?

Ethel Williams: It was a wonderful thing to be able to attend this [sort of meeting] and be with other people. That's what I thought. It was a wonderful experience for me. I left my kids at home and went to see what Dr. King had to say.

Shirley Mills: There was something about his voice that was very powerful. People wanted to hear him.

Annabelle Freeman: If you heard his voice, even on the radio, you stopped what you were doing to listen. He spoke for everyone, on behalf of all the people.

Janice Dickson: He was young, but he spoke for nonviolence. A lot of people agreed with that.

Shirley Mills: Still there were young folk who wanted the opposite. They wanted to fight. Everybody didn't agree.

Annabelle Freeman: Still, everybody respected Dr. King even when they didn't agree. He was a leader. People just wanted to follow him.

Ethel Williams: The closest thing we've had since was Obama. (Everyone agrees.)
They both spoke for the people, those who couldn't speak for themselves.

DYS: What made Dr. King an effective speaker?

Vera Smith: Dr. King was a forceful speaker, powerful, and very clearly articulated. We knew exactly what he was saying. He kind of sounded like a Baptist preacher, which I was used to hearing, and so it made me sit up to listen even more attentively because it was of the style of the church.

C. P. Noble: Dr. King was a motivator who took the movement, the civil rights movement, the voters' rights, the removal of all vestiges of racism, took it to heart and felt called and compelled to be that leader we needed, and as a result of his prayers and his own seeking God's building guiding him as he guided us made him an effective communicator at the cause and motivated us to follow him no matter what. It didn't mean that we cast all caution to the wind, but because we believed so dearly in the cause and the leader that was leading us, we really put everything on the line for their sake.

Joyce German: I think his ability to use language that affected both educated and uneducated people—he had a way of educating the uneducated person and the educated person he had a way of communicating comfortably with, and that's not an easy thing to do.

DYS: If you ever heard him speak in person, do you remember anything in particular about his style or delivery?

Vera Smith: Like I just mentioned, the style seemed like that of a pastor. It is one where you take a text . . . he had scriptural kinds of leanings in what he was saying. He was always leaning towards the Bible, so to me it had more weight than just coming out and saying things that were, you know, of course, correct, but it was more weighty because it was also tied into our scripture.

Ethel Williams: He also understood what his race had been through—the trials and tribulations, and whatever he said, it was just down to earth, and we could understand what he was trying to say to us. We just believed in what he was saying because he was so dynamic.

C. P. Noble: He was spiritual in that he used the word of God. He was intellectual, meaning that he could use quotes from any number of sources. He was scholarly, and yet he was all of that, but so down to earth and able to communicate with any and everybody.

Joyce German: You know, I'm used to Baptist preachers. So he had almost a preacher-like style, but at the same time there was an eloquence to it that augmented that preacher-like style that I was used to.

DYS: Was there any speech or sermon he did that you thought was particularly memorable? If so, why?

Vera Smith: The "I See the Promised Land" speech was one that was almost like he had a premonition . . . that is the one he did right before he was killed—the one where he said that he had seen over into the Promised Land—that one. That one had a great impact on me but after the fact when it appeared to me that he actually foresaw what was going to happen to him, and for that reason, I said, "My goodness—he is, this is something that is beyond this earth." Because it seemed like he had predicted what was going to happen, and he saw the Promised Land, he knew what was going to happen. I was looking at heaven. He probably was also talking about the fact that one day we would all be, we would all get along better than we were at that time. Life and conditions in this country would be better.

Ethel Williams: He was not afraid. It seemed like all fear was gone. Whatever happened, it was alright with him 'cause God was watching over him.

C. P. Noble: Yes, the one in Memphis where he said he was going to the mountaintop, the one he did at the National Mall in D.C.— "I Have a Dream"—those are the most memorable. I don't remember the topics as such, as when he spoke to us in Selma and when I also heard him speak at different rallies in Montgomery, but all of them left us spiritually uplifted and motivated to take part and play our part in the role of our own liberation.

Joyce German: At the time when I was . . . actually when he was speaking in a very routine and regular basis, I don't really think I was really listening. It all became rhetoric to me because I was maybe 15, 16, 17 at the time, and so I wasn't listening. I was listening to tones rather than actual words. I knew that there was something going on, there was some movement going on, and I was listening but I was feeling at the same time, so not particularly. Not any one particularly stands out to me. It was the tone that he took with most of them that really resonates with me.

DYS: Did you ever hear him speak in a way that you thought was ineffective?

Vera Smith: I did not.

Ethel Williams: No.

C. P. Noble: No. Not one time.

Joyce German: Because we didn't necessarily have the same political philosophy as how to get to—I think we were both . . . I think there were divisions, not necessarily divisions, but different groups or pockets of thought about civil rights and how to get to specifically voting rights and those kind of things. I was not of a mindset of nonviolence, and I don't mean that I was a violent person, but Dr. King did promote a lot of nonviolence, and when I saw what was going on as a young, young adult, it was very hard for me to accept being beat on the head.

DYS: Do you recall the kinds of impressions he made on people? Do you recall anything that people said about him as a speaker?

Vera Smith: The things that I heard were positive. I read about other kinds of things that people didn't like, though. There were some who didn't go out to participate 'cause they were, um . . . even though he was not being violent, he did not promote violence, there were some who were afraid to go out there. So they were standoffish about the whole activities, but I personally did not hear anybody just come out and say it.

DYS: So what were they saying?

Vera Smith: That he shouldn't be doing what he's doing. He's gonna make them lose jobs, he's gonna make them lose their homes, he's gonna make things happen to them that were detrimental because the folks in power did not want him out there doing anything like that. Just keep the status quo and be happy with what you have, and so there were folks who were afraid they were going to lose what they had accumulated.

DYS: Did they have any particular opinion about him as a speaker?

Vera Smith: His speaking abilities? All I heard was that he was outstanding. I never heard anybody say anything different.

C. P. Noble: He was a people person. Not only could he speak to any and everybody as far as his speeches and sermons were concerned, he was approachable. He was a people person.

Joyce German: Well, sure. My parents thought that he was just about a savior, and to most of the people in the black community, that were my parents' age and what not saw him as a leader, and he was. I mean, a very effective leader in a sense. Younger people—I'm not sure if we wanted more, or were trying to push past what we saw as almost complacency, but it wasn't complacency—there's always process. Young folks don't understand process, we don't, and I mean that's just kind of slow. I think that's what I personally may have been feeling.

DYS: When did you first become aware of him? What was your first impression of him?

Vera Smith: When the marches started... the boycott in Montgomery, when people stopped getting on the buses. That's when I first heard about him. I was quite young. I don't think I had one [an impression]. I didn't quite understand what was going on at that time. By the time I was getting towards high school and college, we actually started doing the marches in Tuskegee. Then I could understand what he was doing back in the fifties. It was only after I became old enough to participate myself that I understood what he was doing. He was a man ahead of his time, he was strong and not fearful—because those were very fearful times during that period. I remember the mass meetings that were held at Tuskegee, and that was fearful, 'cause they (pointing at Ethel Williams) used to go to the mass meetings, and we would be home with the babysitter or somebody, and there was one of the times, during the bus boycott I think, it had to be in the fifties... that was scary because we would see things, we would hear about crosses being burned in the yards, in some people's yards and at some of the churches, even here in Tuskegee. So it was just scary. You were always afraid someone would come and harm us. I was scared for him too because he was out there leading.

C. P. Noble: I became aware of him as a youngster in Troy, Alabama, while he was leading the bus boycott in Montgomery. I think I was probably in elementary school, somewhere along in there. But I got involved because my hometown was not involved in that type of thing as I was growing up even though it was only about forty-nine or fifty miles away. It almost seemed like we were in a completely different world, but I was very much aware of what he was going about doing, even though I had to watch it on black and white TV. [He was] unusually gifted, unusually powerful, unusually motivating.

Joyce German: I became aware of Martin Luther King through my parents and through speeches that I heard and through rallies because during the time that I was actually coming up, there were a lot of church rallies, a lot of public rallies, and Martin Luther King was in some of them before he became so very prominent. He was in this local area, so I may have had occasion to see him maybe more than once, I'm not sure, but the impact on me in terms of him being there was more that I could see the excitement in my parents and the people who were rearing me at the time, you know, my community, so that excited me because they were excited.

DYS: Do you think there were any other leaders at the time who were as effective as he was as a speaker? If so, who were they?

Ethel Williams: Not at that time. No.

Vera Smith: During the sixties there were some other folk that came out . . .

Ethel Williams: Other ministers . . .

Vera Smith: Like Stokely Carmichael and some of those other folks that came out like the Black Panthers. They had a large following at that time. There were the Black Muslims, and what was the guy's name that got killed? He was assassinated too—a lot of folks listened to him. We didn't, but a lot of folks did listen to him . . . Malcolm X. Malcolm had a . . . his was more forceful and not free of violence, I don't think, and for that reason I didn't go for him. I had been indoctrinated by Dr. King's nonviolence, but there were folks who listened to him and joined up with some of the groups who would do things . . .

Ethel Williams: But he [Malcolm X] did have a change of heart. I think he went to Mecca, and when he came back, he was a different person. That had to do with the reason he was assassinated—because of his change of heart.

C. P. Noble: There were other speakers like Fred Shuttlesworth. Abernathy was his cohort, his partner at that time. He was an effective speaker. There was a Reverend Anderson in Selma, Fred Reese in Selma. I mentioned Shuttlesworth, there was C. T. Vivian. Andrew Young was among them. Jesse Jackson . . . there were a number of other guys, but when Martin spoke, it was like we were given marching orders.

Joyce German: I could listen to Stokely Carmichael even though they tried to paint him as a radical. He was a very eloquent speaker. Malcolm X was also a very eloquent speaker . . . they all had things to say and different perspectives, but things to say.

DYS: Do you recall your reaction to Dr. King's assassination? Were you surprised, or had you feared that such a thing might happen?

Vera Smith: I was surprised, but I always had a fear it might happen, but you never thought it would, you know. I just mostly hoped that it would not happen. It was awful. They canceled school. I was in Baltimore in school, and they canceled everything. I got caught up in the riots. There were riots there and they were shooting all through the buses and all kinds of things, and it was frightening. People were very angry. I was too, but angry to fight us. I was angry at whoever had done this evil deed. And at that time we didn't know who it was.

Ethel Williams: It was a shock. We didn't want anything to happen to him because he was our leader at that particular time.

Vera Smith: Because they had killed John Kennedy, I thought anything was possible. If you can kill the president, almost anyone can be assassinated.

C. P. Noble: I can't say I had premonitions, but I had . . . I guess you could use the word *fears*, 'cause he was exposed a lot, and there were a lot of forces that were trying to take him out. Not only was he talking about civil rights, but then he started talking about the war in Vietnam, all those kinds of things. A number of forces started gathering against him including [those opposing] civil rights. It was hurtful, it was painful to hear of his assassination. It really took the movement down a notch or two. I'm sure that was the intent of the assassination. He didn't live to see the fruits of his labor, but maybe that was just his destiny, to get us, to see the promised land but not to go into it with us. Only God can answer that question.

Joyce German: I think that I wasn't fearful of it, but I don't think I was surprised. I wasn't surprised—I was numbed by it. It wasn't a real surprise to me, it really wasn't. At that point, at such a young age, I had almost become jaded about things that were going to happen, or things that were happening. It was . . . I can't say it was shock 'cause it wasn't shock. It was remorseful and all those things that people feel when you lose someone that you know has been effective in some kind of way. It was a loss that almost was personal.

DYS: Aside from President Obama, have there been any other leaders, and especially speakers, who have impressed you as much as Dr. King did?

Ethel Williams: No.
Vera Smith: I don't know anybody who came close to him.
Joyce German: Actually, Barbara Jordan and Shirley Chisholm were very eloquent speakers to me, especially Barbara Jordan. She always impressed me. Maybe it was because of her heavy voice, I'm not sure. But she always had a way of coming across. I appreciated her eloquence in speaking.

DYS: Pastor Noble, can you tell us a bit about when you were arrested?

C. P. Noble: I was arrested as a part of that group that marched on the County Courthouse in Dallas County in Selma. This should have been the Monday or Tuesday following the bridge crossing as an attempt to still get people the opportunity to go in and register to vote. We were not told we would be arrested, but we were told about the possibility of being arrested. So we went as students protesting along with the citizens of Selma, fully aware of what could happen, so we were arrested and taken, I believe, first to the county jail. We were booked and put in a cell block—I guess that's what you call it, fingerprinted and all that type of thing. A day or two later we were taken out to Camp Selma where we spent—I think it was a work release camp—where we spent the next eight days. There was a bunch of us, students from Selma University, and I guess young people from the high schools around too, and maybe a few older adults. But there was nothing frightening about it. Nobody felt a sense of fear, even knowing that there had been some bloody bloodletting on that Sunday prior to this. We just felt like the civil rights movement was God sent, God directed. There was no fear in that.

RESOURCES

Chronology of Martin Luther King Jr.'s Life

1929	Michael King is born on January 15 in Atlanta, Georgia, to the Reverend Michael King, a minister, and his wife, Alberta, a teacher. The names of both father and son are later changed to Martin Luther King (Sr. and Jr.).
1941	On September 20, King Jr. begins his studies at Atlanta's Morehouse College.
1946	A letter by King, advocating rights for African Americans, is published on August 6 by the *Atlanta Constitution*.
1948	On February 25, King is ordained and becomes assistant pastor of his father's church (Ebenezer Baptist). On June 8, he graduates with a bachelor of arts in sociology from Morehouse. On September 14, he begins studying at Crozer Theological Seminary in Chester, Pennsylvania.
1951	In early May, King graduates from Crozer with a bachelor of divinity degree and gives the valedictory speech. On September 13, he begins studying systematic theology at Boston University.
1953	King marries Coretta Scott, from Alabama, whom he had met in Boston.
1954	On September 1, he begins serving as pastor of the Dexter Avenue Baptist Church in Montgomery, Alabama.

1955	On June 5, he receives his doctorate in systematic theology from Boston University. On November 17, his first daughter (Yolanda) is born. On December 1, Rosa Parks refuses to give up her seat in the white section of a segregated bus in Montgomery. Local women plan a one-day boycott of the bus system for December 5—the day on which the Montgomery Improvement Association is born, with King elected as its president.
1956	On January 27 (according to King), a threatening phone call leads to a spiritual revelation that gives him the strength to persist. On January 30, while King is away speaking at a meeting, his home is bombed. Fortunately, the bomb fails to injure his wife and daughter, and at a speech given from his porch later that night, King advocates a nonviolent response. By mid-November, the U.S. Supreme Court concurs with a lower court ruling that segregation of buses in Montgomery is illegal. By late December, King is one of the first people to ride on the newly desegregated buses.
1957	In January, King helps found the Southern Christian Leadership Conference and is elected its president. In mid-February, he appears on the cover of *Time* magazine. In early March, he attends independence celebrations in the new African nation of Ghana. In mid-May, he speaks to 15,000 people in Washington, D.C., and in mid-June he meets with Vice President Richard Nixon. By late October, his second child, a son, is born.
1958	The U.S. Congress passes major civil rights legislation. Later, along with other civil rights leaders, he meets with President Eisenhower. In mid-September, King publishes his first book, *Stride Toward Freedom*. A

few days later, while signing copies of the book in Harlem, he is stabbed by a deranged black woman and nearly dies.

1959	In early February, King visits India for a month and is inspired to continue his emphasis on nonviolence. He resigns as pastor of Montgomery's Dexter Avenue Baptist Church in order to move to Atlanta and devote more of his energies to the national battle for civil rights.
1960	In early February, King joins his father's Atlanta church as co-pastor while also assuming leadership of the newly founded Southern Christian Leadership Conference. In late May, a white jury in Montgomery finds him innocent of tax fraud charges. In late June, he meets with John F. Kennedy, who is running for president as a Democrat. In late October, King is arrested for participating in a sit-in demonstration at an Atlanta department store. Although sentenced to hard labor on another charge, by the end of the month he is released on bail.
1961	In late January, his third child (a second son) is born. In late May, after violent assaults in northern Alabama on "Freedom Riders" seeking to desegregate buses, King speaks to a large rally in Montgomery. In mid-October he meets with President Kennedy, asking him to issue a proclamation outlawing segregation. In late fall, segregation in interstate travel is banned by the federal government, largely as a result of violence against freedom riders who sought such a ban. In mid-December, King is arrested for trying to desegregate Albany, Georgia.
1962	At the end of July, King is jailed for two weeks in Albany, Georgia, while protesting against segregation

in that city. In late September, he is physically attacked in Birmingham by a member of the American Nazi Party.

1963	In late March, a daughter (the Kings' fourth child) is born. In mid-April, King and others are arrested and jailed in Birmingham, Alabama, sparking large protests. He spends nearly two weeks in jail and writes a famous letter rebuking "moderate" clergy members who had urged him to be more patient and accommodating. In early May, the Birmingham police violently attack civil rights protestors, generating national outrage. By the middle of the month, city officials agree to end much local segregation. Near the end of June, King leads a massive "Freedom Walk" in Detroit. At the end of August, he delivers his famous "I Have a Dream" speech before a huge crowd in Washington, D.C., as part of the largest public demonstration ever held in that city. Shortly thereafter, he meets with President Kennedy and Vice President Johnson. In mid-September, King speaks at the funerals of several young black girls killed in the bombing of a Birmingham church. In early October, Attorney General Robert F. Kennedy gives the FBI permission to listen in on King's home phone conversations. On November 22, President Kennedy (Robert's brother) is assassinated. By the end of December, King is selected as *Time* magazine's Man of the Year for 1963; his photo appears on the cover of the first issue of 1964.
1964	In mid-January, King and other civil rights leaders meet with President Lyndon Johnson, who seeks their support for a proposed War on Poverty. In late March, King has his first and only meeting with Malcolm X, a leader of the Black Muslim movement, whose approach to civil rights issues is less peaceful than King's. In mid-June, King is arrested for seeking service at a

segregated restaurant in St. Augustine, Florida, where local blacks have been campaigning for civil rights. In early July, King is present in the White House to see Johnson sign major civil rights legislation. During that same summer, however, he is stoned by Black Muslims in Harlem, but also assists other civil rights groups in campaigning for civil rights in Mississippi. In mid- November, the FBI director, J. Edgar Hoover, denounces King but then, in early December, meets with him. On December 10, King receives the Nobel Peace Prize in Oslo, Norway, at the unprecedentedly young age of thirty-five. He announces his plans to give the proceeds from the award to civil rights groups.

1965 In early February, King is arrested in Selma, Alabama, while protesting on behalf of voting rights for blacks. In early March, civil rights marchers are beaten by the police in Selma. Ten days later, King and other civil rights advocates lead a weeklong march from Selma to the state capital in Montgomery. Increasingly, King now begins to turn his attention to economic injustice, not simply racial discrimination. In mid-August he announces his opposition to the war in Vietnam.

1966 In late January, King takes up residence in a run-down building in a Chicago ghetto to highlight the issues of poverty and racial bias in housing. By June, he and others are participating in a March Against Fear in the South. By early June, King and others are leading a civil rights campaign in Mississippi and, in early July, he is leading a campaign against racial discrimination in Chicago.

1967 In early April, King prominently denounces the war in Vietnam. After King's conviction for illegally demonstrating in Birmingham is upheld by the U.S. Supreme Court, he spends four more days in a jail there. At the end of November, he announces a Poor People's Campaign to improve the living conditions of all poverty-stricken people, regardless of race.

1968	In late March, King leads protests in support of striking sanitation workers in Memphis, Tennessee. The protest turns violent—the first time this had happened during one of King's protests. On April 3, King delivers his famous "I've Seen the Promised Land" speech. The next day, he is killed by an assassin's bullet while standing outside his motel room. Riots break out throughout the United States. His funeral on April 9, in Atlanta, attracts mourners from throughout the world and his coffin is followed by a huge crowd through the streets of Atlanta.

Works Consulted

Lee, Eli. "Martin Luther King Jr. Changed a Nation in Only 13 Years: A Timeline." https://www.theatlantic.com/magazine/archive/2018/02/martin-luther-king-jr-timeline/552548/. Accessed 22 Oct. 2018.

"Major King Events Chronology 1929-1968." The Martin Luther King, Jr. Research and Education Institute, Stanford University. https://kinginstitute.stanford.edu/king-resources/major-king-events-chronology-1929-1968. Accessed 22 Oct. 2018.

"Martin Luther King Timeline." Datesandevents.org. http://www.datesandevents.org/people-timelines/28-martin-luther-king-timeline.htm. Accessed 22 Oct. 2018.

"Timeline of Martin Luther King, Jr.'s Life." LSU Libraries. https://guides.lib.lsu.edu/c.php?g=353667&p=2385247. Accessed 22 Oct. 2018.

"Timeline: The Life of Martin Luther King Jr." *USA Today*. https://www.usatoday.com/story/news/nation-now/2018/02/02/martin-luther-king-jr-timeline/1061525001/. Accessed 22 Oct. 2018.

Works by Martin Luther King Jr.

Books by King Published in His Lifetime

Strength to Love. Harper & Row, 1963. [Collection of sermons]

Stride Toward Freedom: The Montgomery Story. Harper & Row, 1958. [Autobiography]

The Trumpet of Conscience. Harper & Row, 1968. [Transcription of lectures]

Where Do We Go From Here: Chaos or Community? Harper & Row, 1967. [Sociopolitical commentary]

Why We Can't Wait. Harper & Row, 1963. [Essential writings]

Posthumous Collections of King's Writings, Sermons, and Speeches

Carson, Clayborne, editor. *The Autobiography of Martin Luther King, Jr.* IPM in Association with Warner Books, 1998.

Carson, Clayborne, and Peter Holloran, editors. *The Words of Martin Luther King, Jr.* Newmarket, 1983.

Carson, Clayborne, and Kris Shepard, editors. *A Call to Conscience: The Landmark Speeches of Dr. Martin Luther King, Jr.* Warner Books, 2001.

Washington, James M. editor. *A Testament of Hope.* Harper & Row, 1986.

Volumes from the Ongoing King Papers Project

The Papers of Martin Luther King, Jr. Volume I: Called to Serve, January 1929-June 1951. Edited by Clayborne Carson, Ralph Luker, and Penny A. Russell. U of California P, 1992.

The Papers of Martin Luther King, Jr. Volume II: Rediscovering Precious Values, July 1951-November 1955. Edited by Clayborne Carson, Ralph Luker, Penny A. Russell, and Peter Holloran, U of California P, 1994.

The Papers of Martin Luther King, Jr. Volume III: Birth of a New Age, December 1955-December 1956. Edited by Clayborne Carson, Stewart Burns, Susan Carson, Dana Powell, and Peter Holloran, U of California P, 1997.

The Papers of Martin Luther King, Jr. Volume IV: Symbol of the Movement, January 1957-December 1958. Edited by Clayborne Carson, Susan Carson, Adrienne Clay, Virginia Shadron, and Kieran Taylor, U of California P, 2000.

The Papers of Martin Luther King, Jr. Volume V: Threshold of a New Decade, January 1959-December 1960. Edited by Clayborne Carson, Tenisha Armstrong, Susan Carson, Adrienne Clay, and Kieran Taylor, U of California P, 2005.

The Papers of Martin Luther King, Jr. Volume VI: Advocate of the Social Gospel, September 1948-March 1963. Edited by Clayborne Carson, Susan Carson, Susan Englander, Troy Jackson, and Gerald L. Smith, U of California P, 2007.

The Papers of Martin Luther King, Jr. Volume VII: To Save The Soul of America, January 1961-August 1962. Edited by Clayborne Carson and Tenisha Armstrong, U of California P, 2014.

Bibliography

Baldwin, Lewis V. *Toward the Beloved Community: Martin Luther King Jr. and South Africa*. Pilgrim, 1995.

Bass, S. Jonathan. *Blessed Are the Peacemakers: Martin Luther King, Jr., Eight White Religious Leaders, and the "Letter from Birmingham Jail."* Louisiana State UP, 2001.

Bennett Jr., Lerone. *What Manner of Man*. Johnson, 1964.

Bobbitt, David A. *Rhetoric of Redemption: Kenneth Burke's Redemption Drama and Martin Luther King, Jr.'s "I Have a Dream" Speech*. Rowman & Littlefield, 2004.

Branch, Taylor. *At Canaan's Edge: America in the King Years, 1965-68*. Simon & Schuster, 2006.

———. *The King Years: Historic Moments in the Civil Rights Movement*. Simon & Schuster, 2013.

———. *Parting the Waters: America in the King Years 1954-63*. Simon & Schuster, 1988.

———. *Pillar of Fire: America in the King Years 1963-65*. Simon & Schuster, 1998.

Burns, Roger. *Martin Luther King, Jr.: A Biography*. Greenwood, 2006.

Carson, Clayborne. *Martin's Dream: My Journey and the Legacy of Martin Luther King Jr*. Palgrave Macmillan, 2014.

———. et al. *The Martin Luther King, Jr., Encyclopedia*. Greenwood, 2008.

Chappell, David L. *Waking from the Dream: The Struggle for Civil Rights in the Shadow of Martin Luther King, Jr*. Duke UP, 2015.

Clemons, Michael L., Donathan L. Brown, and William H. L. Dorsey, editors. *Dream and Legacy: Dr. Martin Luther King in the Post-Civil Rights Era*. UP of Mississippi, 2017.

Calloway-Thomas, Carolyn, and John Louis Lucaites, editors. *Martin Luther King, Jr., and the Sermonic Power of Public Discourse*. U of Alabama P, 1993.

Chakrabarty, Bidyut. *Confluence of Thought: Mahatma Gandhi and Martin Luther King, Jr*. Oxford UP, 2013.

Dyson, Michael Eric. *April 4, 1968: Martin Luther King, Jr.'s Death and How It Changed America*. Basic Civitas, 2008.

_____. *I May Not Get There with You: The True Martin Luther King, Jr.* Free, 2000.

Echols, James, editor. *I Have a Dream: Martin Luther King Jr. and the Future of Multicultural America*. Fortress, 2004.

Frady, Marshall. *Martin Luther King, Jr.* Viking Penguin, 2002.

Garrow, David J. *Bearing the Cross: Martin Luther King, Jr., and the Southern Christian Leadership Conference*. Harper, 1986.

Gilbreath, Edward. *Birmingham Revolution: Martin Luther King Jr.'s Epic Challenge to the Church*. InterVarsity, 2013.

Hansen, Drew D. *Dream: Martin Luther King, Jr., and the Speech That Inspired a Nation*. Ecco, 2003.

Harding, Vincent. *Martin Luther King, The Inconvenient Hero*. Orbis, 2008.

Harris, Trudier. *Martin Luther King Jr., Heroism, and African American Literature*. U of Alabama P, 2014.

Holmes, David Glen. *Where the Sacred and Secular Harmonize: Birmingham Mass Meeting Rhetoric and the Prophetic Legacy of the Civil Rights Movement*. Cascade, 2017.

Jackson, Thomas F. *From Civil Rights to Human Rights: Martin Luther King, Jr. and the Struggle for Economic Justice*. U of Pennsylvania P, 2009.

Jones, Clarence B. *Behind the Dream: The Making of the Speech That Transformed a Nation*. Palgrave Macmillan, 2011.

King, Coretta Scott. *My Life with Martin Luther King, Jr.* Henry Holt, 1969.

Laurent, Sylvie. *King and the Other America: The Poor People's Campaign and the Quest for Economic Equality*. U of California P, 2018.

Lewis, David L. *King: A Critical Biography*. Praeger, 1970.

Loritts, Bryan, editor. *Letters to a Birmingham Jail: A Response to the Words and Dreams of Dr. Martin Luther King, Jr.* Moody, 2014.

Mieder, Wolfgang. *"Making a Way Out of No Way": Martin Luther King's Sermonic Proverbial Rhetoric*. Peter Lang, 2010.

Miller, Keith D. *Martin Luther King's Biblical Epic: His Final, Great Speech*. UP of Mississippi, 2012.

―――――――. *Voice of Deliverance: The Language of Martin Luther King, Jr., and Its Sources.* 1992. U of Georgia P, 1998.

Nelson, Vaunda Micheaux. *Dream March: Dr. Martin Luther King, Jr., and the March on Washington.* Random House, 2017.

Oates, Stephen B. *Let the Trumpet Sound: The Life of Martin Luther King, Jr.* Harper & Row, 1982.

Rieder, Jonathan. *Gospel of Freedom: Martin Luther King, Jr.'s Letter from Birmingham Jail and the Struggle That Changed a Nation.* Bloomsbury, 2013.

―――――――. *The Word of the Lord Is Upon Me: The Righteous Performance of Martin Luther King, Jr.* Harvard UP, 2008.

Schlueter, Nathan W. *One Dream or Two? Justice in America and in the Thought of Martin Luther King, Jr.* Lexington, 2002.

Schulke, Flip, editor. *Martin Luther King, Jr.: A Documentary, Montgomery to Memphis.* Norton, 1976.

Selby, Gary S. *Martin Luther King and the Rhetoric of Freedom: The Exodus Narrative in America's Struggle for Civil Rights.* Baylor UP, 2008.

Shelby, Tommie, and Brandon M. Terry, editors. *To Shape a New World: Essays on the Political Philosophy of Martin Luther King, Jr.* Harvard UP, 2018.

Sokol, Jason. *The Heavens Might Crack: The Death and Legacy of Martin Luther King Jr.* Basic, 2018.

Sundquist, Eric J. *King's Dream.* Yale UP, 2009.

Sunnemark, Fredrik. *Inescapable Network of Mutuality: Discursivity and Ideology in the Rhetoric of Martin Luther King, Jr.* Acta Universitatis Gothoburgensis, 2001.

―――――――. *Ring Out Freedom! The Voice of Martin Luther King, Jr. and the Making of the Civil Rights Movement.* Indiana UP, 2004.

Terry, Brandon M., with Barbara Ransby et al., editors. *Fifty Years Since MLK.* Boston Review, 2017.

Waldschmidt-Nelson, Britta. *Dreams and Nightmares: Martin Luther King, Jr., Malcolm X, and The Struggle for Black Equality in America.* UP of Florida, 2012.

Ward, Brian, and Tony Badger, editors. *Making of Martin Luther King and the Civil Rights Movement.* New York UP, 1996.

Witherspoon, William Roger. *Martin Luther King, Jr.: To the Mountaintop.* Doubleday, 1985.

Younge, Gary. *Speech:The Story behind Dr. Martin Luther King Jr.'s Dream.* Haymarket, 2013.

About the Editor

Robert C. Evans is I. B. Young Professor of English at Auburn University at Montgomery, where he has taught since 1982. In 1984, he received his PhD from Princeton University, where he held Weaver and Whiting fellowships as well as a university fellowship. In later years his research was supported by fellowships from the Newberry Library (twice), the American Council of Learned Societies, the Folger Shakespeare Library (twice), the Mellon Foundation, the Huntington Library, the National Endowment for the Humanities, the American Philosophical Society, and the UCLA Center for Medieval and Renaissance Studies.

In 1982 he was awarded the G. E. Bentley Prize and in 1989 was selected Professor of the Year for Alabama by the Council for the Advancement and Support of Education. At AUM he has received the Faculty Excellence Award and has been named Distinguished Research Professor, Distinguished Teaching Professor, and University Alumni Professor. Most recently he was named Professor of the Year by the South Atlantic Association of Departments of English.

He is a contributing editor to the John Donne *Variorum Edition* and is the author or editor of over fifty books (on such topics as Ben Jonson, Martha Moulsworth, Kate Chopin, John Donne, Frank O'Connor, Brian Friel, Ambrose Bierce, Amy Tan, early modern women writers, pluralist literary theory, literary criticism, twentieth-century American writers, American novelists, Shakespeare, and seventeenth-century English literature). He is also the author of roughly four hundred published or forthcoming essays or notes (in print and online) on a variety of topics, especially dealing with Renaissance literature, critical theory, women writers, short fiction, and literature of the nineteenth and twentieth centuries.

Contributors

Jordan Bailey is an independent scholar with a special interest in literary theory and the literature of motherhood. Other interests include teaching, tutoring, and theater.

Raymond Blanton is assistant professor of communication arts in the School of Media and Design at the University of the Incarnate Word in San Antonio, Texas. His research is primarily concerned with the civic and religious dimensions of communication, rhetoric, myth, and media in intellectual history and American culture. In particular, his research considers the mythology of the road in twentieth-century American folk music and the blues through the fieldwork of folklorist Alan Lomax and Samaritan ethics in the civic-sermonic discourse of Martin Luther King Jr. in the American civil rights movement. He has written an array of book chapters on subjects ranging from indigenous culture in film studies to public memory in the Lincoln Memorial and the National Mall as well as loyalty and leadership, millennials, mindfulness and mindset, sacred rhetoric and the American sermon, and interactive nostalgia in *Stranger Things*.

Marshall D. Buford is an independent scholar with extensive background in the military and a special interest in American literature, particularly the writings of Mark Twain.

Sam Dunton is an independent scholar with a special interest in Martin Luther King Jr. A second essay on King has recently been completed and further work is under way.

Dr. Charles Johnson, University of Washington (Seattle) professor emeritus and the author of 23 books, is a novelist, philosopher, essayist, literary scholar, short story writer, cartoonist and illustrator, author of children's literature, and writer of screen- and teleplays. A MacArthur fellow and PhD in philosophy, Johnson has received a 2002 American Academy of Arts and Letters Award for Literature, a 1990 National Book Award for his novel *Middle Passage*, a 1985 Writers Guild award for his

PBS teleplay Booker, the 2016 W. E. B. Du Bois Award at the National Black Writers Conference, and many other awards. The Charles Johnson Society at the American Literature Association was founded in 2003. In November 2016, Pegasus Theater in Chicago debuted its play adaptation of *Middle Passage*, titled Rutherford's Travels. Dr. Johnson's most recent publications are *The Way of the Writer: Reflections on the Art and Craft of Storytelling*, and his fourth short story collection, *Night Hawks*.

Simran Kumari is an independent scholar with special interests in Indian culture and American literature. She is the recipient of numerous academic awards, especially for public speaking. She has worked as a data interpreter for NDTV (the national news channel of India) and has also worked with autistic and mentally disabled children.

Wolfgang Mieder is University Distinguished Professor of German and Folklore at the University of Vermont. While he has published widely on fairy tales, legends, and folksongs as well as literary and philological matters, his major research is paremiology (the study of proverbs). Among his many books are *Proverbs Are Never Out of Season: Popular Wisdom in the Modern Age* (1993), *The Politics of Proverbs: From Traditional Wisdom to Proverbial Stereotypes* (1997), *No Struggle, No Progress: Frederick Douglass and His Proverbial Rhetoric for Civil Rights* (2001), *Call a Spade a Spade: From Classical Phrase to Racial Slur* (2002), *Proverbs: A Handbook* (2004), *Proverbs Are the Best Policy: Folk Wisdom and American Politics* (2005), *Yes We Can: Barack Obama's Proverbial Rhetoric* (2009), *Proverbs Speak Louder Than Words: Folk Wisdom in Art, Culture, Folklore, History, Literature, and Mass Media* (2008), *Making a Way Out of No Way: Martin Luther King's Sermonic Proverbial Rhetoric* (2010), *Behold the Proverbs of a People: Proverbial Wisdom in Culture, Literature, and Politics* (2014). He is also the founding editor of *Proverbium: Yearbook of International Proverb Scholarship* (since 1984) and the chief editor of *A Dictionary of American Proverbs* (1992) and a co-editor of *The Dictionary of Modern Proverbs* (2012).

Keith D. Miller, a professor of English at Arizona State University, wrote *Voice of Deliverance: The Language of Martin Luther King, Jr., and Its Sources* and *Martin Luther King's Biblical Epic: His Final, Great*

Speech. In leading journals and scholarly collections, he has published many essays about the language of King, Fannie Lou Hamer, Malcolm X, Frederick Douglass, C. L. Franklin, and Jackie Robinson. Recently, he assisted Helene Rene Billups Baker in writing her memoir, *My Life with Martin Luther King and Charles Billups: Trauma and the Civil Rights Movement*, which reconstructs the life of an unsung civil rights pioneer who led a crucial march in Birmingham. Luring him into many archives is his current project, a book tentatively titled *Who Wrote the Autobiography of Malcom X?*

Kristine Warrenburg Rome, PhD, is an associate professor of communication at Flagler College. Her research is driven by the problematic concerning the politics of difference. Such politics—of race, class, and gender—resonate in the situational context of communication interaction and create opportunities to re-produce hierarchy and transformation. Her most recent publication, "Counterpublicity and the Trail of Broken Treaties: Why Not 'AIM' for New Sites of Deliberation?" can be found in *Decolonizing Public Address: American Indian Rhetoric and the Struggle for Self-Determination*. Her research has also appeared in *Contemporary Argumentation and Debate* as well as in multiple international argumentation conference proceedings. Her work on Robert F. Kennedy's April 4, 1968, announcement of Martin Luther King Jr.'s assassination, which has been presented at over a dozen national and international scholarly conferences, is still ongoing. She received her BA (communication arts and sciences) from DePauw University, her MA (history) from Butler University, and her PhD (rhetoric and communication ethics) from the University of Denver.

Donna Yvette Smith is an independent scholar with a special interest in African American culture, children's literature, and literature as well as in music composition. She is also interested in eye motifs in literature in general and especially in how eye problems are often depicted negatively in movies and television.

Nicolas Tredell is a writer and lecturer who has published 20 books and over 350 essays and articles on authors ranging from Shakespeare to Zadie Smith and on key issues in literary, film, and cultural theory. His recent books include *C. P. Snow: The Dynamics of Hope*; *Shakespeare: The Tragedies*; *Novels to Some Purpose: The Fiction of Colin Wilson*; *Conversations with Critics*, an updated edition of his interviews with leading literary figures; and *Anatomy of Amis*, the most comprehensive account so far of the fiction and nonfiction of Martin Amis. He formerly taught literature, drama, film, and cultural studies at Sussex University and is currently consultant editor of Palgrave Macmillan's Essential Criticism series, which now numbers 86 volumes, with many more to come. He is a frequent speaker at a wide variety of venues, most recently at the 2018 Literary London Conference at the University of London and the Second International Colin Wilson Conference at the University of Nottingham, UK.

Bryan Warren is an independent scholar with a special interest film, reception studies, and literature, especially drama. Recent publications include essays on the film version of *Into the Wild* and on filmed and theatrical versions of Ralph Ellison's *Invisible Man*.

Colleen Wilkowski, PhD, is a student at Arizona State University. Her scholarship focuses on the rhetoric of civil rights speeches and music. She has presented at national and international conferences for academic organizations such as Rhetoric Society of America, College Composition and Communication, International Society for the History of Rhetoric, American Society for the History of Rhetoric, and Popular Culture Association. She has a book review forthcoming in Rhetoric Review.

Index

Abernathy, Ralph xxxiii, 150, 161, 193, 204, 221
African American xii, xvi, xvii, xviii, xx, xxi, xxii, xxiv, xxv, xxix, xxxi, 4, 11, 12, 17, 21, 28, 35, 52, 74, 85, 102, 104, 105, 107, 108, 111, 112, 114, 121, 146, 163, 179, 192, 194, 196, 197, 198, 206
Albany, GA 10
allegory 30
alliteration 30, 45, 51, 59, 75, 181, 192
All Our Sins Forgiven 230
American dream 18, 45, 120, 121, 122, 124, 126, 137, 141, 142, 171
American history vii, xvi, xix, 28, 133, 198, 230
American Revolution of 1776 104
"American Sonnet" 193
Anderson, Marian xxviii, 105, 107, 108, 113
Antczak, Frederick 27
anthology xi, xii, 9, 179, 214, 216, 217, 219, 220
Aristotle ix, 33, 46, 48, 71, 73, 142, 151
Arnold, Matthew 82
assassination xxxvii, 18, 27, 40, 163, 177, 179, 187, 210, 241
Astrophil and Stella 51, 68
Autobiography of Malcolm X, The xxv, xxix

Baker, Houston, Jr. 170
Baldwin, James 85
Baldwin, Lewis V. 30
Barthes, Roland 71
"Beyond Vietnam" xxxvi
Bible, the x, xxi, xxii, 17, 25, 29, 31, 48, 76, 78, 79, 80, 81, 82, 85, 122, 125, 126, 130, 136, 144, 145, 147, 169, 236
biblical imagery 77, 169
biography vii, xxiv, xxv, 204, 206, 207, 208
Birkenstein, Kathy 100, 101
Birmingham, AL xxiii, xxiv, xxviii, xxxiii, xxxiv, 4, 6, 7, 8, 10, 26, 61, 62, 64, 72, 84, 86, 153, 158, 167, 188, 190, 195, 220, 227, 229, 230
Black America 204
black community 21, 44, 157, 180, 238
Black Liberation Army 232
Black Muslims xxxv, 240
black power movement 163, 164
black slave 37, 92
black theology 26
Blake, William 52, 76, 78
Bobbitt, David A. 133
Bond, Julian 20, 22
Bosley, Harold 23, 100, 101, 213
Boulware, Marcus H. 30
Branch, Taylor 103, 108
Branham, Robert 104
"Brevity" 196
Bryant, William Cullen 98, 216, 221
Buttrick, George xvi, xix

"Call and Response" 191, 193

265

Calloway-Thomas, Carolyn 15, 26, 162
capitalism 173
Carey, Archibald xviii, 108, 109, 111, 114
Carlyle, Thomas 221
Carmichael, Stokely xxxvi, 232, 240, 241
Carson, Clayborne xxvi, xxviii, 15, 16, 68, 86, 110, 114, 129, 222
Carter, Jimmy xxxvii
Chaucer, Geoffrey 142
Chicago, IL xii, xxviii, xxxvi, 114, 149, 162, 171, 177, 227, 231
Christianity 17, 18, 59, 64, 106, 215
Christine, Willie xxx
civil rights vii, viii, x, xi, xx, xxii, xxiii, xxxi, xxxii, xxxiii, xxxiv, xxxv, xxxvi, 3, 4, 5, 6, 7, 10, 11, 30, 42, 43, 44, 83, 88, 99, 103, 108, 116, 117, 132, 133, 136, 139, 140, 143, 149, 150, 158, 160, 163, 170, 180, 194, 195, 197, 198, 199, 200, 202, 203, 208, 211, 214, 220, 227, 228, 229, 230, 231, 233, 234, 235, 237, 241, 243
Civil Rights Act xxxii, xxxv, 44, 138, 170, 173, 231
civil rights movement viii, x, xi, xx, xxii, xxxii, xxxiii, xxxiv, 3, 4, 7, 10, 11, 30, 42, 44, 83, 88, 99, 103, 117, 132, 136, 139, 140, 143, 149, 150, 158, 163, 170, 180, 197, 198, 228, 230, 231, 235, 243
Civil War 3, 9, 29, 78, 85, 104, 105, 106, 107
Clark, Gregory 154
Colonialism 175
communism xxxv
Congress of Racial Equality xxxv
Connor, Eugene "Bull" xxxiv, 7
Cotton, Dorothy 21
Cowper, William 92
Cox, Robert 102
Cullen, Countee 85

D'Aguiar, Fred 191
Daley, Richard 227
Darwinian 34, 39, 40
Daughters of the American Revolution 106, 107
Declaration of Independence 18, 29, 36, 37, 46, 117, 118, 120, 133, 140, 141, 170, 225
deconstruction 34, 53
democracy 6, 39, 118, 119, 121, 122, 125, 135, 141, 155, 173
Detroit race riots of 1943 3
Dickson, Janice 233, 234
discrimination xxxiii, xxxvi, 24, 35, 43, 44, 94, 106, 107, 112, 119, 123, 133, 136, 167, 181, 182, 188, 229
Donne, John 81, 85, 122
Douglass, Frederick ix, xxii, 30, 71, 82, 83, 106, 130, 141, 147, 225
Downward Way 157, 158, 159, 161
Dreamer xii, 226, 227, 230, 231
Du Bois, W. E. B. 229

Dunbar, Paul ix, 71, 82
Dungy, Camille T. 194
DuVernay, Ava 197
Dyson, Michael Eric 110, 164

Ecocritics 34, 49
Edelman, Marian 204
Edwards, J. H. xvii
Eisenhower, Dwight D. xxxii
Eliot, T. S. ix, 71, 84, 86
Ellison, Ralph 85, 154, 162
Emancipation Proclamation xxxiii, 35, 83, 105, 107, 112, 151, 170
Emerson, Ralph Waldo 82
Epictetus ix, 71, 73, 86
Espada, Martín 189
existentialism 60
Exodus xxii, 16, 26, 74, 150, 158, 159, 160, 161, 162

Finney, Nikky 180
Fishman, T. A. 216
Forman, James xxxv
Fosdick, Harry Emerson xvi, 23
Foust, Christina 102
freedom xxi, xxiii, xxxiii, xxxiv, xxxvi, 3, 6, 7, 8, 9, 10, 11, 14, 35, 38, 40, 41, 42, 44, 46, 48, 49, 50, 74, 94, 103, 104, 109, 110, 119, 123, 125, 132, 133, 135, 137, 138, 141, 143, 144, 145, 153, 155, 158, 166, 167, 170, 179, 189, 229
Freeman, Annabelle 233, 234, 235
French Revolution 52

Garrow, David J. 218

German, Joyce 233, 235, 236, 237, 238, 239, 241, 242
"Ghost" 188
Gift of Love, A 53, 55, 57, 58, 59, 60, 68, 72, 73, 74, 75, 76, 77, 79, 80, 81, 82, 86, 162
Gilkes, Cheryl Townsend 217
Graff, Gerald 100
Grange, Lester xxxii
Great Depression 151

Hamilton, J. Wallace xvi
Hamlet 79, 80, 82, 87
Hansen, Drew D. 28, 123, 132, 136, 139, 140
Harlem Renaissance 85
Harrison, Linda K. 28
Harrison, Robert D. 28
Harris, Trudier 179
Hayes, Terrance 193
Hegel, Friedrich 142
heights/depths 57, 63
Hemmans, Martha 20
Henderson, Lollie 233
Hill, Bobby 19
Holocaust, the 180
Hoover, J. Edgar xxxv
Horace 33, 37, 38, 42, 48
Hugo, Victor 221
Human Rights 256
Hurston, Zora Neale 85

"I Have a Dream" viii, x, xviii, xxii, xxiii, xxxiv, 17, 26, 27, 28, 29, 32, 33, 34, 35, 37, 39, 41, 43, 45, 47, 49, 102, 103, 104, 109, 110, 111, 112, 116, 117, 119, 121, 123, 125, 127, 128, 129, 130,

131, 132, 133, 140, 146, 164, 187, 225, 226, 237
"I Have a Scheme" 186, 188
"In a Station of the Metro" 196
India xxi, xxxii, xxxiii, 232
Intertextuality 71, 73, 75, 77, 79, 81, 83, 85, 87
"I See the Promised Land" x, xix, xxxvii, 152, 163, 164, 165, 236
"I've Been to the Mountaintop" xix, 27
"I've Seen the Promised Land" 252

Jackson, Jesse 88, 193, 240
James, William 52, 53, 54, 61
Jet 203, 204, 213
Johnson, Gwen 233
Johnson, James Weldon 13, 221
Johnson, Lyndon Baines xxxiv, 210
Johnson, Mordecai xxi
Jordan, Rosa 6

Kant, Immanuel 142
Kennedy, John F. xxxiii, xxxiv
Kennedy, Robert 206
King 197
King, Coretta Scott xxvi, 12, 198, 200, 216
King, Martin Luther, Jr. vii, xi, xv, xxviii, xxx, xxxvii, 12, 15, 26, 31, 32, 115, 116, 130, 132, 148, 163, 165, 179, 181, 183, 185, 187, 189, 191, 193, 195, 197, 198, 210, 214, 227
King, Michael xxx

King's Dream 29, 32, 130, 132, 138, 148

Lafayette, Bernard 19, 22
Larsen, Nella 85
Les Misérables 40
Lester, Julius 230
"Letter from Birmingham Jail" xxiv, xxxiv, 61, 72, 86
Let the Trumpet Sound 228
Levinas, Emmanuel xi, 163
Levison, Stanley 72, 197
Lewis, John xxxv, 204, 230
LGBTQ 42
liberalism 60, 61
light/dark imagery 58, 59
Lincoln, Abraham xxii, 30, 35, 101, 123, 130, 141, 147, 151, 179, 196
literary criticism viii, 33, 67
Longinus 33, 48
Los Angeles Times 206, 210, 212, 213
Lowell, James Russell ix, 71, 82, 98, 216, 221
Lowery, Joseph 203
Lucaites, John Louis 15, 26, 27, 32, 129, 146
Luker, Ralph 220
Lyrical Ballads 51, 68

Macbeth 80, 87
Mahatma Gandhi xxxiii, 84
Mann, Abby 197, 198, 199, 200, 201, 203, 204, 205, 206, 207, 209, 211, 213
Marriage of Heaven and Hell 52, 67, 68
Mays, Benjamin xxi

McCullough, Lornell 20
McKibben, Bill 216
McPhail, Mark 165
Memphis, TN xi, xxiv, xxxvi, xxxvii, 149, 150, 151, 152, 153, 155, 156, 158, 159, 163, 166, 167, 172, 173, 175, 207, 228, 237
Meredith, James xxvii, xxxvi, 204
metaphor xi, 27, 28, 30, 36, 39, 46, 51, 58, 65, 74, 75, 78, 81, 94, 104, 110, 132, 133, 134, 135, 136, 139, 143, 149, 155, 158, 180, 181, 183, 193
Meteorological imagery 58
metonymy 51
Mighty Stream, The 179
Miller, Ernest xv
Mills, Charles W. 165
Mills, Shirley 233, 234, 235
modernism 170
Moldovan, Russel 17
Montgomery, AL xii, xxi, xxvi, xxxi, xxxii, xxxiii, xxxv, 4, 5, 6, 7, 76, 102, 109, 115, 160, 180, 181, 184, 185, 190, 194, 215, 219, 220, 226, 227, 228, 229, 233, 237, 239
Montgomery bus boycott xxxi, 6, 7, 215, 229
Montgomery Improvement Association xxxi, 5, 219, 228
morality xi, 42, 46, 48, 170, 174, 207
moral law 52, 53, 64, 65
Morris, Calvin S. 18

"Mountaintop" 159
Muhammad, Elijah xxv, xxxvi
multiculturalism 187
Myrdal, Gunnar 121

NAACP xxxi, 106, 108, 117, 203, 204, 229, 231
National Endowment for the Humanities 29
Nation of Islam xxv, xxxvi
Native Americans 42, 181
New Criticism 67
Niebuhr, Reinhold xvi, xxi, 84
nihilism 57
Nixon, E. D. 203
Nixon, Richard M. xxxii
Nkrumah, Kwame xxxii
Nobel Peace Prize xxxv, 226, 228, 231
Noble, C. P. 233, 235, 236, 237, 238, 239, 240, 241, 242
nonviolence ix, xxi, xxxi, xxxiii, 51, 63, 67, 75, 84, 96, 97, 100, 125, 152, 153, 166, 175, 215, 230, 232, 234, 237, 240

Oates, Stephen 228
Obama, Barack 130, 141, 147
"On Being A Good Neighbor" 157
Ong, Walter 12
Orality and Literacy 12, 16
oratory vii, xxi, xxii, 13, 28, 78, 102, 105, 107, 108, 128, 137, 207, 218, 225

parallelism 30, 51, 59, 84
Parks, Rosa xxxi, 4, 5, 15, 180, 183, 194, 203, 219

Parting the Waters 103, 113
patriotism 106, 108
personification 30
pessimism ix, 51, 58, 145
Peters, Ida 201
plagiarism 23, 72
Plato ix, 33, 35, 42, 71, 73, 142, 151, 161, 162
Plessy v. Ferguson 92
Pluralism viii, 33
Poor People's Campaign xxxvi, 171
Postmodernism 34
Pound, Ezra 196
poverty xxxiv, 36, 39, 100, 122, 128, 172
Powell, Adam Clayton 228
Pragmatism 54, 68
preaching viii, xvii, 11, 17, 20, 21, 22, 25, 28, 92, 140, 192
Promised Land x, xix, xxviii, xxxvii, 7, 9, 11, 13, 74, 151, 152, 159, 160, 162, 163, 164, 165, 166, 177, 236
Protestantism xx, xxx

race xxi, 3, 6, 24, 44, 85, 95, 120, 124, 151, 163, 164, 165, 166, 167, 171, 172, 174, 175, 176, 187, 236
racial discrimination xxxiii, 43, 44, 106, 107, 167
racism xi, xx, xxx, 47, 49, 63, 128, 165, 166, 171, 198, 215, 235
radicalism 44, 218
Randolph, A. Philip xxxii, 229
Ray, James Earl xxxvii
Reagan, Ronald xxxvii
"Red Velvet" 180

"Revolutionary Symbolism in America" 10, 15
Richard II 40
Rieder, Jonathan xxvi, 30
Roosevelt, Eleanor 106
Roosevelt, Franklin 151
Roots xxv, xxvii, 30, 162, 197, 200, 213
Rustin, Bayard 72

sacrifice 119
Samaritan Way xi, 149, 151, 153, 155, 156, 157, 159, 161
Sameness 66
Scott, Coretta xxvi, xxx, 12, 15, 198, 200, 216
segregation xxxi, xxxii, xxxiii, xxxiv, 23, 24, 35, 36, 39, 45, 47, 64, 74, 83, 94, 107, 112, 118, 119, 121, 123, 133, 135, 136, 171, 175, 180, 184, 190, 194, 215, 216, 229
Seibles, Tim 188
Selma 197
Selma, AL xxxv, 158
sermons viii, ix, x, xvi, xvii, xviii, xix, xx, xxii, xxiv, xxv, xxvi, 6, 11, 13, 14, 17, 20, 22, 23, 24, 25, 31, 53, 63, 71, 72, 83, 88, 89, 90, 117, 139, 145, 149, 161, 214, 217, 218, 219, 221, 225, 226, 228, 231, 238
Shakespeare, William ix, xvi, xviii, xix, xxvi, 40, 71, 78, 79, 80, 81, 87, 96, 98, 134, 142
Shales, Tom 200
Sharpton, Al 88

Shippy, Dick 209
Shuttlesworth, Fred xxiv, 19, 204, 240
Sidney, Philip 51
simile 30, 51, 183
slavery xviii, xxii, 6, 7, 8, 9, 46, 59, 74, 105, 107, 121, 175, 197
"Sleeping on the Bus" 189
Smith, Cecil 210
Smith, Samuel 102, 104
Smith, Vera 233, 235, 236, 237, 238, 239, 240, 241, 242
social discrimination 182
Solomon, Martha 26
Søren Kierkegaard 60
Southern Christian Leadership Conference xxxii, 18, 229
Southern Negro Leaders Conference xxxii
Spillers, Hortense J. 30
St. Augustine, FL xxxiv, xxxv, 226
Stowe, Harriet Beecher 104
Strength to Love 68, 86, 116, 130, 162
Strickland, Edward 155
Stride Toward Freedom: The Montgomery Story xxxii, 14, 219
structuralism 53
Student Nonviolent Coordinating Committee xxxv, 204
suffering xx, 44, 59, 61, 75, 76, 78, 119, 153, 169
Sundquist, Eric J. 29, 132, 138
symbolism 10, 15

Tennyson, Alfred ix, 71, 81, 82, 87

Testament of Hope, A xii, xxix, 16, 101, 116, 131, 148, 162, 177, 214, 215, 217, 218, 219, 220, 221, 222, 223, 224
"The Preachers Eat Out" 194
They Say / I Say 100, 101
Thoreau, Henry David 82, 87
Thousand Illustrations for Your Sermons, A xviii
Thurman, Howard xxi
Tierce, Mike 219
Till, Emmett 127
Tillich, Paul xvi, 60, 84
Trumpet of Conscience, The 147
Tulsa race riots of 1921 3

Uncle Tom's Cabin 104
universalism 120
Upward Way 3, 11, 14, 155, 158, 159, 161

Vail, Mark 135
"*Vernon Johns*" xxiii, 194, 195
Vietnam War xv, xxxvi, 215
Voice of Deliverance xviii, xx, xxi, xxii, xxviii, 22, 32, 115, 147
Voting Rights Act xxxv, 231

Walker, Wyatt 203
Washington, Booker T. xxx, 44, 225
Washington, James M. xii, 101, 214, 222, 223, 224
Washington Post, The 200, 213, 214, 224
Wells, Ida B. 105
Where Do We Go From Here: Chaos or Community? 72
white racism 49, 165, 171, 198

Why We Can't Wait 72
Wilkins, Roger 214
Wilkins, Roy xxxii, xxxiv
Williams, Ethel 233, 234, 235, 236, 237, 239, 240, 241, 242
Williams, Hosea 204
Wilson, Kirt 102
Winfield, Paul 200, 201, 205, 206
Wordsworth, William 51
World War I 9
World War II 9, 180, 229
Wright, Richard 85

X, Malcolm xxiii, xxiv, xxv, xxvii, xxix, xxxv, 227, 230, 240, 241

Young, Andrew 207, 240
Younge, Gary 30, 31

Zephaniah, Benjamin 186